Trust and Crisis Management in the European Union

Dóra Győrffy

Trust and Crisis Management in the European Union

An Institutionalist Account of Success and Failure in Program Countries

palgrave
macmillan

Dóra Győrffy
Péter Pázmány Catholic University
Corvinus University of Budapest
Budapest, Hungary

ISBN 978-3-319-88733-3 ISBN 978-3-319-69212-8 (eBook)
https://doi.org/10.1007/978-3-319-69212-8

Softcover re-print of the Hardcover 1st edition 2018

Cover illustration: H. Mark Weidman Photography / Alamy Stock Photo

Printed on acid-free paper

This Palgrave Macmillan imprint is published by Springer Nature
The registered company is Springer International Publishing AG
The registered company address is: Gewerbestrasse 11, 6330 Cham, Switzerland

Preface

The book emerged from my earlier research on trust and economic policy as well as my impressions about contemporary Hungarian political and economic developments. As I was observing the impact of the financial crisis on Hungary, I became keenly aware of the importance of institutions and trust in choosing a path to deal with the financial crisis. Examining how other European countries managed the crisis served both as a distraction from focusing on Hungarian developments as well as tests about my ideas concerning the factors that determine the political and economic outcomes of crisis management.

The research started with an article on trust and the emergence of austerity cycles—"The role of expectations in austerity cycles: the political economy of crisis management in Ireland and Greece," which was published in *Acta Oeconomica* in 2014. In a significantly revised form, the article appears in this book. I am grateful for the permission of the publisher as well as the comments from the reviewers.

Following the examination of the role of trust in the Greek and Irish cases, the scope of the research was gradually expanded to include further cases of EU member states, which received international financial assistance—Latvia, Hungary, Romania, Portugal, Cyprus, and Spain. All of these countries struggled with institutional trust, but they still managed to avoid the economic collapse experienced by Greece, as well as the breakdown of institutional checks and balances, which could be observed in Hungary. Their cases show that even in an environment of distrust, there is a path toward economic recovery without falling prey to populism. What are the factors, which made such outcome possible, is the central puzzle of the research.

As the European Union struggles to fight the numerous challenges it is facing, I strongly believe that the lessons of the financial crisis are broader than the eight cases discussed in the book. Strengthening domestic institutions, especially the rule of law, appears to be a key factor in overcoming the distrust resulting from concerns over moral hazard and solidarity among the member states. The book is a contribution to the debate about the future of European integration and underlines the importance of domestic institutional structures in this process.

During the years of research, I incurred a debt of gratitude to a number of people. First and foremost to László Csaba, who encouraged me to write the book, patiently read the entire manuscript, and always gave me valuable feedback. I received helpful remarks on earlier versions of particular chapters from Bruno Dallago, Erik Jones, Júlia Király, István Kónya, George Kopits, János Kornai, Mihály Laki, Péter Mihályi, and Dóra Siklós. I am also grateful to three anonymous referees for their insightful comments on the initial plans of the book as well as the final manuscript. Finally, I would like to thank the help of Rachel Sangster, Thomas Coughlan, Rachel Hurley and Shruti Krishna at Palgrave, who guided me through the publication and editing process. Naturally, all remaining errors are mine.

Budapest, Hungary — Dóra Győrffy
September, 2017

Contents

List of Figures

List of Tables

1

Understanding Success and Failure in Financial Crisis Management

Although the European financial crisis had mostly abated after 2012, the consequences persist long after the speculative attacks ceased. High rates of public debt and unemployment, low level of investment, and large-scale social disappointment characterize numerous member states of the European Union (EU) several years after the crisis. In such an environment, gloomy predictions about the future of Europe have been prevalent even before the migration crisis, Brexit, or the inauguration of Donald Trump as the president of the United States.

As the public discourse became enveloped in despair and angst, a wide discrepancy opened between the short-term fire-fighting efforts of international institutions and the various long-term proposals of analysts about the move toward fiscal and political union in the EU. The divergence among countries, which were most hit by the crisis, the sources of the differences and their implications for building a more resilient EU were mostly neglected in the debate. However, without understanding these national-level issues, it is very difficult to make realistic proposals about further integration.

The major question of this book is very simple: what factors determined the success or failure of financial crisis management in countries which needed international financial support? Success and failure are

D. Győrffy, *Trust and Crisis Management in the European Union*,
https://doi.org/10.1007/978-3-319-69212-8_1

naturally subjective concepts. Here they are understood in both economic and political terms. Economic crisis management can be considered successful if a country is able to return to market financing, its economic growth recovers with declining unemployment and public debt, and its competitiveness is stable or improving.[1] The definition of political success is more complex—in the book it is understood as the ability of the traditional political elite to recover the trust of the public or at least preserve its political power from anti-elite, populist forces. At first sight, the relationship between the two dimensions of success can vary—an economically successful crisis management does not necessarily exclude populist takeover, while the resistance to populism does not imply economic success. The case studies of the book provide ample evidence about how difficult it is to be successful in both dimensions.

The chapter provides an overview of the research. The next section introduces the eight countries under analysis focusing on their economic differences after the crisis. Then a brief literature review is presented about the major debates surrounding financial crisis management in the EU, followed by an elaboration on the theoretical approach taken in the book. The fourth section discusses methodology, and the chapter concludes with an overview about the structure of the book.

1.1 Divergence After Crisis in the EU Program Countries

After the collapse of Lehman Brothers, the global financial crisis swiftly spread to Iceland then to the EU. The first victim was Hungary, which requested financial assistance in October 2008. Latvia and Romania also needed support, and turned to the International Monetary Fund (IMF) in November 2008 and March 2009, respectively. As these countries can be considered emerging economies, their financial trouble and the need for IMF involvement was not completely unexpected. However, euro-zone member states were not supposed to turn to the IMF, and thus although Greece lost access to the financial markets in December 2009, it took months before financial assistance was finally offered in May 2010. Afterward other euro-zone countries followed: Ireland in November 2010, Portugal in April 2011, and finally Spain and Cyprus in June 2012. In the following, these eight countries are referred to as program countries.

By 2016 all program countries could return to market financing with the exception of Greece. However, as shown by Table 1.1 there is a considerable divergence in growth, unemployment, the level of public debt, and the changes in competitiveness among the eight countries.

Economic growth performance is assessed through taking 2004 GDP as the base—while the choice is certainly arbitrary, it seems more appropriate than using the immediate pre-crisis year as in many cases the latter was an indicator of an overheated economy. From Table 1.1 we can see that compared to the EU-28 average, three countries showed exceptional growth performance between 2004 and 2016 in spite of the financial crisis: Ireland, Romania, and Latvia. Greece represents a stark contrast with its 2016 GDP standing only at 80.8 percent of its 2004 level. Portugal is the second worst performer as its GDP stands at the 2004 level. Hungary, Cyprus, and Spain perform around the EU-28 average with their 2016 GDP surpassing the 2004 level by 10–15 percent.

Similar divergence can be observed in terms of unemployment and public debt. On these dimensions the Eastern countries (Hungary, Latvia, and Romania) and Ireland perform better than the Mediterranean countries as they register single-digit unemployment rates and debt levels

Table 1.1 Selected macroeconomic indicators in EU program countries in 2016

	GDP 2016 (2004 = 100)	Unemployment rate in 2016	Public debt as % of GDP in 2016	Competitiveness rank in 2016 (change from 2006/2007)
Cyprus	110.5	13.1	107.8	83 (−28)
Greece	80.8	23.6	179	86 (−21)
Ireland	155.9	7.9	75.4	23 (−1)
Hungary	115.6	5.1	74.1	69 (−22)
Latvia	131.4	9.6	40.1	49 (−4)
Portugal	100.6	11.2	130.4	46 (−6)
Romania	142.2	5.9	54.4	62 (+12)
Spain	111.6	19.6	99.4	32 (−3)
EU-28	114.5	8.5	85.1	N/A

Data sources: GDP, AMECO database; unemployment, European Commission (2017) 14–15; public debt, European Commission (2017) 164–165; competitiveness, WEF (2006, 2016)

below the EU average. Greece fares the worst on these dimensions with 23.6 percent unemployment and public debt at 179 percent of GDP. The other three Mediterranean countries also underperform the EU average with double-digit unemployment rate and debt levels around 100 percent of the GDP with Portugal registering 130.4 percent.

The long-term sustainability of growth performance strongly depends on competitiveness. Table 1.1 shows the ranking of the eight countries in 2016 in the *Global Competitiveness Report* of the World Economic Forum and the change in their ranking from the pre-crisis period. As we can see, the competitive position of Cyprus, Greece, and Hungary deteriorated the most, while Ireland, Latvia, Portugal, and Spain registered only a moderate decline in their ranking. The best performer on this dimension is Romania, which improved its position by 12 places although clearly from a very low initial level.

To summarize the main findings from Table 1.1 we can see that Greece is clearly the worst performer, while Ireland has fared best among the eight countries. Among the remaining countries, the three Eastern countries generally perform better than three Mediterranean states. The central question of the book is what explains these differences.

1.2 Narratives on Crisis Management

During the years of financial crisis management, several narratives emerged about what factors determined the speed of the recovery. While early accounts focused on fundamental factors and the availability of exchange rate adjustment, later the issue of fiscal consolidation became the subject of the most heated debates. Institutions received scant attention during the process.

1.2.1 Fundamental Factors

An evident explanation for variation in the outcomes of crisis management is initial conditions in the economy, most importantly the level of indebtedness. It could be expected that more indebted countries are more likely to be hit by a crisis and struggle more to recover as they have to finance their debt. Figure 1.1 shows three indicators of indebtedness as

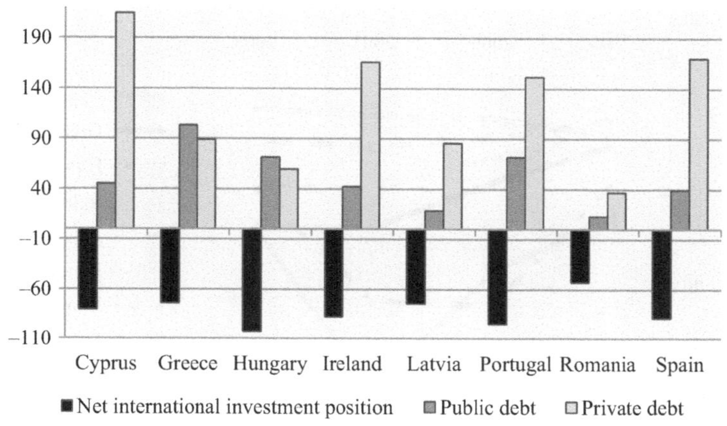

Fig. 1.1 Indicators of indebtedness in EU program countries in 2008 (% of GDP) (Data sources: Net international investment position, Eurostat; Public debt, European Commission 2017: 164–165; Private debt, World Bank databank domestic credit to the private sector variable)

percent of GDP: net international investment position, public debt, and private debt.

As we can see from the figure these variables explain little about the divergence of economic indicators after the crisis. With the exception of Romania, there is relatively little variation on net international investment position, thus it cannot be the explanation for success or failure of crisis management. Low initial level of public debt appears to explain more as Greece, Hungary, and Portugal were the most indebted states, while Romania, Latvia, and Ireland had the lowest initial level of public debt, which probably contributed to their success in managing the crisis. This provides some basis for analysts, who castigated the failure of the Stability and Growth Pact in preventing budgetary imbalances (Larch et al. 2010; Schuknecht et al. 2011; Sinn 2014: 52–58). However, Cyprus and Spain had very similar level of public and even private debt to Ireland, and they appear much less successful in dealing with the crisis.

A related fundamental variable to indebtedness in explaining the crisis is the level of current account deficit as a result of overconsumption due to the availability of credit (Giavazzi and Spaventa 2011; Lane 2012). As shown by Fig. 1.2, all of the countries, which needed financial support, had considerable current account deficits indicating the importance of

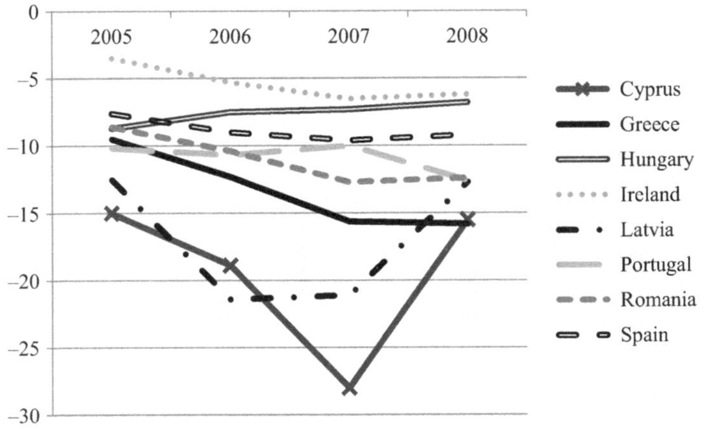

Fig. 1.2 Current account deficit in EU program countries 2005–2008 (% of GDP) (Data: European Commission 2017: 96–97)

this variable.[2] However, in predicting which countries succeed in managing the crisis, this variable is hardly predictive. While Ireland had the lowest level of current account deficit, which fits with its successful recovery from the crisis, the most extreme deficits were registered by Cyprus and Latvia, which showed much better performance following the crisis than Greece or Portugal, which had lower levels of current account deficit during this period.

1.2.2 Exchange Rate Devaluation

As current account imbalances were considered a major reason for the financial crisis, the availability of exchange rate devaluation became a focal point in the discussion. During the early phases of the crisis, several commentators suggested that the possibility for devaluation could restore competitiveness and ease the pain of rebalancing the current account in Greece or in Latvia (Krugman 2011; Hall 2012). In countries, which were not members of the euro-zone, the possibility for devaluation was also viewed as a relatively painless adjustment mechanism and a reason not to introduce the euro.

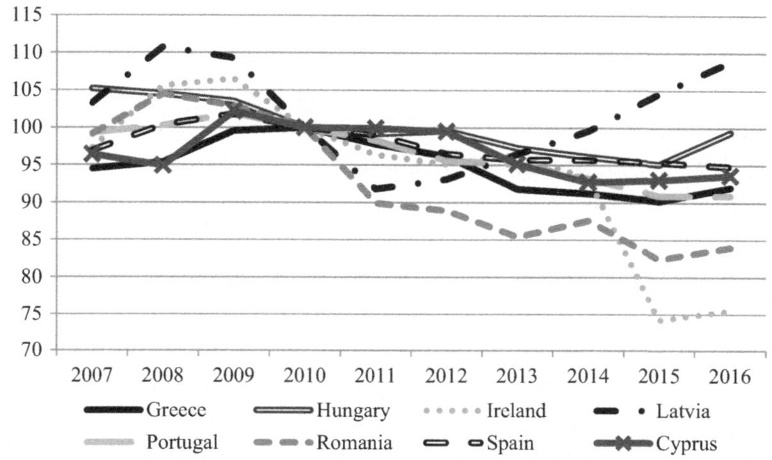

Fig. 1.3 Real unit labor costs in EU program countries 2007–2016 (2010 = 100) (Data: European Commission 2017: 76–77)

Among the six countries examined, only Romania and Hungary could freely determine its exchange rate policy. Both countries experienced significant devaluation—the Romanian currency went from 3.5 lei/euro to 4.59 lei/euro, while the Hungarian currency weakened from 237 HUF/euro to 307 HUF/euro between September 2008 and June 2017.[3] However, Fig. 1.3 shows that in spite of a similar rate of devaluation, real unit labor costs fell sharply only in Romania while remained mostly constant in Hungary. Indeed all euro-zone member states experienced a greater fall in labor costs due to internal devaluation than Hungary.

1.2.3 Austerity

The most serious debates regarding European crisis management related to the impact of fiscal consolidation on growth. Disappointment over the slow economic recovery in the EU, the continued uncertainty on the financial markets as well as the comparably better performance of the United States all contributed to the questioning of the European method of crisis management. The key issue became fiscal consolidation or austerity, which was criticized as self-defeating—the recession due to expenditure cuts leads to both lower tax revenues and higher debt rates and thus necessitates more austerity resulting in an austerity spiral (Krugman 2013).

The debate on austerity was waged in the context of the social consequences of the crisis. While pensioners were largely saved from the consequences of adjustment, the young generation suffered greatly given cuts in family benefits and education. Increase of poverty and unemployment for the youth threatens with a lost generation syndrome with the Southern periphery of Europe being particularly affected (Darvas and Tschekassin 2015). Another important fear is the populist turn in politics and the electoral gains of radical parties. Parallels with the great depression and the rise of fascism are often drawn (Bromhead et al. 2012; Lindvall 2014). Kriesi (2012) warns that a negative spiral could develop as outvoted incumbents are followed by governments, which are also unable to manage the crisis.

The experiences of crisis management questioned the pre-crisis consensus on the growth benefits of expenditure-based consolidations (Giavazzi and Pagano 1990; Alesina and Perotti 1995; Alesina et al. 1998). Several studies suggest that non-Keynesian effects, which can counter the effects of the fall in demand during fiscal consolidations such as increase in confidence, take place primarily during economic booms and are unlikely during periods of global recession especially when interest rates are close to zero (IMF 2010; Perotti 2011). Blyth (2013: 9–10) also calls attention to the problem of the fallacy of composition—"we cannot all be austere at once," implying that when all countries implement fiscal consolidation at the same time, export-led recovery, which characterized the pre-crisis success stories, becomes more difficult for all. The empirical evidence from the current consolidation seems to support the critics of expansionary fiscal consolidations and shows an even larger short-term trade-off between austerity and growth than previously assumed. De Grauwe and Ji (2013) find a strong negative correlation between the size of fiscal consolidation and growth. They also find that in the euro-zone consolidation does not appear to have effects on market confidence as interest rates are negatively related to consolidation efforts.

An important factor in the above debate is the size of the fiscal multiplier—the impact of consolidation on growth. During the early years of the current crisis, the IMF found that the fiscal multiplier equals 0.5, which means that reducing the deficit by 1 percent of the GDP reduces growth by 0.5 percent within two years (IMF 2010: 94). Later Blanchard and Leigh (2013) showed that the size of the multiplier was severely underestimated and is well above unity.[4] In a meta-regression analysis involving 98 countries between 1992 and 2013, Gerchert and Rannenberg (2014) found that fiscal multipliers are higher during economic downturns especially for spending cuts. On the basis of their analysis, they argue that consolidation should take place during economy recovery and should be primarily tax-based. While the longer-term growth aspects might be subject to debate, Mody (2015: 7) argues that the short-term growth consequences of fiscal adjustments are clear. He emphasizes the superiority of the US approach, which followed a more countercyclical policy and allowed greater debt restructuring for households. In defense of the pre-crisis consensus, Alesina et al. (2015) show that the composition of adjustment mattered greatly during the 2009–2013 period, and expenditure-based consolidations were much less harmful for growth than revenue-based ones—and they also do not find sufficient evidence to claim that the recent fiscal adjustment have been more harmful to economic growth than the pre-crisis adjustments. However, they explicitly do not address the issue of the timing of adjustment, and underline the importance of context for the effects of consolidation.

1.2.4 Domestic Institutions

Monastiriotis (2014) made an important contribution to the debate on austerity by providing important insights into the determinants of the relationship between austerity and growth. He showed for the period 2008–2012 that the relationship between austerity and growth disappears once we exclude Greece. Figures 1.4 and 1.5 show the relationship for the period 2008–2014, which is approximately the crisis management period for most EU member states. They confirm the argument that Greece is an extreme case in the austerity and growth

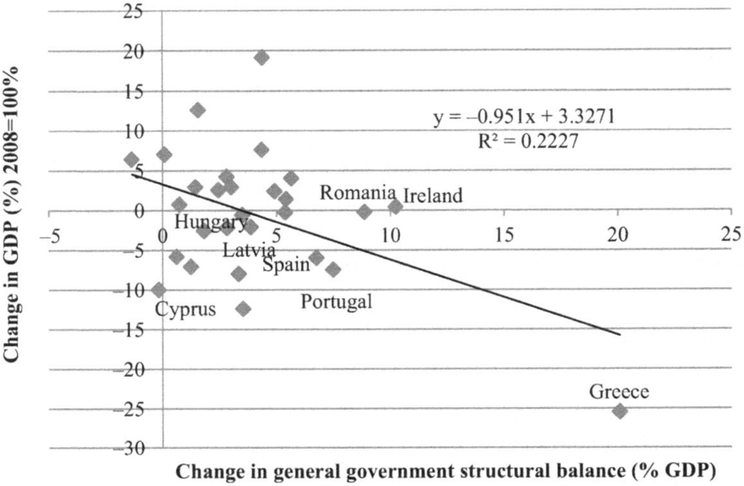

Fig. 1.4 Fiscal tightening and growth in the European Union 2008–2014 (Notes: Fiscal tightening is measured by the difference between the highest level of imbalance during the period 2008–2011 and the balance in 2014. In order to exclude one-off and cyclical factors, the general government structural balance date is used from the IMF World Economic Outlook Database. For measuring change in GDP, the European Commission's AMECO Database is used with 2008 as the starting year)

debate as well as show that once it is excluded from the analysis, we see no relationship between the two phenomena. If we focus only on the eight program countries, the conclusion remains the same—indeed during the period examined, Ireland and Romania implemented the largest consolidation, and they are among the most successful cases of crisis management.

In order to explain the context-dependent relationship between austerity and growth, Monastiriotis (2014) argues that the impact of austerity on growth depends on the openness of the economy and the quality of government—in open economies with high-quality government, successful austerity programs could be implemented without large impact on growth. The openness of the economy can reduce the fiscal multiplier and thus reduce Keynesian effects through two channels: (1) the costs of fiscal austerity can be neutralized by external demand; (2) the wage reduction

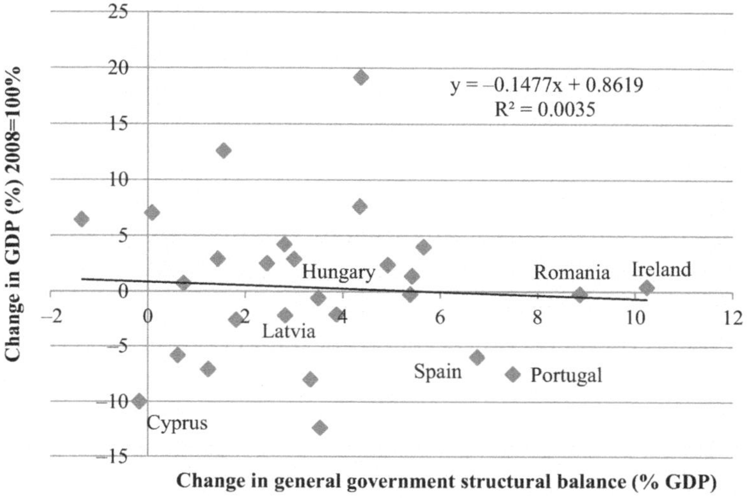

Fig. 1.5 Fiscal tightening and growth in the European Union 2008–2014 (without Greece) (Data: see Fig. 1.4)

coming from austerity provides the most benefits for those with a large export base. High-quality governments "have the ability to design appropriate fiscal measures and implement them in a timely and consensual fashion, through coalition-building and the adoption of non-adversarial policy discourses that justify and legitimize the policy. In such environments, policy exerts a sense of confidence, both domestically and abroad, that raises its credibility thus easing possible concerns about policy reversals and (public or party-political) reform resistances" (Monastiriotis 2014: 82).

The recognition of the importance of domestic institutions in the presence or absence of austerity spiral during the management of the financial crisis recalls earlier research on the difficulties of sustaining a common currency among countries, which show wide divergence in their quality of governance (Boltho and Carlin 2013). Csaba (2014: 28–29) also calls attention to the fact that economic models often disregard factors such as rule of law, security of property rights, independence of the judiciary, democracy, and human rights. In the Eastern (and Southern) parts of the EU, these institutional factors cannot be taken for granted, and they seem to be critical in designing economic policy and the success or failure of crisis management. From a somewhat different perspective, Farkas (2016) also underlines the key role of domestic institutions—she argues that the model of capitalism strongly determined the method of crisis management all across the EU.

The quality of domestic institutions can provide the clue to explain the differences in crisis management outcomes in the eight program countries. The high-quality governance in Ireland resulted in a clearly superior crisis management performance than Greece with its proverbially low-quality administration. The more open economies of the Eastern member states showed faster recovery than the less integrated Mediterranean countries. However, these factors still do not explain the Hungarian case, which registered a considerably weaker recovery than Latvia or Romania in spite of its superior institutions prior to the crisis and its greater level of openness. The case also shows that we cannot take institutional quality as a constant and its changes also require explanation. Since institutions are by their nature political, the politics of crisis management cannot be excluded from the analysis. Thus the main question for the research becomes: how do institutions influence the outcomes of crisis management, and how does crisis management influence institutions?

In order to answer the above question, the following issues need to be addressed in the specific context of individual cases:

- How do institutions shape the negotiations over program conditionality?
- How do institutions influence the implementation of the program?
- How do institutions influence the reception of the program by the public and by the markets?
- How do institutions change during the management of the crisis?
- What is the role of domestic and external actors in institutional change?

Before addressing these issues, a theoretical framework is necessary to explain how institutions govern social relationships and how they contribute to the presence or absence of trust in those relationships.

1.3 Institutions and Trust: The Theory in a Nutshell

A starting point in analyzing success or failure in crisis management is the recognition that the outcome is shaped by a series of relationships in which cooperation is necessary. During the negotiation phase, representatives of the international institutions work together with representatives of the government setting the terms for the agreement. During the implementation of the program, the government has to explain the public the need for painful policies and thus gain the acceptance and cooperation of its constituency. Ultimately it is the confidence of the markets determining whether a country succeeds in returning to the financial markets and attracting investment.

Understanding crisis management as a series of relationships provides a central role for trust as a basis for cooperation. While there are various definitions of trust in the literature, a cross-disciplinary analysis by Rousseau et al. (1998: 395) show a common understanding of the concept as "a psychological state comprising the intention to accept vulnerability based upon the positive expectations of the intentions or behavior of another."[5] The positive expectations can come from the particular social structure (control) or the benign intentions and capability of the other party. As explained by Das and Teng (1998) as well as Möllering (2005), trust and control are part of a duality, which cannot be reduced to one another. Trust cannot be reduced to control, while control cannot be completely given up on the basis of trust. Still, it is easy to see the possibility for control and trust to act as substitutes—the more trusted a partner is, the less control appears necessary. In terms of the program negotiations, a central argument of the book is that the more trust there is among the negotiating partners, the less onerous is the conditionality. During the implementation phase, the more trusted is the government by the public, the less resistance can be expected against the sacrifices necessary during crisis management. Finally, market trust manifests itself in lower risk premium and greater investment.

Institutions enter the picture as a crucial source of trust.

According to the classical definition by Douglass North (1995: 3), institutions are "the rules of the game … humanly devised constraints that shape human interaction" and thus reduce uncertainty in the society. In order to fulfill these functions, institutions can be formal or informal. Formal institutions have a hierarchy "from constitutions, to statute and common laws, to specific bylaws, and finally to individual contracts" (North 1995: 47). These rules are generally written, adopted, and enforced by official bodies such as parliaments, governments, and courts. Informal institutions are unwritten social rules, which are enforced outside of the official channels and transmitted through socialization into the relevant community. They are usually substitutes for formal rules, if the latter are incomplete, their application would be too costly or are implicitly rejected by the relevant actors (Helmke and Levitsky 2004: 730).

From the perspective of economic growth, four sets of institutions are crucial (World Bank 2002): the provision of information for economic actors, the security of property rights, and the enforcement of contracts as well as the maintenance of market competition. These institutions suppose the presence of checks and balances for the state administration, which ensures that the government can commit itself to rules-based policies.

The government's ability to tie its hands through the respect for the rule of law is considered as a crucial source of trust in the research. A basic understanding of the concept is composed of three elements (Tamanaha 2004: 114–126): the government limited by the law, formal legality—public, prospective laws with the qualities of generality, equality of application, and certainty—and rule of law, not men implying the separation of powers and the independence of the judiciary.[6] The importance of limited government for trust is straightforward: only the recognition of the limits of power allows the government to make credible promises. Without such limits the problem of time inconsistency becomes dominant: a decision, which appears optimal at a certain point of time, might not be optimal at a later point of time (Kydland and Prescott 1977). As other actors recognize this reality, they will be unwilling to cooperate with an actor not committed to rules. During the management of crisis the credibility of the commitment of the government to implement conditionality is indispensable for an agreement. For the public the acceptance of sacrifices requires a belief in the commitment of the government to the public good rather than particular interests. The markets expect loans to be repaid and investments to bear profits. If trust is missing because the government is not committed to rules, more control becomes necessary or cooperation will fail.

In the management of financial crises the presence or absence of trust gives rise to self-reinforcing cycles. If a government is committed to rules-based behavior, it is likely to be trusted during the negotiations and is allowed to design its own adjustment plan, which is more likely to be accepted by the public. The implementation of the program fuels market confidence, which helps the program succeeding. Institutions during this process remain stable. If checks and balances on the government do not work properly, distrust dominates the entire process. As the government is not trusted during the negotiations, excessive control becomes necessary—this implies tough conditionality, which is likely to be strongly resisted by the public. As the markets see the resistance, interest rates remain high and investments suffer. The prolonged recovery fuels distrust in institutions, which can come under attack from two fronts—populist forces trying to destabilize the government as well as the government itself, which tries to push through its crisis management measures. In order to stop the deterioration of institutions external forces have to step in—reducing the autonomy of national-level decision-making even further.

In order to see how this theory works in reality, a deeper analysis of the eight cases is necessary.

1.4 Methodology

Researching trust and institutions is notoriously difficult. According to Lyon et al. (2012: 2), there are over 70 definitions of trust in social science. Without an accepted definition, operationalization and measurement are very challenging. The same is true for institutions. In addressing the issue of external incentives to improve institutions, Rodríguez-Pose (2013: 1040) argues that one of the main difficulties is that "measuring what are adequate, solid, and efficient institutions is virtually impossible." At the same time given their importance, researchers should find ways to overcome these problems.

The use of case studies can be very helpful in mitigating the difficulties of conceptualization, operationalization, and measurement. Unlike in quantitative studies, there is no need to reduce a complex phenomenon into a single number (George and Bennett 2005: 50). In assessing the level of trust or institutions, beyond the usual indices and surveys, interviews and the analysis of historical context can be used in parallel. While this approach gives greater weight to the subjective judgment of the researcher, such triangulation of empirical evidence can help to increase the validity and credibility of the research (Rothbauer 2008).

Another important advantage of case studies is the focus on causality, which provides the link between a hypothesized cause and an effect[7] rather than just mere correlation between two variables. The attention to processes, which shape the outcome, allows tracing the impact of the hypothesized causes. A historical analysis of events generally provides a deeper understanding of the causality than the study of one point in time. It is similar to the difference between a movie and a photograph—without understanding the buildup to the main event, it is very difficult to grasp what exactly happened.

While case studies are often criticized for a "confirming bias," which means cases are chosen in order to confirm a certain theory (Flyvberg 2006: 221), in reality a deeper empirical analysis of multiple cases is likely to reveal factors, which are not included into the theoretical framework. While the theory in this book focuses on trust and institutions, the empirical evidence clearly shows that other factors such as power, the particular choices of the elites, or ideology play an important role in the outcomes. A recognition for these factors allow the definition of scope conditions for the theory as well as make us realize that aggregate social phenomena are generally the result of numerous factors at work rather than a single cause. The focus on any single factor requires ceteris paribus conditions. While these are very difficult to attain in social science research, a careful comparison of the evidence from several case studies can help to eliminate competing causal mechanisms as explanation for the outcomes.

The above methodological considerations imply a rather pragmatic approach to researching the management of the financial crisis in the eight countries under consideration. All cases will be examined from a historical perspective with a particular attention to the role of the state in the economy and the quality of institutions. While the historical perspective provides the broader picture of the institutions and the level of trust in the given country, I will not refrain from using aggregate indices to summarize the quality of institutions or the level of trust.

In the aggregate assessment of institutions and trust, two measures will be assessed for each case: the World Governance Indicators (WGI) and the satisfaction with democracy by Eurobarometer. The WGI examines the quality of governance in 213 countries every year based on 31 data sources. The index measures six dimensions of governance: voice and accountability, political stability and absence of violence, government effectiveness, regulatory quality, rule of law and control of corruption. The scores range between −2.5 and 2.5.[8] The satisfaction with democracy of the Eurobarometer is simpler, as is a survey measure based on the following questions: on the whole, are you very satisfied, fairly satisfied, or not very satisfied with the way democracy works in the EU/your country? In the literature both indicators are often criticized as being too general and vague (Canache et al. 2001; Thomas 2010). However, they have the undeniable advantage of making comparison of a wide range of countries possible. In the research they are interpreted along with contextual and historical evidence.

Examining trust during the negotiations with the IMF and the Troika is even more difficult than measuring trust and institutions at the country level. In this case there is not even an imperfect number for assessment. Consequently I rely on various sources of evidence and attempt to provide a narrative about what happened. Official statements are widely available from these meetings. The evaluations by the IMF are particularly helpful as they describe the discussion with authorities as well as the impressions about those discussions. There is also secondary literature about individual countries, where interviews with participating officials are described. Newspapers provide another source of useful insights into the dynamics of the negotiations. Finally, participants often voice their opinions about the events on personal websites such as internet blogs. In assessing the negotiations, there is also some more objective evidence, which includes the length of negotiations or the number of conditions in the program.

The research assesses market trust and economic outcomes in a more conventional manner—long-term interest rates on ten-year government bonds are taken as an indicator for the confidence of the market. In order to trace shifting expectations over individual countries, special attention is paid to the existence of gaps between projections and outcomes through using the IMF World Economic Outlook database. Otherwise, data on macroeconomic aggregates primarily relies on European Commission statistics and occasionally on the databases of the European Central Bank (ECB) and the World Bank.

With all the uncertainties about conceptualization, operationalization, measurement, and causality, the research aims to uncover a wide range of sources and wave them into a coherent narrative. The outcome is an account of processes and tendencies rather than definitive laws in the sense of natural sciences. The scientific value of the narrative depends on its evaluation against competing narratives. An institutional analysis of the financial crisis thus does not aim at presenting the final word about European crisis management, but it is rather an effort to improve on the prevailing narratives, which were presented in the previous section.

1.5 The Structure of the Book

The next chapter provides an overview of the financial crisis in the euro-zone. First it examines the origins of the crisis, then recounts the EU-level steps taken to fight the crisis including the establishment of emergency funds, the interventions of the ECB as well as institutional changes. The second part of the chapter considers those paths, which were not taken during the crisis management—the breakup of the euro-zone, the establishment of Eurobonds, or a transfer union. The main argument of the chapter is that in an attempt to balance considerations of moral hazard and solidarity during the management of the crisis, a strong divide opened between the North and the South of the EU, which presented a rather distrustful environment for crisis management.

The third chapter takes a closer look on the relationship between trust and crisis management. First, it provides an introduction into the concept of trust emphasizing the elements of vulnerability, uncertainty about the future and subjectivity. Then it discusses different forms of interpersonal and institutional trust. The second part of the chapter describes how trust plays a role in the various stages of crisis management—negotiations, implementation, and market reception. The chapter ends with a theoretical framework describing austerity spirals as the outcome of distrust during crisis management.

The fourth chapter applies the theoretical framework to the contrasting experiences of Ireland and Greece. The two countries can be considered as model cases to provide an illustration about how the theory works. The chapter recounts the role of the state in the two countries showing the difference between an outward-oriented economy with high-quality governance, and an inward-oriented country with poor governance. After both needed international financial assistance, these differences proved to be crucial in the management of the crisis. The two cases show how trust at all levels of crisis management results in successful recovery from the crisis in Ireland, while distrust leads to a vicious spiral of recession in Greece.

The fifth chapter uses the experiences of three other Mediterranean countries—Cyprus, Portugal, and Spain—as counterfactual cases for Greece. It asks the question how these countries succeeded in avoiding the fate of Greece despite sharing many similarities with its model of capitalism. The key explanation appears to be a shared elite commitment to the implementation of the program even though the three countries faced a very different set of conditions due to their varied negotiating power. In all three cases, public trust in the elite collapsed, but mainstream parties succeeded in preventing populist challengers taking over the government. However, following the exit from the program, reform fatigue set in indicating the limits of elite-driven reforms during a period of crisis.

The sixth chapter examines the cases of Hungary, Latvia, and Romania, which were the first countries hit by the crisis. At the time, neither of them was in the euro-zone, while low level of trust and weak institutions characterize them similarly to the Mediterranean states. The main question in these cases is to what extent the findings from the euro-zone apply to them as well. The analysis shows that the three countries represent three different models—while Latvia most resembles to the Irish case, Romania shares many similarities with the Mediterranean countries. Hungary is a case by itself—the level of distrust with the international community makes it similar to Greece, but as it successfully avoided a second international assistance program, it could follow a populist adjustment path financed by the global markets and EU transfers. The chapter argues that their greater integration into the global economy strongly influenced the success of the adjustment in these countries.

The seventh chapter asks the question how crisis management is related to the emergence of populism. First it provides a summary of the main findings from the case studies on the relationship between institutions, trust, and crisis management. Then it elaborates on the idea of limited government, which involves the rule of law, international rule of law, size of government, political and civil liberties. By reviewing the changes in these dimensions during the period of crisis management in the eight countries, it categorizes the cases into three groups, which show different characteristics along these lines. The main argument of the chapter is the central argument of the book: a commitment to limited government is associated with both economic success and resistance to populism. In contrast, a steady deterioration of institutions without an elite commitment to checks and balances eventually resulted in the takeover of government by populist forces in Greece and Hungary. While the latter did not experience an economic collapse, its performance is inferior to both Latvia and Romania.

Within the context of discussions of the future of Europe, the last chapter asks how the EU can contribute to the strengthening of institutions at the domestic level. It is argued that precautionary measures are more desirable than strengthening punishment mechanisms—the integration of institutional development into EU competitiveness and regional policy as well as reducing moral hazard on the financial markets are more likely to succeed in building a resilient institutional framework than enhancing Article 7 although that also appears a necessary step. The main conclusion from the chapter is that stronger domestic institutions and higher level of trust are necessary to bridge the gap between concerns of solidarity and moral hazard, which arise from plans about deeper integration.

Notes

1. Sapir et al. (2014) use similar variables to assess the success of crisis management.
2. The relationship between increased debt and current account deficit will be discussed in greater depth in Chap. 2.
3. Data from ECB at: https://www.ecb.europa.eu/stats/exchange/eurofxref/html/index.en.html.
4. This represented an important shift in the IMF position from the defender of the pre-crisis status quo to a more nuanced understanding of fiscal policy. For a detailed analysis of this shift, see Ban (2015).
5. The concept will be explained more in depth in Chap. 3.
6. There will be a deeper discussion of the concept in Chap. 7.
7. Causality is another very difficult philosophical concept not only for the social sciences. In the research I follow Gerring's approach, who argues that a minimal definition of a cause is that "X may be considered a cause of Y if (and only if) it raises the probability of Y" (Gerring 2005: 169).
8. For a deeper discussion of the WGI methodology, see Kaufmann et al. (2010).

References

Alesina, Alberto, and Roberto Perotti. 1995. *Fiscal expansions and fiscal adjustments in OECD countries*. NBER Working Paper No. 5214.

Alesina, Alberto, Roberto Perotti, and Jose Tavares. 1998. The political economy of fiscal adjustments. *Brookings Papers on Economic Activity* 29 (1): 197–266.

Alesina, Alberto, Omar Barbiero, Carlo Favero, Francesco Giavazzi, and Matteo Paradisi. 2015. *Austerity in 2009–2013*. NBER Working Paper No. 20827.

Ban, Cornel. 2015. Austerity versus stimulus? Understanding fiscal policy change at the International Monetary Fund since the Great Recession. *Governance* 28 (2): 167–183.

Blanchard, Oliver, and Daniel Leigh. 2013. *Growth forecast errors and fiscal multipliers*. IMF Working Paper No. 13/1. Cambridge, MA: National Bureau of Economic Research.

Blyth, Mark. 2013. *Austerity: The history of a dangerous idea*. Oxford: Oxford University Press.

Boltho, Andrea, and Wendy Carlin. 2013. EMU's problems: Asymmetric shocks or asymmetric behavior? *Comparative Economic Studies* 55 (3): 387–403.

Bromhead, Alan de, Barry Eichengreen, and Kevin H. O'Rourke. 2012. *Right-wing political extremism in the Great Depression.* Discussion Papers in Economic and Social History No. 95. Oxford: University of Oxford.

Canache, Damarys, Jeffery J. Mondak, and Mitchell A. Seligson. 2001. Meaning and measurement in cross-national research on satisfaction with democracy. *Public Opinion Quarterly* 65 (4): 506–528.

Csaba, László. 2014. Developmental perspectives on Europe. *Society and Economy* 36 (1): 21–36.

Darvas, Zsolt, and Olga Tschekassin. 2015. *Poor and under pressure: The social impact of Europe's fiscal consolidation.* Bruegel Working Paper No. 2015/04.

Das, T.K., and Bing-Sheng Teng. 1998. Between trust and control: Developing confidence in partner organizations in alliances. *Academy of Management Review* 23 (3): 491–512.

European Commission. 2017. *Statistical annex of European economy, Spring.* Brussels: Commission of the European Communities Directorate General for Economic and Financial Affairs.

Farkas, Beáta. 2016. *Models of capitalism in the European Union: Post-crisis perspectives.* London: Palgrave Macmillan.

Flyvberg, Bent. 2006. Five misunderstanding about case-study research. *Qualitative Inquiry* 12 (2): 219–245.

Gechert, Sebastian, and Ansgar Rannenberg. 2014. *Are fiscal multipliers regime-dependent? A meta regression analysis.* IMK Working Paper No. 139. Available: http://www.boeckler.de/pdf/p_imk_wp_139_2014.pdf. Accessed 2 July 2017.

George, Alexander, and Andrew Bennett. 2005. *Case studies and theory development in the social sciences.* Cambridge, MA: MIT Press.

Gerring, John. 2005. Causation: A unified framework for the social sciences. *Journal of Theoretical Politics* 17 (2): 163–198.

Giavazzi, Francesco, and Luigi Spaventa. 2011. Why the current account may matter in a monetary union: Lessons from the financial crisis in the euro area. In *The euro area and the financial crisis*, ed. Miroslav Beblavy, 199–221. Cambridge: Cambridge University Press.

Giavazzi, Francesco, and Marco Pagano. 1990. *Can severe fiscal consolidations be expansionary? Tales of two small European countries.* NBER Working Paper No. 3372.

Grauwe, Paul De, and Yuemei Ji. 2013. Panic-driven austerity in the eurozone and its implications. *VoxEU*, February 21. Available: http://www.voxeu.org/article/panic-driven-austerity-eurozone-and-its-implications. Accessed 2 July 2017.

Hall, Peter A. 2012. The economics and politics of the euro crisis. *German Politics* 21 (4): 355–371.

Helmke, Gretchen, and Steven Levitsky. 2004. Informal institutions and comparative politics: A research agenda. *Perspectives on Politics* 2 (4): 725–740.

IMF. 2010. Will it hurt? Macroeconomic effects of fiscal consolidation. In *World Economic Outlook –October 2010*, 93–124. Washington: IMF.

Kaufmann, Daniel, Aart Kraay, and Massimo Mastruzzi. 2010. *The Worldwide Governance Indicators: Methodology and analytical issues*. World Bank Policy Research Working Paper No. 5430.

Kriesi, Hanspeter. 2012. The political consequences of the financial and economic crisis in Europe: Electoral punishment and popular protest. *Swiss Political Science Review* 18 (4): 518–522.

Krugman, Paul. 2011. Can Europe be saved? *New York Times*, January 12.

———. 2013. How the case for austerity has crumbled. *The New York Review of Books* 60 (10). Available: http://www.nybooks.com/articles/archives/2013/jun/06/how-case-austerity-has-crumbled/?pagination=false. Accessed 2 July 2017.

Kydland, Finn E., and Edward Prescott. 1977. Rules rather than discretion: The inconsistency of optimal plans. *Journal of Political Economy* 85 (3): 473–491.

Lane, Philip R. 2012. The European sovereign debt crisis. *Journal of Economic Perspectives* 26 (3): 49–68.

Larch, Martin, Paul Van den Noord, and Lars Jonung. 2010. *The stability and growth pact: Lessons from the Great Recession*. Munich Personal RePEc Archive Paper No. 27900. Available: https://mpra.ub.uni-muenchen.de/27900/1/MPRA_paper_27900.pdf. Accessed 2 July 2017.

Lindvall, Johannes. 2014. The electoral consequences of two great crises. *European Journal of Political Research* 53 (4): 747–765.

Lyon, Fergus, Guido Möllering, and Mark Saunders. 2012. Introduction: The variety of methods for the multi-faceted phenomenon of trust. In *Handbook of research methods on trust*, ed. Fergus Lyon, Guido Möllering, and Mark Saunders, 1–18. Cheltenham/Northampton: Edward Elgar.

Mody, Ashoka. 2015. *Living (dangerously) without a fiscal union*. Bruegel Working Paper No. 2015/03.

Möllering, Guido. 2005. The trust/control duality: An integrative perspective on positive expectations of others. *International Sociology* 20 (3): 283–305.
Monastiriotis, Vassilis. 2014. (When) does austerity work? On the conditional link between fiscal austerity and debt sustainability. *Cyprus Economic Policy Review* 8 (1): 71–92.
North, Douglass C. 1995. *Institutions, institutional change, and economic performance*. Cambridge: Cambridge University Press.
Perotti, Roberto. 2011. *The austerity myth: Gain without pain?* NBER Working Paper No. 17571.
Rodríguez-Pose, Andrés. 2013. Do institutions matter for regional development? *Regional Studies* 47 (7): 1034–1047.
Rothbauer, Paulette. 2008. Triangulation. In *The SAGE encyclopedia of qualitative research methods*, ed. Lisa Given, 893–894. Thousand Oaks: SAGE.
Rousseau, Denise M., Sim B. Sitkin, Ronald S. Burt, and Colin Camerer. 1998. Not so different after all: A cross-discipline view of trust. *Academy of Management Review* 25 (3): 393–404.
Sapir, André, Guntram B. Wolff, Carlos de Sousa, and Alessio Terzi. 2014. *The Troika and financial assistance in the euro area: Successes and failures*. Study on the request of the Economic and Monetary Affairs Committee. Available: http://www.bruegel.org/publications/publication-detail/publication/815-the-troika-and-financial-assistance-in-the-euro-area-successes-and-failures/. Accessed 2 July 2017.
Schuknecht, Ludger, Philippe Moutot, Philipp Rother, and Jürgen Stark. 2011. *The Stability and Growth Pact – Crisis and reform*. ECB Occasional Paper No. 129. Frankfurt: European Central Bank.
Sinn, Hans-Werner. 2014. *The euro trap: On bursting bubbles, budgets and beliefs*. Oxford: Oxford University Press.
Tamanaha, Brian. 2004. *On the rule of law: History, politics, theory*. Cambridge: Cambridge University Press.
Thomas, M.A. 2010. What do the Worldwide Governance Indicators measure? *European Journal of Development Research* 22 (1): 31–54.
WEF. 2006. *The global competitiveness report 2006/2007*. Geneva: World Economic Forum.
———. 2016. *The global competitiveness report 2016/2017*. Geneva: World Economic Forum.
World Bank. 2002. *World development report: Building institutions for markets*. Washington, DC: World Bank.

2

A Bird's-Eye View of Crisis Management in the Euro-Zone

Before understanding how trust played a role in crisis management in countries, which needed international financial assistance, it is important to understand the European context. What were the roots of the crisis in the euro-zone? How did the EU respond? What are the paths not taken? Which actors were empowered or disempowered by the crisis? These issues lingered in the background of every individual program negotiation.

The chapter provides a bird's-eye narrative about the main dilemmas associated with crisis management. It recounts the unpreparedness of the EU to respond to the crisis, the political difficulties of offering financial assistance in a transparent manner, and the crucial role played by the ECB in halting the crisis by managing expectations. As German policy-makers attempted to balance the persistent moral hazard problems in the EMU (Economic and Monetary Union), a new framework for economic governance emerged, which further de-politicized economic policy and provided greater surveillance power to the technocrats in the European Commission over elected national officials. The experiences of the crisis strongly increased distrust between the North and the South of the EU—while the former begrudged the financial contributions it had to make during the crisis and worried

D. Győrffy, *Trust and Crisis Management in the European Union*,
https://doi.org/10.1007/978-3-319-69212-8_2

about moral hazard, the latter felt bitter about the conditionality and the apparent lack of solidarity.

The structure of the chapter is the following. The next section will discuss the roots of the financial crisis in the euro-zone followed by a brief timeline about its main events. Afterward the chapter provides an overview about the main measures adopted to contain the crisis and then lists some of those measures, which are often seen as solutions but have not been implemented. In the fourth section, the various responses are jointly evaluated, and the dilemma between moral hazard and solidarity is discussed.

2.1 The Road to the Crisis

The roots of the euro-zone financial crisis have been widely debated. Jones (2015) offers an overview of four competing narratives on the roots of the crisis: sudden stop of capital flows, competitiveness problems in the periphery, government financial imbalances, and growing household debts. He argues that while these explanations are not necessarily contradictory, the emphasis on one or another explanation shapes the policy responses to the crisis—from a political economy perspective "the policy that shunts the burdens of adjustment elsewhere seems the most 'logical' to adopt" (Jones 2015: 818). Based on comparative evidence on the main narratives of the European financial crisis, he concludes that the sudden stop explanation has the most explanatory power.

The immediate cause of the eruption of financial crisis might well be the reversal of capital flows. At the same time, we cannot forget about the deeper causes of the crisis, which led to sudden stop in some countries but not in others. We should also remember that financial crises are dynamic incidents, and no explanation can disregard their temporal dimension. If we look at crises from the time vulnerabilities build up to the eruption, we can integrate the various explanations of the crisis into a coherent narrative, and we do not have to make an either-or choice of explanations, which would oversimplify a complex phenomenon.

Existing theories of financial crisis, which were built on cases other than the ones under scrutiny, offer a method to analyze the European financial crisis from a dynamic perspective. The primacy of finance is well supported by these theories. On the basis of historical evidence Kindelberger and Aliber (2005) as well as Reinhart and Rogoff (2009) argue that monetary expansion is the root cause of crises. Increased credit supply leads to a process, when asset prices are less and less determined by fundamental factors and are rather driven by expectations about their future price. As asset bubbles emerge, the vulnerability of the economy to crisis increases. This stage is characterized by growing indebtedness, underpricing of risks as well as scams and swindles (Kindelberger and Aliber 2005: 165–171). The crisis hits after an unfavorable shock occurs, investors' expectations change, and the general selling of assets leads to a self-reinforcing fall in prices. In the following this model will be applied to explain the origins of the European financial crisis.

2.1.1 Monetary Expansion: The Unintended Consequences of the Euro

One of the major reasons for the establishment of the euro was that in the single market different currencies function as non-tariff barriers and hinder free movement. This is particularly true of capital movements. With the introduction of the euro, capital became widely available for all EMU member states—without appropriate pricing of country risks. At the time, this was not seen problematic: the European Commission considered interest rate convergence as a natural outcome of the euro. It expressed concerns only with regard to the persistent inflation rates and the divergence in real interest rates across the euro-zone (European Commission 2008: 77–78). However, in retrospect, it is clear that the nominal convergence in interest rates meant that the institutions established for the euro-zone were unable to provide either bureaucratic or market discipline for individual member states.

Although there was a no-bailout clause included into the Maastricht Treaty,[1] ex post it is clear that this clause was not credible. Following the introduction of the euro up until the eruption of the crisis, there was slight difference between the long-term interest rates in the GIPS countries[2] and Germany (Fig. 2.1). Since the fundamental macroeconomic

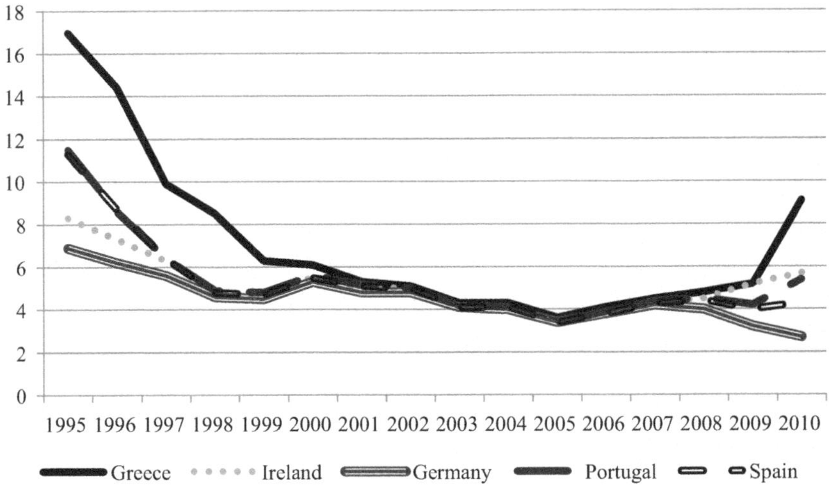

Fig. 2.1 Long-term interest rates (%) in Germany and the GIPS countries 1995–2010 (Data: European Commission 2017: 106)

indicators differed widely in these countries, and we cannot assume that professional investors were unaware of this fact, the explanation for interest rate convergence lies elsewhere.

The first possibility is that markets believed that the Stability and Growth Pact will enforce financial discipline in the member states; thus markets do not have to be concerned about it. While this might have been reasonable prior to 2003, following the non-enforcement of the pact in the case of France and Germany, this belief could not be rationally held. As noted by Chang and Leblond (2015: 630), neither this event nor the change of rules in 2005 caused any market reactions.

The second possibility is that the enormous liquidity, which characterized the financial markets during this period,[3] made market actors insensitive to risks. While this probably played an important role, countries outside the euro-zone did not register an almost complete interest rate convergence with Germany as did Greece.[4]

A third possibility is that markets treated the euro-zone as a single market and held the expectation that if one member gets into trouble, others will come to rescue. This expectation was rather well-founded once we consider that after the establishment of the single market, the increasing concentration in the banking sector led to the emergence of too-big-to-fail banks all across the EU, which could count on public bailouts (Goldstein and Véron 2011: 13). The perception of low risk was further reinforced by international regulations—there is no reserve requirement for holding bonds of advanced OECD (Organization for Economic Co-operation and Development) countries since these are considered risk-free (Gros 2013). This regulation makes lending to advanced countries very attractive to meet capital requirements, even at interest rates, which are lower than what would be justified by a country's fundamentals (Bartha and Schelke 2015: 834). The ECB also treated all euro-area government debt equally, and allowed their use as collateral without any haircut (Brunnermeier et al. 2016: 99–100). Finally, the construction of the ECB system also allowed unlimited overdraft facilities in the form of emergency liquidity assistance (ELA), which made it likely that the ECB could facilitate as a lender of last resort in case of a crisis (Sinn 2014: 258). Together these factors sent a message to investors that lending to euro-zone countries was safe.

The second and third possibilities complement each other well, and lead investors toward taking greater risks. This implies that serious moral hazard emerged in the system, which means that the risks and benefits of an investment are not held by the same actor—while investors heap any profits, the risks are born by the taxpayers. In retrospect it is also clear that expectations about a bailout were largely justified.

The absence of either market or bureaucratic discipline[5] exacerbated one of the fundamental problems of the euro-zone—given the divergence in the rates of economic growth, interest rates set by the ECB proved to be too low for certain countries such as Ireland, and led to negative real interest rates for an extended period. This means that it was perfectly rational to consume any income in the present and take loans since the money would be worth less in the future. Increasing indebtedness was encouraged in all sectors of the economy—state, companies, and households. The availability of credit was an important objective of the establishment of the euro-zone, but in retrospect it is clear that it had severe unintended effects.

2.1.2 Emergence of Vulnerabilities: Competitiveness Problems in the Periphery

During the early years of the euro, there was a general sentiment that the common currency will force structural reforms, and competitiveness will improve in all participating member states. This was the perspective of TINA (There Is No Alternative)[6]: with the loss of independent monetary policy, adjustment to asymmetric shocks necessitates structural reforms.[7]

The possibility for seemingly unlimited indebtedness significantly eased the pressure for reforms. The availability of credit led to the overheating of the economies of the periphery and provided the illusion of growth. Facilitating such credit boom appeared much more rewarding politically than implementing long-term oriented reforms, which are painful in the short term. In an OECD report just before the crisis (OECD 2007), the neglect of recommendations for structural reforms was a prominent theme.

During the overheating of an economy consumption surges and the increased demand leads to a rise in prices and wages. In the course of this process bubbles can emerge on the real estate or other markets. The increase of wages above productivity leads to the loss of competitiveness vis-à-vis foreign trade partners and becomes manifest in the growing current account deficit.[8] The need to finance this deficit makes the country vulnerable to the sentiments of international financial markets.

The evolution of wages and the current account in Germany and the GIPS countries are shown by Figs. 2.2 and 2.3. As we can see Fig. 2.2, Germany kept its wages relatively stable during this period. This was due to the implementation of the so-called Hartz reforms, which lowered taxes on capital and labor, weakened labor market regulations, and drastically reduced support for long-term unemployment (Scharpf 2011: 175–176). In the periphery countries, we can observe a steady increase in wages, which led to a loss of competitiveness and a deteriorating current account balance.

The differences in the current account balance created a peculiar circulation of money in the European financial system: countries with a surplus invested their excess capital into the periphery countries, which

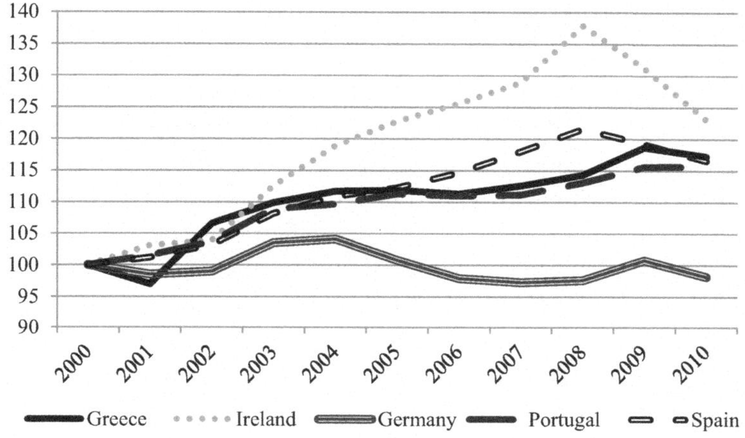

Fig. 2.2 Nominal unit labor costs in Germany and the GIPS countries 2000–2010 (2000=100) (Data: European Commission 2010: 98)

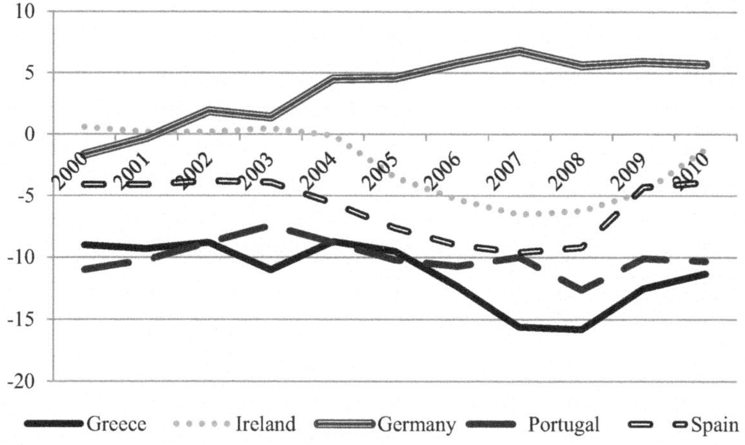

Fig. 2.3 Current account balance in Germany and the GIPS countries 2000–2010 (% of GDP) (Data: European Commission 2017: 96)

could then finance their current account deficits. This interdependence between lenders and borrowers is another unintended consequence of the euro. In 2008 the exposure of French and German banks to the GIPS countries and Italy amounted to 31 percent and 24 percent of their respective GDP (Sinn 2014: 93).

2.1.3 The Eruption of the Crisis

In spite of the existence of serious financial imbalances, the spread of crisis to the euro-zone took many observers by surprise.[9] The Greek crisis started in October 2009 over a year after the collapse of Lehman Brothers when it became evident that the budgetary position of Greece is significantly worse than it was believed—the deficit reached 13.6 percent of GDP instead of 3.7 percent, while the public debt stood at 115 percent of GDP (Aslund 2010: 93). Following these announcements investors lost their belief that Greece can finance its debts, and the risk premium increased significantly (Fig. 2.1)—the country was essentially shut out of the international financial markets.

Although Greece would have needed immediate relief, as a euro-zone member state it was unprecedented to turn to the IMF for help. Instead it took until May 2010 for the EU to put together a financial assistance program (Aslund 2010: 93–95). The lack of prompt response to the evolving crisis led to sustained uncertainty on the markets, and the crisis spread to Ireland then to Portugal, which had to sign a program in November 2010 and May 2011 respectively. However, these responses proved unsuccessful to calm the markets, and in the summer of 2011 European interbank lending rates rose significantly especially for Italy and Spain. The solution was provided by the forceful interventions of the ECB, which brought periphery bonds and provided support to the banking system of the periphery. Still, Spain was forced to sign a program in June 2012 to support its failing banking system. By the end of 2012, the crisis receded, and the 2013 banking crisis in Cyprus did not cause fears similar to the Greek crisis in 2010.

The euro-zone successfully withstood the crisis in spite of the constant criticism of various observers. In the following section, I provide an overview about the main measures taken to address the crisis.

2.2 Crisis Management in the EU

One of the major weaknesses of the euro-zone, which was revealed by the financial crisis, was the lack of crisis management methods. Prior to 2008 an invisible impossible trinity dominated the thinking on the euro-zone, when rules of "no exit, no bail-out and no default" coexisted (Benczes 2013). As countries gave up their monetary sovereignty when joining the EMU, they would have to leave the EU to reintroduce their own currency. The no-bailout clause has been already mentioned in the previous section. The idea of no default meant that there was no institution in place, which could have dealt with a default of a member state—the founders seemed to think such an event was impossible.

Together the three rules explain why it was so difficult to address the Greek crisis early on—Greece could not be bailed out either by other member states or the ECB; it could not default on its debt and it could not leave the euro-zone either. As it became immersed in crisis, a reassessment of the rules became necessary. Since there was no roadmap about how to manage the crisis, the solutions emerged gradually through agreements at European summits and interventions by the ECB. In the following, a brief account is provided about the main steps, which were taken to contain the crisis.

2.2.1 Establishment of Emergency Funds

The first major step to fight the crisis was taken in May 2010 with the establishment of the European Financial Stability Facility (EFSF), which aims to preserve the financial stability in the euro-zone and provide assistance to troubled countries, which cannot raise funds from the markets because of a severe loss of confidence.[10] The EFSF can issue bonds to raise capital on the financial markets up to €440 billion. The bonds are backed by guarantees of the member states in proportion to their share in the reserves of the ECB. Access to the funds is subject to strict conditionality.

In January 2011 another emergency fund was created by the EU, the European Financial Stability Mechanism (EFSM), which could be used by all EU countries in case of financial difficulties. The total amount of resource in this fund is €60 billion backed by the budget of the EU as collateral. Similarly to the EFSF, access to this fund is subject to strict conditionality.

The EU has finally set up a permanent rescue facility, the European Stability Mechanism (ESM) in 2012 as a successor to EFSF. Together with the EFSM, they are able to access €700 billion,[11] composed of €80 billion from member state contribution and raising funds from the financial markets on the basis of guarantees by member states. While there have been considerable fears that the German constitutional court declares the project as unconstitutional because of the lack of democratic control over taxpayers' money, the September 2012 decision of the court gave green light to the fund (Sinn 2014: 269).

These emergency funds filled an important gap in the institutional structure of the EMU and made the bailing out of troubled countries possible in an orderly manner. Given their design and strong conditionality, they are the least likely to give rise to moral hazard problems.

At the same time, the size of these funds is clearly insufficient if larger countries need assistance—the debt level of Italy or France is over €2000 billion.[12] The limitation of resources also implies that the danger of a speculative attack cannot be excluded—in case of a loss of confidence investors may try to get rid of the bonds before the fund is completely exhausted. As De Grauwe (2012) called attention, such expectations can easily become self-fulfilling prophesies. A further difficulty of these funds is that as the number of countries, which need to be rescued, increases, the number of countries, which have to bear the burden of rescuing them, decreases. In light of this danger, Moody's downgraded the outlook for Germany from stable to negative in July 2012.[13]

Given the problems of size as well as the time necessary to establish the funds, other interventions were needed in order to fight the ongoing financial crisis. Such emergency measures came from the ECB.

2.2.2 The Interventions by the ECB

The loss of confidence on the markets triggered several different interventions by the ECB from the outbreak of the crisis.[14] The two major measures were the various bond purchase programs and the long-term refinancing operations, which were aimed to help the troubled euro-zone countries.

In 2010 the ECB introduced its Securities Markets Program (SMP) and began buying government bonds from periphery countries, which could not raise financing on the market at a reasonable interest rate. SMP holdings reached €218 billion by December 2012.[15] The move appeared contradictory with the mandate of the ECB, which explicitly excludes the possibility of buying up government debt. Although in February 2012 the program was suspended, responding to market and member state pressure, in September 2012 the president of the ECB, Mario Draghi, announced the start of a new unlimited bond purchase program called Outright Monetary Transactions (OMT), which was designed to lower the borrowing costs of countries in trouble.[16] The move proved to be very effective to calm the markets without the ECB having to buy any new government bonds (Sinn 2014: 260).

The ECB also provided liquidity support to troubled European banks in the form of long-term refinancing operations (LTROs). In December 2011 and February 2012, €429.2 and 529.5 billion credit was given at a 1 percent interest rate to 523 and 800 European banks for a period of three years.[17] Most of these funds went to banks on the periphery. However, according to Sinn (2014: 255) these moves only boosted capital flight and were akin "to attempting to extinguish fire with gasoline." The accelerating capital flight showed up in the euro settlement system (TARGET—Trans-European Automated Real-time Gross Settlement Express Transfer System). While these balances do not matter until the euro-zone remains intact, if a country leaves the euro-zone, defaulting on these claims becomes a possibility. High TARGET imbalances can thus improve the bargaining power of troubled member states (Brunnermeier et al. 2016: 343). As Sinn (2014: 259) argues this "basically amounted to lending the printing press from the North to the South (and West) of the euro-zone."

The interventions of the ECB probably went against the no-bailout clause of the Maastricht Treaty,[18] and they certainly did not help to alleviate the problem of moral hazard in the euro-zone. At the same time, it is also clear that after the announcement of OMT, the crisis finally abated (Chang and Leblond 2015: 648).

2.2.3 Institutional Reforms

The establishment of rescue funds and the interventions of the ECB were emergency reactions to the ongoing crisis. However, given the persistent competitiveness problems in the periphery, the EU also implemented several institutional changes, which aimed to improve economic governance.[19]

In September 2010 the European semester was decided upon in order to increase economic surveillance and coordination. The major objective of this process, which integrates the surveillance over fiscal policy and structural programs, is to provide feedback on national measures prior to making the decision. The program gives a large role to the European Commission, which evaluates the national programs.

A second major initiative was the Euro-Plus Pact, which was adopted in March 2011. The aim of this program is to harmonize economic policies in the EU[20] in the fields of competitiveness, employment, fiscal sustainability, financial stability, and tax policies. The method of enforcement is the open method of coordination, which basically means that compliance with the objectives is largely voluntary. The first report on progress was issued in November 2011 (Schmieding et al. 2011), and a clear divergence was already noted among participating countries—those, which needed financial bailout made substantial progress, while others, which had been lagging behind but did not need a rescue package, such as France or Italy, did not make progress.

A more comprehensive institutional change was the adoption of the so-called Six-pack, which entered into force in December 2011. The pack strengthens the enforcement of the Stability and Growth Pact (SGP) through earlier and quasi-automatic sanctioning. The major novelty of the Six-pack is the introduction of a macroeconomic surveillance mechanism,[21] where non-compliance can also lead to fines. The mechanism was introduced in order to increase the credibility of the commitment toward financial stability in the member states. At the same time, there are at least three major criticisms against it. First, it is highly questionable whether countries at different level of development need the same thresholds (Neményi and Oblath 2012: 652). This could easily lead to the renewal of debate on the economic foundation of the rules, which was one of the major issues in the earlier SGP. This leads to the second problem about the limits of our knowledge. Prior to the crisis, there were serious debates about whether there exist asset price bubbles at all,[22] and now we pretend to know the precise indicators of bubbles and use these as basis for possible punishment. This is particularly questionable in light of the poor performance of early warning mechanisms in predicting financial crises.[23] Finally as Scharpf (2011: 189) calls attention, in contrast to debt and fiscal deficit, governments have no direct influence over the measures of macroeconomic imbalances, which also seriously questions whether punishment for them is realistic.

The Six-pack was followed by the Fiscal Compact[24] in March 2012 in order to enshrine fiscal discipline in member states. The new rule practically outlaws deficits by envisaging strict punishment for structural deficits over 0.5 percent.[25] It also requires signatories to insert an amendment about fiscal responsibility into their constitution. Similarly to the Six-pack, the major aim of this measure is to signal commitment to fiscal discipline by member states. At the same time, there are very serious problems with the economic foundation of these rules. According to Sawyer (2012) empirical evidence does not support that greater deficits necessarily lead to unsustainable debt path, while calculation of the structural deficit is not uncontested given the debates about how to calculate potential growth upon which this indicator is based.

The last major institutional change is the establishment of a banking union, which was agreed upon in July 2012 (European Council 2012). As recounted by Brunnermeier et al. (2016: 212), the idea of a banking union emerged in the 1980s, but Hans Tietmeyer, then president of the Bundesbank, feared that "supervision by the central bank would implicitly signal a bailout guarantee and hence lead to moral hazard problems." The financial crisis after 2008 changed these calculations. After the ESM was established to assist domestic banking systems through recapitalization, it became imperative for the EU to be able to independently verify the balance-sheet quality of participating financial institutions (Brunnermeier et al. 2016: 218). Banking union was also seen as necessary to break the vicious link between banking and sovereign debt crises (Rynck 2016: 127). In June 2012 an agreement was reached at the European summit about the creation of a banking union. Most progress to date occurred on the area of single supervision with harmonized rules and direct supervisory powers given to the ECB (Rynck 2016: 124). The second pillar of the banking union, the single resolution mechanism entered into force in August 2014 and aims to ensure rapid and effective resolution of failed banks (Brunnermeier et al. 2016: 220). The third pillar of the banking union would be a common deposit insurance, but given the resistance of Germany little progress has been made so far.

Overall we can conclude that the responses to the crisis strongly reflect the circumstances under which they were introduced. Their adoption does not indicate the existence of a clear roadmap but rather suggests a trial and error process in order to calm the markets. When evaluating this process, it is insufficient to consider only the measures, which were adopted. To gain a clear picture, we also have to consider the roads, which could have been taken but were rejected. In the following section I will provide an overview about the major rejected measures: exit from the euro-zone, Eurobonds, and transfer union.

2.3 Rejected Measures of Crisis Management

2.3.1 Exit from the Euro-Zone

In light of the Greek crisis there was a widespread opinion that it would be better for all to let Greece exit the euro-zone.[26] The major reason for exit from a Greek perspective was the possibility for independent monetary policy and the devaluation of the exchange rate, which could help to restore competitiveness. A weaker exchange rate and the financing constraint could greatly constrain imports, stimulate exports, and thus improve the current account. Once a troubled country left the euro-zone, an argument could be made that the credibility of the zone increases, and the remaining member states understand the consequences of financial laxity.

The advantages of a possible exit however are greatly outweighed by the probable losses. The collapse of the exchange rate could lead to a debt explosion given the public and private debt in foreign currency. This would be followed by a series of defaults in the private sector, and debt restructuring for the public sector.[27] These events imply the collapse of the banking sector, which would need to be rescued. The only method to do this would be printing money, which in turn leads to high inflation with far-reaching consequences—credit crunch, erosion of the value of savings, as well as the increase in radical uncertainty with the weakening coordination function of the price mechanism. According to IMF calculations, these processes could lead to a 10 percent fall in GDP during the first year (IMF 2012: 46). An even more important consideration than the loss in GDP is that the move would not solve the structural problems of the Greek economy.[28] Furthermore the economic crisis would unlikely to remain economic and could easily turn into a severe political crisis, where the weakness of the state could lead to violence and a civil war in the worst-case scenario.

The exit of Greece would not be without costs to other member states either. The exposure of euro-zone countries to Greece was around €300 billion in 2012. Somewhat surprisingly it was shown that the loss would be lowest to the greatest creditor, Germany, since it could borrow at low or negative interest rates (Alcidi et al. 2012: 5). The largest loss would have to be borne by the other Mediterranean countries, because they would be hit not only by a loss of confidence but would also need to refinance the money, which went to the rescue packages. This would be very expensive because of the high interest rates they face on the markets. Given these considerations it is unsurprising that the exit of Greece was seen as a possible Lehman Brothers moment for Europe. Indeed, as recounted by Brunnermeier et al. (2016: 262–264) US officials were strongly involved in convincing Angela Merkel that allowing Grexit carried too much risk to take.

2.3.2 Eurobonds

Although the European Council has declared that the common issuance of debt by members of the euro-zone is a long-term goal for the euro-zone (European Council 2012), the idea has faced strong resistance from the Northern countries. While the establishment of the ESM can be viewed as a limited form of Eurobonds, a full-fledged implementation of such plan seems to be far away. According to Claessens et al. (2012: 4), the issuance of Eurobonds would solve three major problems in the euro-zone:

1. Fiscal risk-sharing and discipline: common issuance of debt would imply the sharing of financial risks, which would allow the periphery to access credit at a lower risk premium. The related institutions, such as a European Treasury, could exert disciplinary force on the member states.

2. Financial stability: the common issuance of debt would make it possible to separate banking and fiscal problems. It would also make liquidity available in the case of a crisis, which would reduce speculative pressures.
3. Monetary transmission: the common issuance of debt would improve monetary transmission mechanisms and would foster deeper financial integration.

The major counterargument to Eurobonds is the moral hazard problems associated with such a move. This means that the debt is paid back by someone other than the debtor. Such a setup provides incentives for irresponsibility, which is the reason why there was a no-bailout rule in the original structure of the euro-zone. The possibility of cheap loans also allows the postponement of structural reforms—in a very similar manner to the interest rate convergence prior to the crisis. Finally spending public money to finance other countries is contrary to democratic principles and the constitution of several member states (Csaba 2012: 69).

Given the moral hazard problems associated with Eurobonds, their potential design is extremely important. Currently there are several ideas, which aim to protect against moral hazard issues such as differentiating among debts based on debt stock or maturity, as well as establishing institutions, which would constrain access to the common bond.[29] In the official plan of the European Council (2012), Eurobonds can be created only after establishing joint financial supervision, integrated budgetary policies, and deeper coordination of economic policies.

Overall there are strong arguments in favor of the common issuance of debt. At the same time given the associated dangers of moral hazard, in countries, which are most expected to contribute to the costs, there has been strong opposition to the idea.[30]

2.3.3 Transfer Union

The third solution, which also faces strong resistance, is increasing the size of the European budget, which means that a growing proportion of revenues and expenditures would be decided at the supranational level.

There is a proposal to pay certain social security benefits, such as unemployment insurance, from the EU budget (Guérot and Klau 2012: 5). This could counter the tendency that during a recession the state budget deteriorates significantly—its revenues fall, while its expenditures such as unemployment insurance increase. A similar logic is behind the idea of a European deposit insurance scheme, which is partly accomplished by the establishment of the ESM. From the perspective of resolving the crisis, the strongest argument in favor of such solutions is the strengthening of the criteria of optimal currency areas: a transfer of funds from prospering to crisis regions helps the adaptation to asymmetric shocks. Currently this takes place only to a limited extent via the regional and cohesion funds.

Besides the theoretical benefits of the idea, the disadvantages of such solutions are also evident. Most importantly, the incentive for structural reforms is greatly reduced in the periphery, and transfer dependence could be the outcome. The experiences of East Germany illustrate how this problem leads to lasting backwardness (Busch and Müller 2004). A similarly important question is democratic legitimacy, which was also mentioned in the case of Eurobonds—questions of taxation and spending reflect value choices, which cannot be separated from democratic control. Without a real political union the centralization of revenues and expenditures would cause serious tensions among culturally different member states.

The move toward political union is also one of the long-term goals of the European Council (European Council 2012). However, its reality was well reflected in the debate over 2014–2020 budget of the EU—net contributors were adamant to cap the EU budget at 1 percent of EU GNI (Gross National Income).[31]

2.4 Dilemmas of Moral Hazard and Solidarity

The review of accepted and rejected solutions shows that there is enormous resistance in creditor countries to any proposal, which favor open redistribution. At the same time, it is also evident that the eventual solutions still result in considerable redistribution in an opaque manner and contrary to the original design of the euro-zone. As argued by Hall (2012: 366–367), "at each step, the response to this crisis has resembled a giant co-ordination game, in which the benefits of reaching agreement outweigh the costs of failing to do so, but any specific agreement distributes the relevant benefits and risks differently."

The problems associated with moral hazard, which was a major cause of the crisis, persist. The promises of the ECB of unlimited liquidity help sustaining the financing of troubled countries but at the same time reduce the incentives for structural reforms. European decision-makers are clearly aware of the problem of moral hazard—in the Northern countries, which bear the burden of crisis management, there is strong political pressure to discipline debtor countries (Streeck and Elsässer 2016: 13).

Beyond the conditionality of the financial assistance programs, institutional reforms were implemented to discipline debtor countries. While the Commission took a backseat to France and especially Germany during the management of the crisis (Brunnermeier et al. 2016: 18–20), the new institutional framework greatly increases its surveillance powers over national economic policies (Savage and Verdun 2016). The Commission's ability to interfere with domestic economic policies is also enhanced by the reversed qualified majority voting on sanctions, which insulates its decisions from national veto, as well as the greater scope of the macroeconomic imbalance procedure in comparison to the Stability and Growth Pact (Dawson 2015: 979–980). The new economic governance mechanisms provide no role for the European Parliament, as it does not have to co-adopt the recommendations of the Commission leading to questions about political accountability (Dawson 2015: 983).

The above implies that we are witnessing the further de-politicization of economic policy and the strengthening of supranational features. De-politicization means that decisions are not made by democratically elected officials, who are accountable to their electors, but rather by competent bureaucrats, who rely on scientific evidence. Legitimacy in this case originates not from the input side but rather from the output side, which means that the bureaucracy can provide efficient answers to difficult problems (Scharpf 1999: 11–12). The emphasis on output-oriented legitimacy is not necessarily a bad idea. Rothstein and Teorell (2008: 169), for example, argue that it is actually much more important than the input side. However, when results are not forthcoming, the loss of legitimacy can undermine governance and endanger the union.

De-politicization also implies different things for the Southern and Northern countries with highly asymmetrical power relations. While creditor countries are unlikely to be disciplined by these new mechanisms (Dawson 2015: 982), they have to bear the costs of the various support programs in the name of solidarity. On the other side, Southern countries are faced with the fact that elections do not matter as policies remain the same (Featherstone 2016: 56).

The dilemmas associated with moral hazard and solidarity led to resentment in the North and the South as well as disillusionment from the European project. As the North wanted to gain control over how its money is spent, the South expected solidarity in the face of crisis. Individual negotiations took place in this environment, and trust became a critical factor in the discussions. This is the subject of the next chapter.

Notes

1. Article 125(1) of the Treaty on the Functioning of the European Union asserts: "The Union shall not be liable for or assume the commitments of central governments, regional, local or other public authorities, other bodies governed by public law, or public undertakings of any Member State, without prejudice to mutual financial guarantees for the joint execution of a specific project." Text available: http://eur-lex.europa.eu/legal-content/EN/TXT/?uri=celex%3A12012E%2FTXT. Accessed: 2 July 2017.
2. The acronym signals the troubled countries of the euro-zone, and includes Greece, Ireland, Portugal, and Spain. Cyprus is not included here as it joined the EU only in 2004. In Chap. 5 it will be included into the analysis.
3. The origins of enormous liquidity during this period have been widely debated. A particularly influential explanation was the global savings glut hypothesis, which attributed low interest rates in the United States and possibly in other Western countries to excess savings in emerging economies (Bernanke 2005). However, when testing competing hypotheses,

Bracke and Fidora (2008) found that loose monetary policies in developed countries carry more explanatory power. Shin (2012) attributes the liquidity to the leveraging and deleveraging cycle in the global banking system.

4. The lowest interest rates could be observed in 2005—long-term interest rate stood at 3.4 percent in Germany and 3.6 percent in Greece, but they were still 6.6 percent in Hungary and 5.2 percent in Poland (European Commission 2017: 106–107).
5. As the European Commission was unable to enforce fiscal discipline, Kopits (2017: 219–220) underlines that IMF surveillance of euro-area countries was also rather lax, and the fund seemed complacent given the low level of interest rates.
6. The slogan is attributed to Margaret Thatcher, who used it to argue that there is no alternative to global capitalism and neoliberal policies. See Flanders (2013).
7. On the relationship between the euro and structural reforms see the analysis by Duval and Elmeskov (2006).
8. This mechanism is also discussed by Lane (2012): 52.
9. The cases below will be discussed more in the depth in the following chapters.
10. Unless noted otherwise, the following description is based on Kuenzel (2011).
11. Data is from EMS website at: https://www.esm.europa.eu/about-us/history#context. Accessed: 2 July 2017.
12. In 2016 gross public debt stood at €2147 billion in France and €2217 in Italy (AMECO database).
13. See the announcement by Moody's at: https://www.moodys.com/research/Moodys-changes-the-outlook-to-negative-on-Germany-Netherlands-Luxembourg--PR_251214. Accessed: 2 July, 2017.
14. For a thorough discussion of the various programs of the ECB to manage the financial crisis, see Brunnermeier et al. (2016): 325–367.
15. See the statement by ECB: http://www.ecb.europa.eu/press/pr/date/2013/html/pr130221_1.en.html. Accessed: 2 July 2017.
16. See the transcript of the press conference where Mario Draghi announced the program: https://www.ecb.europa.eu/press/pressconf/2012/html/is120906.en.html. Accessed: 2 July 2017.
17. Data is from ECB monthly bulletin available at: https://www.ecb.europa.eu/pub/pdf/other/mb201203_focus03.en.pdf?633af8e40f98a75808996a7857cbbd93. Accessed: 2 July 2017.

18. While the numerous programs for assistance especially the bond-buying programs speak for themselves, there is a rather substantial controversy over whether the ECB has indeed overstepped its mandate. For an elaborate discussion on the debate, see Sinn (2014): 282–293.
19. Unless noted otherwise, the source of the description of reforms is Kuenzel (2011).
20. The Czech Republic, Hungary, Sweden, and the UK did not sign the pact mostly citing the infringement of national sovereignty as a reason.
21. The procedure consists of the following ten indicators with indicative thresholds (Ecofin 2012):
    1. Three-year backward moving average of the current account balance in percent of GDP, with a threshold of +6 percent and −4 percent
    2. Net international investment position in percent of GDP, with a threshold of −35 percent
    3. Five-year percentage change of export market shares measured in values, with a threshold of −6 percent
    4. Three-year percentage change in nominal unit labor cost, with thresholds of +9 percent for euro-area countries and +12 percent for non-euro-zone countries, respectively
    5. Three-year percentage change of the real effective exchange rates based on HICP/CPI deflators, relative to 35 other industrial countries, with thresholds of −/+5 percent for euro-area countries and −/+11 percent for non-euro-area countries, respectively
    6. Private sector debt in percent of GDP with a threshold of 160 percent
    7. Private sector credit flow in percent of GDP with a threshold of 15 percent
    8. Year-on-year changes in the house price index relative to a Eurostat consumption deflator, with a threshold of 6 percent
    9. General government sector debt in percent of GDP with a threshold of 60 percent
    10. Three-year backward moving average of the unemployment rate, with a threshold of 10 percent
22. According to the Greenspan doctrine, which was the dominant approach toward bubbles prior to the crisis, bubbles do not exist; if they do, we do not see them while growing; if we did, we could not do anything; if we could, there would be more harm than benefit. For a more thorough discussion, see Mishkin (2011): 17–21.

23. For an overview of performance, see Berg et al. (2004).
24. Officially the Treaty on the Stability, Coordination, and Governance in the Economic and Monetary Union.
25. Structural deficit means that deficit is calculated not from the actual but from the potential growth rate.
26. See, for example, Feldstein (2010), Krugman (2015), or Sinn (2014): 346–352.
27. On the possible consequences of default, see Alcidi et al. (2012).
28. A deeper analysis of the structural problems of Greece will be given in Chap. 4.
29. Claessens et al. (2012) give a thorough overview about the different proposals.
30. See, for example, the letter of 172 German economists in Frankfurter Allgemeine Zeitung on 5 July 2012. Available: http://www.faz.net/aktuell/wirtschaft/protestaufruf-der-offene-brief-der-oekonomen-im-wortlaut-11810652.html. Accessed: 2 July 2017.
31. See Kilnes and Sherriff (2012) for an assessment of the positions on the budget.

References

Alcidi, Cinzia, Alessandro Giovannini, and Daniel Gros. 2012. *'Grexit': Who would pay for it?* CEPS Policy Brief No. 272. Available: http://www.ceps.eu/book/'grexit'-who-would-pay-it. Accessed 2 July 2017.

Aslund, Anders. 2010. *The last shall be the first: The East European financial crisis 2008–10*. Washington, DC: Peterson Institute for International Economics.

Barta, Zsófia, and Waltraud Schelkle. 2015. At cross-purposes: Commercial versus technocratic governance of sovereign debt in the EU. *Journal of European Integration* 37 (7): 833–846.

Benczes, István. 2013. The impossible trinity of denial: European economic governance in a conceptual framework. *Transylvanian Review of Administrative Sciences* 9 (39): 5–21.

Berg, Andrew, Eduardo Borensztein, and Catherine Pattillo. 2004. *Assessing early warning systems: How have they worked in practice?* IMF Working Paper No. 04/52.

Bernanke, Ben. 2005. *The global saving glut and the U.S. current account deficit.* Remarks at the Sandridge Lecture, Virginia Association of Economists,

Richmond, March 10. Available: http://www.federalreserve.gov/boarddocs/speeches/2005/200503102/. Accessed 2 July 2017.

Bracke, Thierry, and Michael Fidora. 2008. *Global liquidity glut or global savings glut? A structural VAR approach*. Working Paper No. 911. Frankfurt-am-Main: European Central Bank.

Brunnermeier, Markus K., Harold James, and Jean-Pierre Landau. 2016. *The euro and the battle of ideas*. Princeton/Oxford: Princeton University Press.

Busch, Ulrich, and Christian Müller. 2004. *Despite or because? Some lessons of German unification for EU enlargement*. Swiss Institute for Business Cycle Research Working Papers No. 87.

Chang, Michele, and Patrick Leblond. 2015. All in: Market expectations of eurozone integrity in the sovereign debt crisis. *Review of International Political Economy* 22 (3): 626–655.

Claessens, Stijn, Ashoka Mody, and Shahin Vallee. 2012. *Paths to eurobonds*. Bruegel Working Paper No. 2012/10.

Csaba, László. 2012. Revisiting the crisis of the EU: Challenges and options. *Zeitschrift für Staats- und Europawissenschaften* 10 (1): 53–77.

Dawson, Mark. 2015. The legal and political accountability structure of 'post-crisis' EU economic governance. *Journal of Common Market Studies* 53 (5): 976–993.

De Rynck, Stefaan. 2016. Banking on a union: The politics of changing eurozone banking supervision. *Journal of European Public Policy* 23 (1): 119–135.

Duval, Romain, and Jorgen Elmeskov. 2006. *The effects of EMU on structural reforms in labour and product markets*. European Central Bank Working Paper No. 596.

Ecofin. 2012. *Scoreboard for the surveillance of macroeconomic imbalances*. European Economy Occasional Papers No. 92. Brussels: Directorate General for Economic and Financial Affairs.

European Commission. 2008. *EMU@10: Successes and challenges after ten years of Economic and Monetary Union*. Brussels: Directorate General for Economic and Financial Affairs.

———. 2010. *Statistical annex of European Economy, Spring*. Brussels: Directorate General for Economic and Financial Affairs.

———. 2017. *Statistical annex of European Economy, Spring*. Brussels: Directorate General for Economic and Financial Affairs.

European Council. 2012. *Towards a genuine economic and monetary union*. Report by President of the European Council Herman Van Rompuy. EUCO 120/12. Available: www.consilium.europa.eu/en/workarea/downloadasset.aspx?id=17220. Accessed 2 July 2017.

Featherstone, Kevin. 2016. Conditionality, democracy and institutional weakness: The euro-crisis trilemma. *Journal of Common Market Studies* 54 (S1): 48–64.

Feldstein, Martin. 2010. Let Greece take a eurozone 'holiday'. *Financial Times*, February 16.

Flanders, Laura. 2013. At Thatcher's funeral, bury TINA, too. *The Nation*, April 12. Available: https://www.thenation.com/article/thatchers-funeral-bury-tina-too/. Accessed 28 July 2017.

Goldstein, Morris, and Nicholas Véron. 2011. *Too-big-to-fail: The transatlantic debate*. Bruegel Working Paper No. 2011/03. Brussels: Bruegel.

Grauwe, Paul De. 2012. Why the EU summit decisions may destabilise government bond markets. *VoxEU.org*, July 2. Available: http://www.voxeu.com/article/why-eu-summit-decisions-may-destabilise-government-bond-markets.

Gros, Daniel. 2013. Banking union with a sovereign virus: The self-serving treatment of sovereign debt. *Intereconomics* 48 (2): 93–97.

Guérot, Ulrike, and Thomas Klau. 2012. *After Merkozy: How France and Germany can make Europe work*. ECFR policy Brief No. 56. Available: http://ecfr.eu/page/-/ECFR56_FRANCE_GERMANY_BRIEF_AW.pdf. Accessed 2 July 2017.

Hall, Peter A. 2012. The economics and politics of the euro crisis. *German Politics* 21 (4): 355–371.

IMF. 2012. *Greece: Request for extended arrangement under the extended fund facility—Staff report*. IMF Country Report No. 12/57. Washington, DC: IMF.

Jones, Erik. 2015. Getting the story right: How you should choose between different interpretations of the European crisis (and why you should care). *Journal of European Integration* 37 (7): 817–832.

Kilnes, Ulrika, and Andrew Sherriff. 2012. *Member states' positions on the proposed 2014–2020 EU budget*. Briefing Note No. 37. Maastricht/Brussels: European Centre for Development Policy Management.

Kindleberger, Charles P., and Robert Z. Aliber. 2005. *Manias, panics and crashes: A history of financial crises*. 5th ed. Hobokan: Wiley.

Kopits, George. 2017. The IMF and the euro area crisis: The fiscal dimension. In *The IMF and the crises in Greece, Ireland and Portugal*, ed. Moises Schwartz and Shinji Takagi, 209–253. Washington, DC: IMF Independent Evaluation Office.

Krugman, Paul. 2015. Ending Greece's bleeding. *New York Times*, July 5.

Kuenzel, Robert. 2011. The EU's comprehensive policy response to the crisis. *Quarterly Report on the Euro Area* 10 (1): 7–14.

Lane, Philip R. 2012. The European sovereign debt crisis. *Journal of Economic Perspectives* 26 (3): 49–68.

Mishkin, Frederic S. 2011. *Monetary policy strategy: Lessons from the crisis*. NBER Working Paper. No. 16755.

Neményi, Judit, and Gábor Oblath. 2012. Az euró bevezetésének újragondolása [Rethinking of the introduction of the euro]. *Közgazdasági Szemle* 59 (6): 569–684.

OECD. 2007. Taking stock of structural policies in OECD countries. In *Economic Policy Reforms: Going for growth 2007*, 3–28. Paris: OECD.

Reinhart, Carmen M., and Kenneth S. Rogoff. 2009. *This time is different: Eight centuries of financial folly*. Princeton: Princeton University Press.

Rothstein, Bo, and Jan Teorell. 2008. What is the quality of government? A theory of impartial government institutions. *Governance* 21 (2): 165–190.

Savage, James, and Amy Verdun. 2016. Strengthening the European Commission's budgetary and economic surveillance capacity since Greece and the euro area crisis: A study of five directorates-general. *Journal of European Public Policy* 23 (1): 101–118.

Sawyer, Malcolm. 2012. *The contradictions of balanced structural government budgets*. Available at SSRN: http://ssrn.com/abstract=2078818.

Scharpf, Fritz W. 1999. *Governing in Europe: Effective and democratic?* Oxford: Oxford University Press.

———. 2011. Monetary union, fiscal crisis and the preemption of democracy. *Zeitschrift für Staats- und Europawissenschaften* 9 (2): 163–198.

Schmieding, Holger, et al. 2011. *The 2011 Euro Plus monitor: Progress amid the turmoil*. Hamburg/Brüsszel: Berenberg Bank and Lisbon Council.

Shin, Hyun Song. 2012. Global banking glut and loan risk premium. *IMF Economic Review* 60 (2): 155–192.

Sinn, Hans-Werner. 2014. *The euro trap: On bursting bubbles, budgets and beliefs*. Oxford: Oxford University Press.

Streeck, Wolfgang, and Lea Elsässer. 2016. Monetary disunion: The domestic politics of euroland. *Journal of European Public Policy* 23 (1): 1–24.

3

Trust and Crisis Management

As we could see from the previous chapter, crisis management involved a series of actors at the European level, who had to cooperate to resolve the crisis. National-level crisis management also requires the participation of various actors. During the negotiations creditors and borrowers have to agree on the conditionality of the program, which guarantees the repayment of the debt. In the implementation phase, the government has to convince the public that the required sacrifices are justified and worthwhile. As returning to market financing is a primary objective of any financial support program, the opinion of the markets matter greatly in the success of the program.

In every phase of crisis management, trust is critical. The main objective of this chapter is to provide an introduction to the concept and show how its various forms play a role during the different phases in crisis management. The discussion serves as the theoretical basis for the empirical chapters, and shows that in the absence of trust, punitive conditionality, resistance of the population, and lack of confidence from the markets can lead to austerity spirals and the failure of crisis management.

The first part of the chapter focuses on the concept of trust. It starts with a basic definition emphasizing the crucial importance of vulnerability and uncertainty. This is followed by a discussion on interpersonal and

D. Győrffy, *Trust and Crisis Management in the European Union*,
https://doi.org/10.1007/978-3-319-69212-8_3

institutional trust as well as an ethical assessment of trust. In the second part of the chapter the role of trust is analyzed during the negotiation, implementation and reception phases of international financial support programs. The chapter ends with a theoretical model for austerity spirals.

3.1 What Is Trust?

The concept of trust is most often introduced within a prisoners' dilemma framework. Table 3.1 shows such a game.

As we can see in such situations, cooperation yields only the second highest payoff (2, 2). The individually most advantageous payoff occurs when one party cooperates while the other defects (−4, 6). Since this is clear to both players, in a one-shot game the expected outcome is 0, 0, which is significantly worse than the cooperative outcome.

The game assumes simultaneous choice, but in numerous social decisions choices are—if A decides to cooperate as the first player, he becomes extremely vulnerable to B, who has a significant incentive to defect. The decision to cooperate in such situations requires good reasons.

What could be good reasons for cooperation? Acting upon trust assumes two things: the willingness of the other party to cooperate as well as the ability to live up to his or her commitments (Ullman-Margalit 2004: 63). In order to achieve cooperation, actors have to signal their intent and capacity to others. According to the classics of game theory, repeated games can spontaneously give rise to cooperation as both players recognize its benefits.[1] Another possibility is building reputation, which also implies repeated games but with different actors. Those actors, who have a reputation for cooperation, can count on the cooperation of others.

Table 3.1 Prisoners' dilemma

		B	
		Cooperate	Defect
A	Cooperate	2, 2	−4, 6
	Defect	6, −4	0, 0

Reputation thus secures credibility, which inspires trust.[2] Credibility can also be achieved by other means such as a commitment—when one actor signals commitment to a certain decision, uncertainty is significantly lessened (Shelling 1963: 24). Such commitment can be made credible by the involvement of external enforcement, such as the state, which can retaliate for non-cooperative behavior.

The conditions, which provide incentives to cooperation, however do not imply certainty about the action of the other party. There can be circumstances, which lead to the abuse of trust. The mere fact of sequential decision-making implies a future event for the first player. However, as the future is essentially uncertain, we can have only some expectations about it with more or less probability. This implies that the most significant characteristic of actions based on trust is vulnerability to the abuse of trust (Seligman 2000; James 2002). Given the presence of vulnerability, acting on trust always requires courage—in the words of Guido Möllering, trust is always a leap of faith (Möllering 2006: 105).

The persistence of vulnerability, the uncertainty of the future, and the significance of faith all call attention to the importance of subjectivity when analyzing trust. Acting from a place of vulnerability always carries risk, and it is a subjective judgment based on personal experiences to what extent someone is willing and able to become vulnerable in any type of relationship. When someone is full of fear, his or her trust had been abused multiple times in the past and has limited tolerance for uncertainty, a trusting attitude is much less likely to emerge than in a case when a person is able to deal with uncertainty. The non-rational aspects of trust naturally do not mean that rationality can be discarded when analyzing trust, but they do imply that the concept cannot be analyzed within a strictly rational framework.

3.2 Interpersonal Trust

In everyday life trust means a characteristic of an interpersonal relationship. The most basic definition of the concept implies that A trusts B to do X (Levi 1998: 78). From an analytical perspective whether A and B know each other has crucial importance. Eric Uslaner differentiates between particular and general trust. Particular trust is present when trust is based upon membership in a certain group, while we talk about generalized trust when people believe that those outside such groups can be trusted as well (Uslaner 1999: 126–127). In order to understand financial crisis management, the discussion of a third type of trust is necessary—trust within the elite, which is treated as a special case of particular trust.

3.2.1 Particular Trust

The basis for particular trust is familiarity. This can mean a personal relationship with family or friends, where repeated situations provide strong incentives for cooperative behavior. A personal relationship however is not necessary for particular trust—having a shared identity or membership in the same ethnic, religious, or professional group might be sufficient. In such situations trust is based upon the assumption that members of the group share the norms concerning cooperation.

Everyone needs particular trust, as the desire to belong is a natural drive in humans. However, from a societal perspective trusting only people in the same group has negative implications. Often it is a reaction to real threats from people outside the group—in dictatorships individuals generally withdraw to their narrow social circle or family, where they can feel safe. In other cases, trusting only group members is the manifestation of category-based trust, which relies on stereotypes, and goes together with distrust toward people outside the group. A differentiation between "us" and "them" prevails within the society (Larson 2004: 43). This attitude can easily turn into amoral familialism, when in the interest of the family or a small group the public good is sacrificed.[3] Terrorist cells or the mafia exhibits this type of trust.

3.2.2 Trust Within the Elite

In the management of a financial crisis, trust within the elite[4] has an important role to play not only during the negotiation, but also the implementation phase of international financial assistance programs.

When we talk about trust within the political elite, it is necessary to differentiate between competitive and non-competitive actors. Competing parties prior to the election are unlikely to choose cooperation in a prisoners' dilemma situation. Under normal conditions, within the context of political competition, trust can be interpreted as a recognized commitment to the rules of the game, which are set in the constitution.[5] However, when faced with a natural or other catastrophe such as a financial crisis, some cooperation can be normatively expected—for example, not campaigning against program conditionality.

During the negotiations of international financial assistance programs we generally see or at least should see non-competitive elites, where trust can be the basis of mutually beneficial cooperation. The roots of trust among non-competitive elite actors are similar to the roots of particular trust—a history of regular interaction and cooperation, shared professional identity, and a shared worldview strongly contributes to the presence of trust. Rothstein (2000: 483) also emphasizes the role of shared collective memories, while Sabatier and Jenkins-Smith (1988) underline the importance of shared ideas about the economy and society.

3.2.3 Generalized Trust

When social science researchers talk about social trust, they refer to generalized trust, which means that people trust others outside their own social group. In the various social surveys such as World Values Survey, generalized trust is usually measured by the question: "Generally speaking, would you say that most people can be trusted or that you need to be very careful in dealing with people?" The larger is a community, the more important it is to be able to trust strangers, which makes it possible to cooperate. For a market economy this is especially important as it allows business transactions among strangers (Arrow 1972).

Generalized trust strongly affects economic performance through various channels. Trusting people need less assurances to cooperate thus they face lower transaction costs from monitoring and contract enforcement (Fukuyama 1996: 27). Solving collective dilemmas in high-trust environments is also less costly as the fear of free riding is lower, thus cooperation is easier (Whiteley 2000: 451). Numerous empirical analyses support these assumptions, and show that higher social trust correlates with better growth performance.[6]

There is substantial debate about the origins of generalized trust. On the basis of US experiences, Uslaner (2002: 112–113) argues that trusting people are generally optimistic, feel control over their lives, and grew up in a family where trust was present. Education is also important—the more educated a person is, the more likely he or she will be characterized by generalized trust.[7] Finally, in the United States, ethnic background also plays an important role—blacks are less likely to trust than whites.[8] Micro-level analyses however do not answer the questions, why some societies exhibit higher level of trust than others. In order to explain this there are two main contending theories: participation in civil society and the quality of institutions.

On the basis of Northern and Southern Italy, Putnam (1994) argues that participation in civic associations is decisive in the emergence of generalized trust. In the past two decades numerous criticisms were addressed to his results. Most importantly, the direction of causation can be questioned—presumably those, who exhibit higher levels of trust toward strangers, are the ones, who join civic associations in the first place. Thus the question, where this trust comes from remains. Second, not every civic association is benign, and it is unclear, how some civic associations build trust, while others do not (Rothstein and Stolle 2008).

According to Offe (1999: 73–75), the role of institutions in the development of generalized trust originates from a substitution effect: in the absence of personal relationship, institutions can guarantee truth telling, keeping of promises, fairness, and solidarity. Ensuring these values is the joint effect of a set of institutions. The knowledge of truth and facts are made possible by the freedom of the press, open court procedures, strict accounting rules, and independent professional associations. The keeping of promises is guaranteed by official contracts, which are enforced by an independent judicial system, while in politics free elections play this role. Fairness is served by equality before the law as well as general elections, when everyone has one vote. Finally, redistribution serves the decrease of inequality of life chances, which contributes to feelings of solidarity.

Rothstein and Stolle (2008) point out that in the emergence of generalized trust it is not the government and other representative bodies which play a crucial role, but rather it is the impartial state administration which provides various services to citizens. They argue that trust in the police and the courts is much more important than the popularity of parliament or the government.

Institutions can directly contribute to generalized trust, but they can also have an important indirect effect through the shaping of inequalities, which is the single most important macro-level factor in regressions about generalized trust—stronger than various indicators of welfare and income (Uslaner 2002: 236). Policies, which reduce the inequality of incomes and opportunities, are able to raise the level of generalized trust. Excessive inequalities lead to the polarization of society, as feeling of a shared fate vanishes (Rothstein and Uslaner 2005: 47).[9] However, in order to have effective policies for the reduction of inequality, trust in institutions is also necessary.

3.3 Institutional Trust

The concept of institutional trust primarily focuses on formal institutions and also involves the organizations, which are responsible for adopting, applying, and enforcing the laws—such as parliaments, governments, and courts.

Trust in institutions is very different from trust in interpersonal relationships. Acting upon trust always assumes some kind of intention of the other party, and only persons rather than institutions can have any kind of intention. When discussing institutional trust, an often used term is confidence, which means than an institution is capable of fulfilling its public role (Ullman-Margalit 2004: 77). Another often used term is legitimacy, which can be formal or ethical. On this issue an important distinction is made by Rosanvallon (2008: 3–4), who defines legitimacy in a strictly procedural manner, while trust is an extension of legitimacy into the ethical and substantial dimension—a belief in the integrity of decision-makers and their commitment to the public good.

The major paradox of institutional trust is that one cannot trust the state since it can abuse its power, while the state needs trust as this is necessary for citizens to follow the law and pay their taxes.

Unlike the case of interpersonal trust, the relationship between state and citizens is a highly unequal one as the state has monopoly over violence. Given the possibility for abusing this power, the natural attitude toward the state is distrust rather than trust (Hardin 2006: 40). Consequently the basic condition for trust in institutions is the presence of democracy and rule of law, which constrains the state in the abuse of power (Hoskin 2014: 177).[10] In the US constitution, distrust is institutionalized in the system of checks and balances (Rose 2005: 75). Trust in the state thus means a belief that given the constraint on its power, the state restrains from the abuse of its monopoly over violence and works in the interest of public good.

While the state can be trusted if it works within the rule of law, particular institutions need impersonality and impartiality to deserve trust. Ullman-Margalit (2004: 77–78) calls attention to an interesting paradox about impartiality: institutional trust implies that an institution fulfills its tasks regardless of which of its employees is responsible for the issue. However, once trust becomes personal and our business depends on who handles it, the institution ceases to be impartial, and the majority, who do not have immediate access to decision-making, loses its trust in it.

3.3.1 The Roots of Institutional Trust

In the establishment of institutional trust, impartiality is the key condition. According to Rothstein and Teorell (2008), impartiality on the output side of governance is analogous to free and fair elections on the input side. It means that "when implementing laws and policies government officials shall not take into consideration anything about the citizen / case that is not beforehand stipulated in policy or the law" (Rothstein and Teorell 2008: 170). Such a definition not only rules out all forms of corruption, "but also practices such as clientelism, patronage, nepotism, political favoritism, discrimination and other forms of 'particularisms'" (Rothstein and Teorell 2008: 171). This is consistent with the classical definition of justice as fairness proposed by Rawls in his veil of ignorance analogy (Rawls 1999: 118) as well as Harsányi when talking about "uncertain prospects" (Harsányi 1953: 434–435). Both authors emphasize that in cases when one does not know his or her place in society, impartial norms are the most desirable.

The empirical research about institutional trust largely supports the theoretical considerations. In his work on the origins of legitimacy, Gilley (2009: 41) finds that the five most important determinants of legitimacy are general governance, income level, gender equality, welfare level, and economic governance. In assessing the Eurobarometer indicator satisfaction with democracy, Wagner et al. (2009) also find that economic governance (measured by growth, unemployment, and inflation) and institutional quality (rule of law, corruption, size of the shadow economy, working of checks and balances) are strong predictors of satisfaction.

The empirical results also show that institutional trust is not simply a function of the level of development. According to the comparative analysis of Medve-Bálint and Boda (2014), in Western and East Central Europe there is a considerable correlation between trust and GDP per capita. However, when they examine the egocentric indicator of institutional trust at the individual level, they arrive to an interesting result—while in Western Europe higher GDP per capita indeed yields high level of institutional trust, in East Central Europe it is not the case. In those countries people with lower income exhibit high level of trust, while the trust of high-income groups in the state is lower. Ultimately trust correlates most significantly with the subjective assessment of the state of the national economy rather than individual incomes. This implies that incomes do not determine institutional trust; instead the decisive factor is perceptions on the quality of governance.

3.3.2 The Consequences of Institutional Trust

Institutional trust is no less important for economic outcomes than interpersonal trust. As discussed above, institutional trust hinges primarily on the perception of impartiality of state institutions. This certainly cannot be taken for granted. As Francis Fukuyama explains, humans are social animals and privilege their kin for biological reasons. In modern states impersonal structures emerged, where positions depend on merit, education or technical knowledge (Fukuyama 2015: 10). However, there is always pressure to revert back to privileging kinship and friends, and Western societies are not immune from these pressures. In such cases of political decay, government efficiency decreases, and the economy cannot remain unaffected.

When trust in the impartiality of state institutions declines, and actors observe partiality on the basis of family relation or party factions, several consequences follow.[11] As the state is seen as serving particular interests, voluntary compliance with the laws declines. Regular and widespread rule evasion leads to a dysfunctional institutional system, where institutions cannot fulfill their role in shaping expectations, which leads to considerable uncertainty. Heightened uncertainty implies increased transaction costs in the economy due to questions about the enforcement of contracts and property rights. Widespread rule evasion by citizens provokes the state to implement stricter regulation and enforcement, which can slow down transactions as well as make them more expensive. In order to hasten such transactions, circumventing regulations is usually a tempting option. The outcome is a vicious cycle of corruption, stricter regulation, and distrust. Empirical analyses (Aghion et al. 2010) have found a strong negative correlation between the extent of state regulation and generalized trust—lower level of trust correlates with more regulation. These developments have a clear negative effect upon doing business.

As it has been mentioned during the discussion of generalized trust, institutional trust is also crucial for policies aimed to reducing social inequalities. Empirical studies show that support for redistribution is greater in countries, where institutional trust is high (Rothstein 1998; Rudolph and Evans 2005). This is not very surprising since extensive redistribution requires high tax revenues, which people are unwilling to pay to corrupt and incompetent governments.[12] However, there is a serious consequence—a trap can easily emerge among inequality, distrust, and poorly functioning institutions. While the upper classes can secure their position through various channels of corruption, for the lower classes evading the law feels morally justified as they observe that corruption and rule breaking is necessary for success (Rothstein and Uslaner 2005: 71).

Finally, in the presence of uncertainty, as people lose their belief in the value of hard work as a road to success, political campaigns are more likely to be waged upon short-term, populist agendas rather than long-term policy issues. The strategy can include attacks on free trade, deficit spending, and tax cuts without matching expenditure cuts. All of this is detrimental to sustainable economic performance, but they can be particularly harmful in periods of financial crisis, when significant sacrifices are required from the population.

3.3.3 Market Confidence

The confidence of the markets can be interpreted as a special case of institutional trust. It means the trust of companies, which invest and create jobs as well as the trust of creditors, who finance those activities.

When making an investment decision, companies plan for the long term with the purpose of earning profit. In order to make such a decision, they need a largely predictable environment, where property rights and enforcement of contracts are guaranteed. In the absence of these conditions, companies become very careful in making long-term investment decisions.

Institutional trust also plays an important role in the financing of country debt. The importance of trust comes from multiple equilibriums in the sustainability of debt: if investors are certain that a county can repay its debts, then lower interest rates ensure that this will be the case. On the other hand, if investors have doubts about repayment, the resulting higher interest rates indeed endanger sustainability.[13] The presence or absence of trust can thus lead to self-fulfilling processes, which are critical from the perspective of financial stability.

In the decisions, economic actors' past behavior and the evaluation of credit rating agencies play an important role. The latter can also be used as indicators for trust. However, there are also non-rational aspects of trust, which Keynes (1936: 161–162) called animal spirits: "a spontaneous urge to action rather than inaction, and not as the outcome of a weighted average of quantitative benefits multiplied by quantitative probabilities." In the waves of optimism and pessimism, the media, fashions, and investor herd behavior all play a part.[14] These can exaggerate the weight of certain opinions, thus objective performance and subjective judgment can deviate from one another—with the latter eventually affecting the former. This shows the critical role of discourses and narratives in various societies.

3.4 The Ethical Assessment of Trust

Trust is a clearly normative, value-loaded concept, thus in explaining the phenomenon, we cannot abstract away from its ethical implications. In a low-trust environment, where cooperation outside the family faces enormous obstacles and taxes are avoided, it is a regular policy advice to increase trust in society. How to understand such statements? In a more general manner—what is the ethical significance of trust?

In answering the above question, Ullman-Margalit (2004: 60–61) starts with a differentiation between trust and distrust. She argues that while the two concepts exclude one another, they do not exhaust all possible state of affairs. Trust and distrust are the two ends of a scale, and in between them there is a large area where there is neither trust nor distrust as maybe we do not know anything of the other. When we consider the ethical implications of trust, we cannot avoid the question, which end of the scale we are talking about.

Trust is clearly not an ethical value in cases when we know that the other is not trustworthy, prone to abuse, or does not have the capacity to live up to his or her commitments. In such cases trust is naïveté and carelessness, and it is certainly not ethically desirable. Applying this insight to finance, we can state that it is certainly not desirable to lend to borrowers, who clearly cannot pay back their debt.

On the other end of the scale, it is also clear that if the other is trustworthy and capable, with a cooperative past, trust is a justifiable expectation. In such cases distrust cannot be justified, it is the questioning of the benevolence of the other, which is malignant suspiciousness. The loss of possible benefits from cooperation is harmful to both parties. When even good borrowers are unable to get credit at reasonable rates, we talk about market failure.

The issue is more complicated in the gray areas between trust and distrust, which allow arguments for both trusting and not. While action based on trust carries risks, not trusting provides some sort of security. In an interpersonal relation, there can be two arguments for considering trusting behavior an ethical value. First, trust and distrust are both reflexive—trust produces trust, while distrust produces distrust, thus opting for trust increases the chances of the evolution of cooperation. Second, acting upon trust implies assuming vulnerability and showing courage—indicating openness to the other person. This kind of openness characterizes usually those who are trustworthy themselves.[15] Thus with the exception of cases, where distrust is certainly justified, trust is an ethically desirable attitude. Its moral significance is also underlined by Eric Uslaner, who shows that in the United States, trusting people are more likely do voluntary work, donate more money, and are tolerant with others (Uslaner 2008).

However, when in the later chapters the issue of trust building is emphasized, it will not mean the increase of interpersonal trust and a proposal for people to trust and take risks. This is a personal problem and belongs to the field of psychology. At the macro-level trust is strongly related to the trustworthiness of institutions, which influence interpersonal relationships via various channels. Building trust in society thus implies increasing the trustworthiness of the state and the conduct of policies, which contribute to generalized trust. The system of checks and balances, stable public policies, reducing excessive inequalities, and increasing the equality of life chances through investing into education are all steps toward building public trust. Their absence provides fertile ground for distrust both in interpersonal and business relationships.

Lacking trust was an often-voiced factor in the management of the EU financial crisis. In the next three sections I will show how trust matters in the negotiation, implementation, and reception phase of financial assistance programs.

3.5 Trust and Crisis Management: The Negotiation of Program Conditionality[16]

Before addressing the role of trust in the various phases of a financial assistance program, it is important to understand who the main actors are and what is the usual practice of designing and implementing such programs.

3.5.1 The Establishment of the Troika

The negotiations with euro-zone countries were somewhat more complicated than usual IMF program negotiations. During the early period of the crisis, as Greece lost access to the financial markets, leading EU authorities, the Commission, the ECB, German or French policy-makers strongly resisted the idea to involve the IMF in providing financial support to euro-zone member states (Brunnermeier, James and Landau 2016: 297). However, as market pressure intensified and the practical aspects of financial assistance became clearer, the resistance faded. As argued by Schwarzer (2015: 609–610), the IMF had superior technical expertise on the fields of designing and implementing stabilization programs as well as systemic surveillance for financial stability. The IMF also had an active interest in getting involved as it was losing influence and tried to repair its image after the failures of managing the Asian crisis (Schwarzer 2015: 620). As the IMF became included into euro-zone crisis management, the Troika was formed, which meant that the stabilization programs were negotiated jointly by the Commission, the ECB, and the IMF. They were strongly relying on the IMF practice of lending.

3.5.2 The IMF Practice of Lending

When a country asks for assistance during a financial difficulty, the fundamental problem of asymmetric information arises, which characterizes all financial transactions. The borrower knows more about her situation than the lender, and thus after receiving the funds a moral hazard problem appears. The borrower may also have incentives to use the funds differently then negotiated with the lender or not pay back the funds. Such risks are generally handled by collateral or an interest premium in the markets. However, since countries in trouble cannot pledge internationally valuable collateral and the necessary risk premium might be prohibitive, the IMF imposes conditionality, which ensures the repayment of loans as a substitute for collateral (Kahn and Sharma 2005: 121).

Conditionality generally involves three areas (Smaghi 2015: 763): fiscal policy to correct budgetary imbalances, financial sector stability to absorb potential losses to the balance sheet, and structural reforms to improve growth potential. Crisis management in the euro-zone was special in the sense that unlike in other crises, monetary policy could not be subject to conditionality as it is conducted by the ECB.

It is also important to emphasize that conditionality in itself does not necessarily solve the problem of moral hazard associated with lending. Unlike a private institution, the IMF cannot just walk away from the program and cut the losses (Kahn and Sharma 2005: 122). This is why country ownership of the program is critical—it aligns the incentives of lenders and borrowers. Ownership means "the extent to which a country is interested pursuing reforms independently of any incentives provided by multinational lenders" (Drazen 2002: 37). This idea has been emphasized particularly strongly since the 1990s (Brunnermeier, James and Landau 2016: 288).

In examining the relationship between conditionality and ownership Drazen (2002: 40) calls attention to a basic tension between conditionality and ownership: why is conditionality needed if the conditions are in the best interest of the country as argued by the IMF? In order to answer this puzzle, Drazen focuses on conflict of interests not between lenders and borrowers but rather among interest groups in the domestic countries—by imposing certain conditions on a country, the multinational lenders strengthen domestic forces interested in reforms and weaken groups opposing reforms.

Still, the IMF has designed several mechanisms, which are meant to strengthen domestic ownership of programs. The most important ones are encouraging countries to design their own programs, streamlining structural conditionality to provide more room for democratic decision-making, adopting floating tranche conditionality and focusing on outcomes rather than policies (Khan and Sharma 2005: 125–128).

3.5.3 The Significance of Trust During the Negotiations of Financial Assistance Programs

The negotiation of financial assistance in the euro-zone involved the Troika and various national governments. Trust among members of the Troika was critical to agree on the negotiating positions, while trust between the Troika and the borrower government strongly shaped the content and evaluation of the program.

Members of the Troika worked together well, and trust did not become an issue although there were some differences on policy. As explained by Lütz and Kranke (2014), the IMF delegates had greater flexibility during the negotiations, while European Commission officials were bound by EU legislation, and focused on fiscal rules more strongly. There were also differences in specific policies—the IMF was more focused than the Commission on structural reforms; it was more pessimistic about the European banking sector, and it pushed harder for debt restructuring in the Greek case (Brunnermeier, James and Landau 2016: 301–303). Still, members of the Troika shared the objective of halting the European crisis and prevent defaults. They could also not risk to be played out against one another during negotiations, so they agreed on a united front during each negotiation (Lütz and Kranke 2014: 318).

Trust was however a crucial issue between the Troika and the negotiating government. While the IMF practice of lending has a number of methods to ensure compliance, these still do not solve the essential problem of moral hazard and negate the importance of trust between lender and borrower. The Troika has to agree to home-grown programs in order to ensure the repayment of loans. A certain amount of trust is necessary regarding the promise that the program will be implemented and will produce the targeted outcomes. Floating tranche conditionality ensures the continued incentive to implement the program and produce the outcome, but there is still substantial judgment involved. As described above, the Troika cannot easily walk away from programs and has a clear interest in their success. This also questions conditionality of outcomes since unexpected events can take place, which might make the terms of the original contract unrealistic. Judgment and politics play a great role in assessing such situations. In these cases trust among actors is critical.

The roots of such trust are multiple and include prior history of successful cooperation as well as a belief in the capability and willingness of the administration to design and implement a successful program. Finally, as described in the theoretical framework on the origins of trust, in a bureaucracy ideational commonality is crucial. Therefore capable administrations, which share the fundamental outlook of Troika officials, are likely to get more freedom in designing their programs and have more room for mistakes than those, which have a poor history of cooperation, unable to design an acceptable program and do not share the economic philosophy of the Troika.

3.6 Public Attitudes and Implementing the Financial Assistance Program

Ownership and the domestic design of a stabilization program do not occur in a vacuum. Domestic conditions are decisive during both stages. The public needs to believe that the sacrifices are worthwhile. A major advantage of public trust is to serve as "a reserve of support that enables a system to weather the many storms when outputs cannot be balanced off against inputs of demands" (Easton 1965: 273). This implies that when potentially difficult changes have to be made, the government is able to implement first-best measures, even if they might be painful for the population in the short term. In such a scenario, the perception of the public about the competence and integrity of the government makes the demands for sacrifice acceptable.

Thinking in the long term and accepting sacrifices is a decisive factor in the design of stablization program and the amount of protest a government has to face in imposing hardship on the population. In a low-trust environment, lack of credibility in the promises of the government implies that the long-term benefits of the reforms will not be believed while the short-term sacrifices will be felt immediately. This creates enormous resistance to fiscal stabilization and structural change thus increasing the costs of adjustment (Győrffy 2009, 2013).

In terms of fiscal consolidation this means that in a low-trust environment the method of consolidation is likely to be suboptimal—the primary motive in the decision over consolidation methods is likely to be short-term political rather than long-term economic. Short-term political perspective is likely to opt for raising taxes rather than cutting revenues—especially cash transfers, which are most visible for the public. Even if expenditure cuts take place, public investments are the most likely targets. As discussed in Chap. 1, in the 1990s such consolidations had clearly inferior results to expenditure-based strategies.

Trust in government generally depends on perceived intentions and capabilities (Rosanvallon 2008: 3–4). Both factors are critically affected by earlier periods of consolidation—memories of success or unnecessary hardship are likely to play an important role for public support. If the public does not believe that the policies are designed for the common good but rather focus on particular interest groups, they are unlikely to accept the sacrifices asked. In this context the fairness of adjustment is critical—if an effort is made to distribute the burdens fairly, public support for the adjustment is more likely. According to Stix (2013), the concern for fairness is present both among the current generation and in the intergenerational context. He also found that the low credibility of success for the plans lowers public support. Some degree of systemic trust thus seems critical for international financial assistance programs to yield the expected results.

3.7 The Market Reception of the Financial Assistance Program

The major aim of financial assistance programs is to help countries return to market financing. In order to achieve this, trust in the capability of repaying the loans is necessary. However, as mentioned in the section on market trust, a given set of fundamentals might be consistent with multiple equilibria, which means that if investors believe in a country's ability to repay its loans, it can, but if they lose this belief, a self-fulfilling crisis can take place. The presence of animal spirits can give rise to cycles of confidence when increasing prices increase confidence reinforcing the rise in prices.

While animal spirits play an important role in creating boom and bust on the financial markets, rational bases for trust cannot be dismissed. Countries with a history of serial default and high inflation face serious constraints in gaining market access and exhibit features of debt intolerance, which means they might face a loss of confidence at much lower levels of debt than developed countries (Reinhart et al. 2003). Present policies also influence market perceptions. One of the main claims of the literature on expansionary fiscal consolidations is that painful expenditure-based consolidations signal the commitment of policymakers to stabilization and thus increase market confidence (Alesina et al. 1998; Ardagna 2004).

One of the ways IMF lending is supposed to work is through catalyzing private lending—it is believed that once a country achieves the seal of approval for its adjustment program, markets are more likely to believe in its success than otherwise. Belief in the success of the program in turn reduces the burden of adjustment on the debtor country. However, as Cottarelli and Giannini (2006) acknowledges, empirical evidence for such effect is small. By reviewing the possible channels through which this effect might work (provision of assistance, information, commitment technology, screening device, and liquidity), they note the uncertainty regarding the conditions for such methods to work, which include the problems noted above regarding IMF lending—asymmetric information, potential for breaching the contract, and the role of judgment over non-compliance.

The above problems imply that markets are also paying attention to domestic factors, which influence the behavior of policy-makers. In case of strong resistance and lack of public support for the program, concerns of sustainability might emerge.

3.8 Trust and Austerity Spirals

Based on the above discussion, we can conclude that the major mechanism for austerity spirals and the failure of crisis management is the lack of credibility of the government. When negotiating a stabilization program, the Troika is likely to require more control over a government with low credibility implying tougher and more severe conditions than a government with credibility. The tougher conditions increase public resistance, which in turn lower market confidence. All these factors contribute to program failure: tougher conditions are more difficult to fulfill, greater public resistance increase the incentives for non-compliance, while lack of market confidence increase the need for adjustment. Failure of the program further reduces the credibility of the government and thus the cycle is reinforced. A graphic representation of this phenomenon is shown by Fig. 3.1.

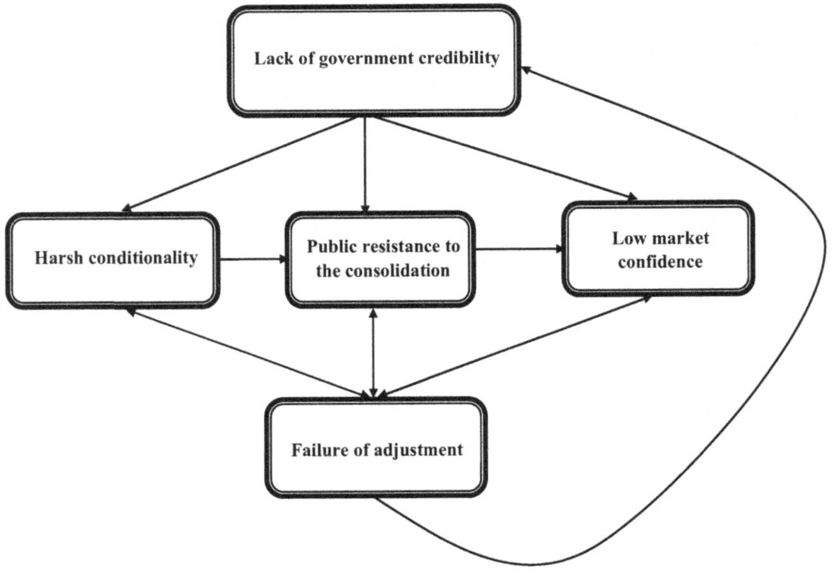

Fig. 3.1 Lack of trust and austerity spirals

* * *

The main objective of the chapter was to provide an overview about the problem of trust and how it could play a role in the management of the European financial crisis. The concept of trust is far from straightforward and at different stages of crisis management, different types of trust are relevant. While during the negotiation phase interpersonal trust within the elites play a key role, in the implementation and reception phases institutional trust is critical. In the long-term prospects of the economy the level of generalized trust plays a significant role.

This chapter also showed why distrust is not conducive to successful crisis management. Distrustful negotiations make the conditionality harsher, the promises more difficult to keep, which in turn worsens the reception by the market and makes the return to market financing more unlikely.

However, one cannot talk about crisis management in general, and there have been substantial differences among the countries which needed financial support in the EU. In the next chapter the theoretical model developed in this chapter is illustrated by the cases of Ireland and Greece.

Notes

1. In the case of repeated games, the winning strategy is TIT FOR TAT, which starts with cooperation but punishes non-cooperative behavior (Axelrod 1984).
2. Trust and credibility are often mentioned together. The difference between them is the subject: if A is credible, B trusts him. However, given the importance of subjectivity, it has to be emphasized that trust and credibility do not necessarily go together—A might be credible but B might still not trust him because he had bad experiences in the past.
3. See the classic elaboration of this problem in Italy by Banfield (1958).
4. The concept of political elite in itself requires explanation. In the following I rely on the classic definition of Wright Mills, who defines it as the power elite, which "is composed of men whose positions enable them to transcend the ordinary environments of ordinary men and women; they are in positions to make decisions having major consequences" (Mills 1956/2000: 4). People belonging here are leading politicians, heads of major state institutions, prominent businessmen, and opinion leaders. Decisions on the economy are

also often influenced by the representatives of intergovernmental institutions.

5. This guarantees that the losers accept the outcome even if they lost—since they do not lose everything and they retain the chance to win next time (Anderson et al. 2005). When even such basic trust is lacking, incentives emerge to act outside the constitutional framework.
6. See, for example, Algan and Cahuc (2010), Horvath (2013), Knack and Keefer (1997), Zak and Knack (2001).
7. This finding is qualified by Charron and Rothstein (2016), who argue that it is present only in a high-quality institutional environment. On the basis of date from 24 countries, they argue that the impact of education on trust disappears when the quality of institutions is low.
8. The importance of ethnic background in generalized trust is supported by other studies as well, such as Guiso et al. (2006).
9. In the past years, economic research has shown increasing attention to inequalities as evidenced by the best-selling volume of Thomas Piketty (2014) as well as the Nobel prize of Angus Deaton. Inequality is a systemic characteristic of market economies, which provide strong incentives to compete and innovate. Some degree of inequality is thus necessary for motivating performance. The question is when inequality can be considered excessive. In a review essay of Piketty's book, Kornai (2015) lists numerous cases when great wealth is ethically justifiable or at least acceptable—such revolutionary innovators, managers of giant corporations, or stars in various fields. However, he also mentions several cases, when great wealth cannot be justified from an ethical perspective: those committing tax fraud, the mafia, or people designing Ponzi schemes. Inequality is often the result of exclusive institutions, which are described by Acemoglu and Robinson (2012). When talking about excessive inequalities, we are describing exclusive institutions and the poor chances for social mobility—rather than unequal performance on a competitive market.
10. A more precise definition and a deeper discussion concerning the rule of law will be given in Chap. 7.
11. These are described more in depth in Győrffy (2013): 28–33.
12. For a monographic exposition of the relationship between trust and tax compliance, see Braithwaite (2009). Recent surveys include Kastlunger et al. (2013) as well as Kogler et al. (2013).
13. For a formal presentation of this statement, see Obstfeld (1996).

14. For an extensive analysis, see the classic work of Shiller (2000).
15. The joint analysis of trust and trustworthiness indicate that trustworthiness and trusting behavior goes hand in hand. See Glaeser et al. (1999).
16. An earlier version of this part was published in Győrffy (2014): 485–489.

References

Acemoglu, Daren, and James Robinson. 2012. *Why nations fail: The origins of power, prosperity, and poverty*. New York: Crown Business.

Aghion, Phillippe, Yann Algan, Pierre Cahuc, and Andrei Shleifer. 2010. Regulation and distrust. *Quarterly Journal of Economics* 125 (3): 1015–1049.

Alesina, Alberto, Roberto Perotti, and Jose Tavares. 1998. The political economy of fiscal adjustments. *Brookings Papers on Economic Activity* 1: 197–266.

Algan, Yann, and Pierre Cahuc. 2010. Inherited trust and growth. *American Economic Review* 100 (5): 2060–2092.

Anderson, Christopher J., Andre Blais, Shaun Bowler, Todd Donovan, and Ola Listhaug. 2005. *Losers' consent: Elections and democratic legitimacy*. Oxford: Oxford University Press.

Ardagna, Silvia. 2004. Fiscal stabilizations: When do they work and why. *European Economic Review* 48 (5): 1047–1074.

Arrow, Kenneth. 1972. Gifts and exchanges. *Philosophy and Public Affairs* 1 (4): 343–362.

Axelrod, Robert. 1984. *The evolution of cooperation*. New York: Basic Books.

Banfield, Edward. 1958. *The moral basis of a backward society*. Glencoe: The Free Press.

Braithwaite, Valerie. 2009. *Defiance in taxation and governance: Resisting and dismissing authority in a democracy*. Cheltenham/Northampton: Edward Elgar.

Brunnermeier, Markus K., Harold James, and Jean-Pierre Landau. 2016. *The euro and the battle of ideas*. Princeton/Oxford: Princeton University Press.

Charron, Nicholas, and Bo Rothstein. 2016. Does education lead to higher generalized trust? The importance of quality of government. *International Journal of Educational Development* 50: 59–73.

Cottarelli, Carlo, and Curzio Giannini. 2006. Bedfellows, hostages, or perfect strangers? Global capital markets and the catalytic effect of IMF crisis lending. In *IMF-supported programs: Recent staff research*, ed. Ashoka Mody and

Alessandro Rebucci, 202–227. Washington, DC: International Monetary Fund.
Drazen, Allen. 2002. Conditionality and ownership in IMF lending: A political economy approach. *IMF Staff Papers* 49 (S1): 36–67.
Easton, David. 1965. *A systems analysis of political life*. New York: Wiley.
Fukuyama, Francis. 1996. *Trust: The social virtues and the creation of prosperity*. London: Hamish Hamilton.
———. 2015. *Political order and political decay*. London: Profile Books.
Gilley, Bruce. 2009. *The right to rule: How states win and lose legitimacy*. New York: Columbia University Press.
Glaeser, Edward, David Laibson, Jose A. Scheinkman, and Christine L. Soutter. 1999. *What is social capital? The determinants of trust and trustworthiness*. NBER Working Paper No. 7216.
Guiso, Luigi, Paola Sapienza, and Luigi Zingales. 2006. Does culture affect economic outcomes? *Journal of Economic Perspectives* 20 (2): 23–48.
Győrffy, Dóra. 2009. Structural change without trust: Reform cycles in Hungary and Slovakia. *Acta Oeconomica* 59 (2): 147–177.
———. 2013. *Institutional trust and economic policy: Lessons from the history of the euro*. Budapest/New York: CEU Press.
———. 2014. The role of expectations in austerity cycles: The political economy of crisis management in Ireland and Greece. *Acta Oeconomica* 64 (4): 489–509.
Hardin, Russel. 2006. *Trust*. Cambridge: Polity Press.
Harsányi, John. 1953. Cardinal utility in welfare economics and the theory of risk-taking. *Journal of Political Economy* 61 (5): 434–435.
Horvath, Roman. 2013. Does trust promote growth? *Journal of Comparative Economics* 41 (3): 777–788.
Hoskin, Geoffrey. 2014. *Trust: A history*. Oxford: Oxford University Press.
James, Harvey S. 2002. The trust paradox: A survey of economic inquiries into the nature of trust and trustworthiness. *Journal of Economic Behavior and Organization* 47 (3): 291–307.
Kahn, Mohsin, and Sunil Sharma. 2005. IMF conditionality and country ownership of adjustment programs. In *IMF-supported programs: Recent staff research*, ed. Ashoka Mody and Alessandro Rebucci, 119–130. Washington, DC: International Monetary Fund.
Kastlunger, Barbara, Edoardo Lozza, Erich Kirchler, and Alfred Schabmann. 2013. Powerful authorities and trusting citizens: The slippery slope framework and tax compliance in Italy. *Journal of Economic Psychology* 34: 36–45.

Keynes, John M. 1936. *The general theory of employment, interest and money.* New York: Harcourt, Brace.

Knack, Stephen, and Philip Keefer. 1997. Does social capital have an economic payoff? A cross-country investigation. *Quarterly Journal of Economics* 112 (4): 1251–1288.

Kogler, Christoph, Larissa Batrancea, Anca Nichita, Jozsef Pantya, Alexis Belianin, and Erich Kirchler. 2013. Trust and power as determinants of tax compliance: Testing the assumptions of the slippery slope framework in Austria, Hungary, Romania and Russia. *Journal of Economic Psychology* 34: 169–180.

Kornai, János. 2015. So what is capital in the twenty-first century? Some notes on Piketty's book. *Capitalism and Society* 11 (1): Article 2.

Larson, Deborah Welch. 2004. Distrust: Prudent, if not always wise. In *Distrust*, ed. Russel Hardin, 34–59. New York: Russel Sage Foundation.

Levi, M. 1998. A state of trust. In *Trust and governance*, ed. Valerie Braithwaite and Margaret Levi, 77–101. New York: Russel Sage Foundation.

Lütz, Susanne, and Matthias Kranke. 2014. The European rescue of the Washington consensus? EU and IMF lending to Central and Eastern European countries. *Review of International Political Economy* 21 (2): 310–338.

Medve-Bálint, Gergő, and Zsolt Boda. 2014. The poorer you are, the more you trust? The effect of inequality and income on institutional trust in East-Central Europe. *Czech Sociological Review* 50 (3): 419–453.

Mills, Wright C. 1956/2000. *The power elite.* Oxford: Oxford University Press.

Möllering, Guido. 2006. *Trust: Reason, routine, reflexivity.* Amsterdam: Elsevier.

Obstfeld, Maurice. 1996. Models of currency crises with self-fulfilling features. *European Economic Review* 40: 1037–1047.

Offe, Claus. 1999. How can we trust our fellow citizens? In *Democracy and trust*, ed. Mark E. Warren, 42–87. Cambridge: Cambridge University Press.

Piketty, Thomas. 2014. *Capital in the twenty first century.* Cambridge, MA: Belknap Press.

Putnam, Robert. 1994. *Making democracy work. Civic traditions in modern Italy.* Princeton: Princeton University Press.

Rawls, John. 1999. *A theory of justice.* Rev. ed. Cambridge, MA: The Belknap Press of Harvard University Press.

Reinhart, Carmen M., Kenneth S. Rogoff, and Miguel A. Savastano. 2003. Debt intolerance. *Brookings Papers on Economic Activity* 34: 1–74.

Rosanvallon, Pierre. 2008. *Counter-democracy: Politics in an age of distrust.* Cambridge: Cambridge University Press.

Rose, Richard. 2005. Giving direction to government in comparative perspective. In *Institutions of American democracy: The executive branch*, ed. J. Aberbach and M. Peterson, 72–99. Oxford: Oxford University Press.

Rothstein, Bo. 1998. *Just institutions matter: The moral and political logic of the universal welfare state.* Cambridge: Cambridge University Press.

———. 2000. Trust, social dilemmas and collective memories. *Journal of Theoretical Politics* 12 (4): 477–501.

Rothstein, Bo, and Dietlind Stolle. 2008. The state and social capital: An institutional theory of generalized trust. *Comparative Politics* 40 (4): 441–459.

Rothstein, Bo, and Jan Teorell. 2008. What is the quality of government? A theory of impartial government institutions. *Governance* 21 (2): 165–190.

Rothstein, Bo, and Eric Uslaner. 2005. All for all: Equality, corruption and social trust. *World Politics* 58 (1): 41–72.

Rudolph, Thomas J., and Jillian Evans. 2005. Political trust, ideology, and public support for government spending. *American Journal of Political Science* 49 (3): 660–671.

Sabatier, Paul A., and Hank Jenkins-Smith. 1988. An advocacy coalition model of policy change and the role of policy orientated learning therein. *Policy Sciences* 21: 129–168.

Schwarzer, Daniela. 2015. Building the euro area's debt crisis management capacity with the IMF. *Review of International Political Economy* 22 (3): 599–625.

Seligman, Adam. 2000. *The problem of trust.* Princeton: Princeton University Press.

Shelling, Thomas. 1963. *The strategy of conflict.* Cambridge, MA: Harvard University Press.

Shiller, Robert J. 2000. *Irrational exuberance.* New Jersey: Princeton University Press.

Smaghi, Lorenzo B. 2015. Governance and conditionality: Toward a sustainable framework? *Journal of European Integration* 37 (7): 755–768.

Stix, Helmut. 2013. Does the broad public want to consolidate public debt? The role of fairness and policy credibility. *Kyklos* 66 (1): 102–129.

Ullmann-Margalit, Edna. 2004. Trust, distrust and in between. In *Distrust*, ed. Russel Hardin, 60–81. New York: Russel Sage Foundation.

Uslaner, Eric M. 1999. Democracy and social capital. In *Democracy and trust*, ed. Mark E. Warren, 121–150. Cambridge: Cambridge University Press.

Uslaner, Eric. 2002. *The moral foundations of trust*. Cambridge: Cambridge University Press.

———. 2008. Trust as a moral value. In *The handbook of social capital*, ed. Dario Castiglione, Jan W. van Deth, and Guglielmo Wolleb, 101–121. Oxford: Oxford University Press.

Wagner, Alexander F., Friedrich Schneider, and Martin Halla. 2009. The quality of institutions and satisfaction with democracy in Western Europe – A panel analysis. *European Journal of Political Economy* 25 (1): 30–41.

Whiteley, Paul. 2000. Economic growth and social capital. *Political Studies* 48 (3): 443–466.

Zak, Paul J., and Stephen Knack. 2001. Trust and growth. *Economic Journal* 111 (470): 295–321.

4

Institutional Capacities and Crisis Management in Greece and Ireland

The tragedy of Greece and the success of Ireland represent the polar opposites in European crisis management.[1] They are representative cases for the importance of trust during the negotiations, implementation, and market reception of international financial assistance programs. While distrust in all relevant relationships plagued the efforts of Greece, competence and widespread confidence accompanied Irish steps to manage the crisis. The two cases show the crucial importance of institutional quality in crisis management—while the high-quality administration in Ireland was able to devise, negotiate, and implement its own program for getting out of the crisis, poor capacities in Greece resulted in increasingly intrusive requirements in the successive financial assistance programs.

The structure of the chapter is the following. The next section provides an introduction into the functioning of the state in Ireland and Greece followed by a discussion on the roots of their financial crisis. The third section portrays the stark contrast between the program negotiations of the two countries and then the next two sections recount the implementation and market reception of the programs. The last part of the chapter shows the outcomes of crisis management, and the final section concludes.

D. Győrffy, *Trust and Crisis Management in the European Union*,
https://doi.org/10.1007/978-3-319-69212-8_4

4.1 State and Market in Ireland and Greece

The state plays an important role in the economy in both Ireland and Greece, but the philosophy behind the interventions is vastly different.

4.1.1 The Irish Developmental State

During the 1990s Ireland was often referred to as the "Celtic Tiger"—between 1995 and 2000, Ireland recorded close to 10 percent average growth rate[2] which reminded the world to the economic performance of East Asian tigers such as Taiwan, Singapore, or South Korea. The resemblance to successful South Asian economies was also underlined by reference to the concept of developmental state, a strong export orientation and investment into education. According to O'Riain (2000: 158), Ireland is a "flexible developmental state, [which] is defined by its ability to nurture post-Fordist networks of production and innovation, to attract international investment, and to link these local and global technology and business networks together in ways that promote development." Following decades of protectionist policies, the country turned toward export orientation from the 1960s (Powell 2003: 433). Attracting foreign direct investment (FDI) in order to become competitive on the global market was a conscious policy choice, and the Industrial Development Agency (IDA) targeted specific sectors to come to Ireland (Barry 2006). An important reason for the success of an FDI-led growth strategy is the investment into human capital. A low-cost, English-speaking workforce was one of the major advantages of Ireland in attracting investment from the United States. The quality of this workforce was further improved by conscious government policy—starting in the 1960s, a system of regional technical colleges was developed producing engineering, science, and computer graduates, who made Ireland particularly attractive for high-tech investment (Barry 2007).

The real birth of the Celtic Tiger however came with the Social Pact in 1987, which put an end to the macroeconomic imbalances, which came from the Keynesian-inspired responses to the oil crises in the 1970s. With the agreement of social partners, the government implemented an expenditure-led fiscal consolidation and reduced its level of debt from close to 110 percent to 36 percent of GDP by 2000.[3] After cutting both expenditures and taxes, state redistribution fell sharply from over 50 percent to 30 percent of GDP[4] during the same period resulting in a liberal regime of low taxes and needs-based social policies.

As the size of the state was reduced, Ireland increased its attractiveness to FDI with very low corporate taxes—the rate was cut from 40 percent to 24 percent by 2000, then lowered further to 12.5 percent in 2003 (Powell 2003: 437). The attractiveness of the country for investment was further enhanced by institutional reforms, which aimed to increase economic freedom, meaning the ability of actors to engage in mutually advantageous transactions. These imply removing restrictions on trade, capital flows, and protecting property rights, as well as ensuring legal security and the rule of law (Powell 2003: 438). The favorable institutional framework combined with a neocorporatist system of labor relations resulted in a stable and peaceful environment for business planning (Boltho 2000). In the 1990s the country experienced a large boom in FDI, especially in electronics and financial services. Between 1989 and 1998, employment in foreign-owned manufacturing sector increased by 24.8 percent, while in financial and internally traded services, it rose by 384.5 percent. What made Ireland special is that the FDI-dominated segment of the economy did not remain isolated and a strong indigenous industry could also develop in parallel (Ó Riain 2000: 160).

While the Irish state has been very active in establishing the conditions for successful integration into the global economy, its direct participation in the economy through state-owned enterprises (SOEs) is limited. According to Forfás (2010: 3) SOEs produced 5.8 percent of GDP in 2008 and employed 41,000 people or 2 percent of the total employed population. Their role is to provide key infrastructure and services at competitive prices for the Irish economy primarily in the fields of energy, water, waste, transport, and broadband networks (Forfás 2010: 8).

The Irish state has been very successful in ensuring the competitiveness in the global economy. In the two decades following the original social pact, Ireland emerged from the periphery of Europe to a model case of development. Just before the crisis, in 2007, GDP per capita adjusted for purchasing power parity stood at 147 percent of EU average, second in the EU after Luxembourg.[5]

4.1.2 State Intervention in Greece

The activism of the Greek state in managing the economy presents a sharp contrast to the Irish flexible developmental state. Greece left behind a seven-year right-wing military dictatorship in 1974. The following decades were dominated by two major parties: New Democracy (ND) founded by Constantine Karamanlis and the Panhellenic Socialist Movement (PASOK) founded by Andreas Papandreou. While in the 1970s the ND government committed itself to West European integration, the Papandreou government, which came to power in 1981, had an inward-oriented economic agenda, in which the state played a key role.

Papandreou opposed the accession to the European Communities (EC) and played on nationalist sentiments by presenting the EC, the United States and the North-Atlantic Treaty Organization (NATO) as "an unholy trinity threatening Greek democracy and the well-being of the Greek people" (Pappas 2010: 1247). Once he got into power, the state was radically expanded. His first step was to increase state wages by 88 percent, pensions by 76 percent. He created a large number of new state agencies, which provided safe and high-paying jobs to his followers (Chrysoloras 2013: 12). While the public sector employed 350,000 people in 1981, by 1992 the number grew to 616,000 (Iokamidis 2001: 77). In this system the main incentive to join a party was to get a job in the state apparatus (Chrysoloras 2013: 13). Since the expansion of the state took place without corresponding increase in taxation, fiscal deficit remained high during the entire period. As a result public debt grew from 27 in 1981 to 74.8 percent of GDP by 1991.[6]

In the 1990s the accession process to the Economic and Monetary Union periodically stopped the further accumulation of debt. The ND government between 1990 and 1993 attempted to implement reforms including privatization of state enterprises as well as a reduction of fiscal deficits. These measures were highly unpopular, and in 1993 the PASOK government came back to power (Chrysoloras 2013: 13). However, under the premiership of Costas Simitis, they did not change course, and

Greece successfully introduced the euro in 2001—although in retrospect we know that the country never reached the 3 percent deficit threshold.[7]

Following the introduction of the euro, fiscal deficits returned. Greece gained substantially from the decline of interest rates with the introduction of the euro—while in 1992 long-term interest rates stood at 24.1 percent, by 2005 they declined to 3.6 percent.[8] As a result, in spite of stagnant public debt, debt service declined from 10.7 to 4.4 percent of GDP between 1995 and 2006.[9] This also implied that budgetary consolidation could take place without structural reforms and the government was able to raise wages and social benefits.[10] The expansion of the state is also shown by employment figures—by 2009 government employment reached 1,200,000 out of a labor force of around 5,000,000 (Visvizi 2012: 18). In 2010 there were 74 SOEs in Greece valued at €44 billion (OECD 2010: 7).[11]

The expansion of the state also implied extensive state regulation of business. Product and labor market regulations have been long considered as the most extensive in the EU (Iokamidis 2001: 77). This is supported by the research on administrative costs, which were the highest in the EU prior to the crisis (European Commission 2006). The overregulation of the private sector provides enormous opportunities for corruption and the functioning of a shadow economy, which is around 30 percent of the official economy in Greece (OECD 2010: 10).

The weakness of the institutional structure shows up in competitiveness rankings. Just before the crisis, in 2007, the *Doing Business* survey ranked Greece 109 out of 175 countries, while Ireland was 10th (World Bank 2007: 6). The Greek ranking was by far the worst place among EU countries. The World Governance Indicators also show the substantial difference between the quality of governance in the two countries as Ireland performs significantly better than Greece in all dimensions (Fig. 4.1).

Lack of competitiveness and weak institutions were reflected in FDI inflows. According to UNCTAD (2012) while Greece has a 1.9 percent share of EU GDP, in terms of FDI, its share is only 0.5 percent. Even by 2010 the stock of FDI was only 11.6 of the GDP—while 121 percent in Ireland (UNCTAD 2011).

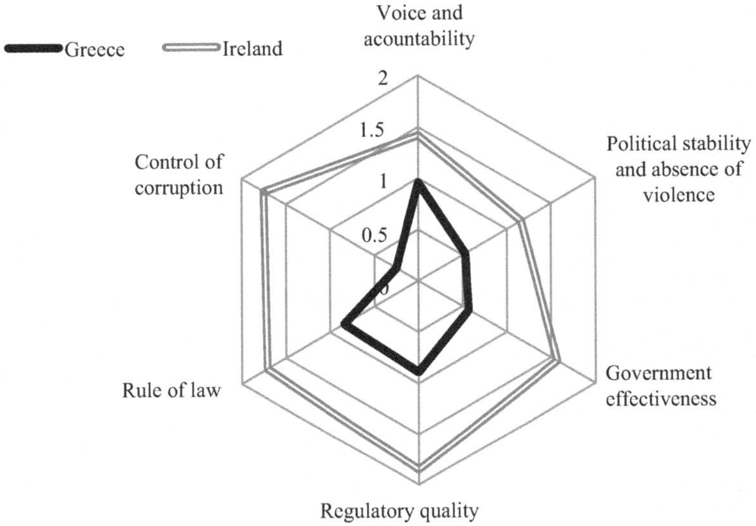

Fig. 4.1 World Governance Indicators in Ireland and Greece in 2007 (Data: World Governance Indicators at: www.govindicators.org)

In spite of the dismal competitiveness indicators and lack of FDI, between 2000 and 2007 growth rate averaged over 4 percent.[12] Growth was driven by the large-scale public investments in preparation for the 2004 Olympic Games as well as the inflow of cheap credit, which fueled consumption (Chrysoloras 2013: 17). This meant an economic structure where private entrepreneurship was stifled by regulations, while growth was primarily based on consumption financed by public spending and high wages—in the Greek GDP, the share of consumption has been close to 70 percent since the 1990s, which is much higher than the 55–57 percent average of the euro-zone.[13] At the same time, exports were only 22.5 percent of GDP in 2007, which is in sharp contrast to the Irish 80.7 value.[14]

Based on this overview we can see that periods of high growth in Greece reflected large-scale state spending rather than integration into global markets. Legitimacy of the government was based on providing jobs, high wages, and transfers. The private sector had to suffer from inefficient state services but was appeased by leniency on tax enforcement.[15] This setup meant a very different environment and mindset for the various actors than the Irish one, which became crucial during the management of the financial crisis.

4.2 The Road to Crisis

4.2.1 Crisis in Greece

As emphasized by Visvizi (2012: 16–17), exposure of Greek banks to toxic assets were minimal, thus the country was relatively unaffected during the first phase of the crisis. It was only during the first half of 2010 when Greek spreads sharply shot up.

According to Gibson et al. (2011: 9–10) as well as Visvizi (2012: 21), a major reason for the loss of confidence was the revision of deficit data by the newly elected PASOK government in October 2012—the 2009 fiscal deficit data was revised to 12.7 percent of GDP, more than double of the 6 percent original projection of the previous government. This was followed in December by the admission that public debt reached €300 billion well over 100 percent of the GDP. The two announcements were quickly followed by downgrades from the major rating agencies. Afterward interest rates rose sharply and Greece lost access to the international financial markets.

While the data mostly supports the above interpretation, Jones (2012: 13) argues that investors long knew about the fundamental Greek problems and calls attention to the early events of 2009: following a slight upward revision of the deficit data, interest rates started to rise but came down eventually. He attributes this turn to the calming influence of the German finance minister, Peer Steinbrück, a Social Democrat, who declared that "no government participating in the euro would be allowed to go bankrupt." The response to the market anxieties at the end of 2009 was entirely different. The 2009 elections in Germany were used by the Christian Democrats to end their grand coalition with the Social Democrats and form a new center-right government with the liberal Free Democratic Party. The new government took a tougher line on bailing out other countries, and this position was made clear by Angela Merkel at the March 2010 European Council. As Merkel stated that "any bailout would come as a last resort," money flew out of Greece (Jones 2012: 14).

The two accounts about the outbreak of the Greek crisis are not necessarily at odds—while the first focuses on the domestic origins of the panic, the second is concerned with the response at the euro-zone level and the resulting collapse in market confidence. Since Greece was unable to raise financing, it had to ask for international assistance. Being in the euro-zone turned out not to be a guarantee against experiencing financial crisis, and this had important consequences for Ireland as well.

4.2.2 The Crisis in Ireland

While the fiscal problems of Greece were well known, the crisis in Ireland appeared more surprising. According to the IMF (2015: 6) "Ireland's long history of economic success may have contributed to the fact that risks were largely not recognized or downplayed, both by domestic and foreign observers." The large-scale real estate bubble in the country mostly emerged unnoticed.

Similarly to other cases of bubbles, the origins of the Irish crisis can be traced back to easy monetary conditions. Between 1999 and 2008, real interest rates were negative implying that the interest rate set by the ECB was too low for Ireland, which had an inflation rate higher than the euro-area average. The resulting negative real interest rates strongly encouraged borrowing, which was made even easier given the enormous inflows of foreign savings following the introduction of the euro (Honohan 2009: 210). The availability of cheap credit led to an easing of lending standards, which made mortgages available to those segments of the population, which did not have access before—100 percent loan-to-value ratios were not unusual, making negative equity widespread once prices started to decline (Honohan 2009: 216). Given the widespread increase in credit, housing prices soared, which started a bubble—expectations about further price increases were built up into current prices, and investment into real estate increased further. There were clear signs of overheating of the economy as a result of buoyant investment, rising private consumption, erosion of wage moderation due to emergent labor shortages as well as government policy, which involved both increased spending and tax cuts.[16]

As there was no intervention to stop the growing bubble,[17] from 2001 onward the Irish growth model began to change, and construction took over the lead from exports—it peaked at 24.5 percent of GNP in 2006

(NESC 2009: 18). Employment in construction illustrates the fast growth of the sector—between 1993 and 2007, it more than doubled growing from less than 6 percent to over 13 percent as share of total employment (Honohan 2009: 212).

The sharp rise in domestic demand also drove up wages, which led to inflation. This was disastrous in the euro-zone given the lack of recourse to devaluation. As labor costs increased, Ireland's competitiveness was steadily declining on the international markets, which was reflected in a worsening current account position—the regular 2–3 percent surplus characterizing the 1990s turned into a deficit over 5 percent by 2007.[18]

Vulnerability to crisis was further exacerbated by the fiscal policy of the government. Starting from the 1990s, a substantial shift took place in the composition of tax revenue: the share of cyclically sensitive taxes such as stamp duties, capital gains tax, and corporation tax increase from 8 percent to 30 percent (Regling and Watson 2010: 27). In explaining this shift, Dellepiane and Hardiman (2010: 10) point to the role of social partnership in wage-setting—through the reduction of personal income tax, trade union members could enjoy an increase in real wage, while the government could collect revenues from the boom in housing. The reliance on revenues from the housing sector might be an explanation why the government also took actions to fuel the boom—the ceiling on the income tax deductibility of mortgage interest for owner-occupied real estate was increased in 2000, 2003, 2007, and 2008 (Honohan 2010: 31).

Given the interests of governments and households, the reluctance of the regulatory authorities to "ruin the party" becomes understandable. However, once the crisis hit, the pitfalls of this arrangement became evident overnight. As Honohan (2010: 32) argues, the bubble would have burst even without the international crisis as real estate prices had been falling for 18 months prior to the collapse of Lehman Brothers. The banks involved in real estate lending were thus on the road to insolvency. The contribution of the international crisis to the domestic problems was that soft landing became impossible.

Once the international financial markets froze and the banks could not roll over their short-term debt, immediate government intervention became necessary for saving the financial system. Measures included the blanket guarantee to depositors and creditors of six domestic banks in September 2008, the nationalization of Anglo-Irish Bank, the recapitalization of the two largest banks (Allied Irish Bank, Bank of Ireland) as well as the establishment of the National Asset Management Agency (NAMA). The total costs of these measures were over 40 percent of the GDP at €64 billion (Hardiman and Regan 2013: 10). At the same time, the international crisis depressed foreign trade as well, thus domestic and external demand both collapsed leading to a sharp fall of GDP—a drop of 4.4 percent in 2008 followed by 4.6 percent in 2009—and an increase in unemployment to over 12 percent.[19] The subsequent collapse of revenues and the rise in expenditures together with the costs of bank consolidation resulted in a fiscal deficit of 32.1 percent of GDP in 2010, while public debt surpassed 100 percent by 2011 from 23.9 percent in 2007.[20] All these developments led to doubts about Ireland's ability to pay its liabilities, and a vicious cycle of high interest rates and increased skepticism about debt service developed. Ireland had to ask for international financial assistance in November 2010.

4.3 Negotiating the Financial Assistance Program

In spite of their very different economic systems, in 2010 both Greece and Ireland had to turn to the Troika and implement considerable financial stabilization measures. Understanding the political economy considerations behind the negotiation and implementation of the program on the basis of the theoretical framework will take us closer to understand why a severe austerity spiral developed in Greece and not in Ireland.

4.3.1 Greece

Trust was low toward Greece from the beginning of the negotiations. The country had regularly falsified statistics,[21] and the outbreak of the crisis was viewed as a just punishment for this practice. Even in March 2010, Angela Merkel denied the possibility of a Greek bailout noting the no-bailout clause of EU and called Greece to fulfill its duties and restore its lost credibility.[22]

Following months of inaction and high level of uncertainty on the global financial markets, the Troika agreed to provide Greece a €110 billion support program over three years in May 2010. Euro-zone member states contributed €80 billion of the loan, while the IMF financed the remaining €30 billion within the context of a standby agreement. The package was conditional upon the implementation of a large fiscal consolidation—18 percent of GDP between 2010 and 2014—as well as structural reforms including pension reform, labor, and product market liberalization.[23] While the size of fiscal adjustment was not unprecedented, Ardagna and Caselli (2012: 7–8) argue that two factors made it extremely unlikely to succeed: the scale of recession in Greece and around the world, as well as the lack of recourse to exchange rate adjustment—both of these factors were present during similar scale fiscal consolidations and eased the pain of adjustment.

While Greece implemented substantial adjustment cutting wages and pensions as well as raising taxes,[24] by 2011 it became evident that the program is unlikely to succeed and Greece is unable to return to market financing. According to Ardagna and Caselli (2012: 21), there were two major reasons. First, the revision of the 2009 deficit from 14 to 16 percent meant a much larger need for adjustment than thought during the planning of the program. Second, the Irish crisis implied continued market uncertainty, which made it impossible to return to market financing. Visvizi (2012: 29–30) also notes the worse than expected downturn, which led to the country missing the deficit target (Table 4.1). Furthermore, she also argues that the excessive focus on fiscal balance yielded the wrong set of policies—while Greece suffered severe structural problems from excessive state intervention, most measures focused on raising expenditures and fighting tax evasion, which further worsened the business environment and led to the collapse of investments. At the same time, privatization, which would have been a clear way to raise revenue and improve productivity, was not even considered (Visvizi 2012: 33).

Following the signing of the program and the austerity measures, the Greek economy kept shrinking, which made consolidation all the more painful. At the same time, the crisis in the euro-zone reached further

Table 4.1 Fiscal primary balance criteria and performance in Greece and Ireland (% of GDP)

	2009	2010	2011	2012	2013	2014	2015	2016	2017
Greece 2010	8.6	−2.4	−1	0.9	3.2	5.9			
Greece 2012	−10.6	−5	−2.4	−1	1.8	4.5			
Greece 2015							−0.25	0.5	1.75
Greece actual	−10.1	−5.3	−3	−3.8	−9.1	0.3	−2.3	3.9	2[a]
Ireland 2010	−12.2	−29	−6.8	−4.1	−1.5	1.2	3.2		
Ireland actual	−11.8	−29.3	−9.3	−3.9	−1.4	0.2	0.7	1.7	1.6[a]

Source: European Commission (2010: 13) European Commission (2011: 29), European Commission (2012b: 16), European Commission (2017: 162)
[a]Forecast

countries, and given the anxiety over the Irish then the Portuguese situation, Greece was unable to return to the international financial markets in 2011. Investors did not believe it would be able to finance its liabilities and thus it was not. The insistence of Germany on private sector involvement in the management of crisis made investors even more weary (Ardagna and Caselli 2012: 22).

While the need for a second program was evident during early 2011, a new agreement was signed only in February 2012. Distrust among the partners was a clear reason for this delay. Greece was an ideal target for being a scapegoat. Added to its history of populist policies and statistical manipulation, the country missed the deficit targets during the first two years of the program by a large margin (Table 4.1). Furthermore, an intensification of mutual resentment took place between Greece and its creditors, especially Germany. While Greeks blamed Germans for imposed enormous austerity on the country in return for financial assistance, Germans saw Greeks protesting and negating the conditions, while they are asked to pay.[25] In a survey conducted in January 2012, only 30 percent of the 5000 respondents supported unchanged or greater participation of Germany in the European rescue funds (Bechtel et al. 2012).

Prior to signing the second program, further deterioration of trust took place among the negotiating partners. The painful adjustment led to widespread protests in Greece. For domestic political reasons, the prime minister, George Papandreou, proposed a referendum on the program conditions—he wanted to implicate the opposition party New Democracy in order to mitigate the political costs of the conditions. Under pressure from his European partners threatening of EU exit, he was forced to cancel the referendum and resign. He was replaced by former ECB Vice President Loukas Papademos, who received a temporary mandate as head of a grand coalition government (government of national unity) until the elections scheduled for May 2012. However, uncertainty persisted, and there was increasing speculation of Greece leaving the euro-zone—the term Grexit was born.[26]

The second program of €130 billion was finally signed in February 2012, and the Troika believed that the Greek government committed itself to the conditions and needed to be given a chance to implement them (IMF 2017b: 11). The program was accompanied by private sector involvement in debt reduction, which essentially meant the write-down of 53.5 percent of Greek public debt.[27] The conditions of the agreement were even stricter than the previous one—they aimed at achieving a primary surplus target of 4.5 percent of GDP by 2014 and a debt rate under 120 percent by 2020 (European Commission 2012b: 16). As emphasized by Ardagna and Caselli (2012), these conditions were much tougher than any previous fiscal consolidation in the OECD countries during the previous 40 years. Structural reform conditionality also became much stricter, and extremely detailed measures were prescribed on the areas of public sector functioning, labor and product markets, financial system, and the judiciary. The measures included a 22 percent cut in minimum wage, fully decentralized wage bargaining, and a 150,000 cut in public sector employment by 2015. The government also committed itself to an ambitious privatization program of €50 billion.[28] The IMF ex post report on the program attributes the extremely detailed structural conditionality to two factors: the country had weaker conditions to start with, and the detailed measures aimed to ensure implementation (IMF 2017b: 28).

The deal was signed amid the run-up to the elections in May. In the campaign, the major opposition party, the Coalition of the Radical Left (SYRIZA) called for the revision of the agreement. The difficulties of forming a government were shown by the impasse after the May elections and the necessity of a second round in June. After the elections three pro-euro parties (New Democracy, PASOK, and Democratic Left) formed a government, whose first promise to the electorate was the renegotiation of the employment conditionality in the program.[29]

At this point the Troika took a tough stance and required significant measures on the expenditure side in return for continuing financial assistance. Cuts in the government wage bill, pensions, and social benefits could not be avoided anymore, and by November 2012 Greece actually performed better than the target (European Commission 2012c: 23). In return for compliance the Troika extended the deadline of bringing down the deficit below 3 percent by two years until 2016. Furthermore, it also eased the terms of lending amounting to a new €40 billion loan although no one dared to call it a third program.[30] As a condition for these relief measures, the medium-term fiscal plan of 2013–2014, which was signed in November 2012, focuses mainly on the expenditure side—out of the €13.4 billion adjustment, €11.25 billion was on the expenditure side (European Commission 2012c: 30).

During the following year and a half, the government worked toward the implementation of the program, and signs of recovery became visible by mid-2014 (IMF 2017b: 14). However, the population grew tired of the recession and austerity, and the promise of SYRIZA to end austerity and still remain in the euro-zone was increasingly popular. In January 2015 Alexis Tsipras became prime minister and declared "an end to the vicious cycle of austerity" (Featerstone 2016: 51).

Tsipras' promise was based on the expectation that Grexit could be very costly for the EU—in 2012, in a confidential report, the IMF calculated that the costs would exceed €1 trillion (IMF 2012: 1), while Petersen and Böhmer (2012) argued that although Grexit in itself would not be a major economic catastrophe, if a domino effect follows, and Portugal, Spain, and Italy also leave the euro, the losses would be €17.2 trillion for the euro area until 2020. The Greeks also gave geopolitical threats to the EU ranging from the invasion of jihadists from the South to a possible turn toward Russia or China (Tsebelis 2016: 30). The aggressive and threatening negotiation strategy was accompanied by various insults on European leaders by Tsipras and Yanis Varoufakis, the Greek finance minister (Featherstone 2016: 53).

Threats and insults to negotiation partners are certainly not conducive to trust. They were especially ill-advised in this case, as Greece was undoubtedly the more vulnerable party. The second program expired in early 2015, and it was clear that the country could not return to market financing. Given the impasse with creditors, fears of Greek default and Grexit resurfaced again, and led to an acceleration of deposit withdrawal—in the first half of 2015, banks lost 27 percent of their deposits (IMF 2017a: 12). Banks had to rely on ELA, which made the country dependent on the ECB. Once the ECB froze ELA in June 2015, Greece had to close banks and impose capital controls to limit the outflow of money. They also defaulted on an IMF loan due that month. In trying to avoid the humiliation of an agreement bringing more austerity, Tsipras called a referendum for 5 July, when over 60 percent of the voters rejected the proposed conditionality of the new program. However, the vote was not the rejection of the euro, but rather a (false) belief that it was possible to negotiate a different program. As the threat of exit from the euro area became real, one week after the referendum, the government had to sign a punitive agreement, in order "to exorcise any impression that SYRIZA's irresponsibility had produced rewards" (Featherstone 2016: 55).

The agreement provided up to €86 billion loan through the ESM and with the possibility of later IMF involvement. The conditionality of the third program reflects the experiences of the first two agreements. While in the first and second programs the emphasis was on numerical conditions and detailed structural reforms, respectively, the third program focuses on implementation.[31] Several conditions are so-called prior actions, which were the conditions for signing the agreement. For other structural conditions, the program prescribes that the international best practice has to be implemented, and it makes consultation with the relevant international organization (ECB, IMF, World Bank, or the OECD) mandatory. The European Commission also founded a new body, the Structural Reform Support Service, in order to assist Greece in institutional reforms. The specific conditionality of the program also shifted somewhat. Beyond the earlier elements of fiscal and financial stability as well as labor and product market reforms, modernizing the Greek state received greater emphasis. The measures include the de-politicization of the state administration, the strengthening of the judiciary and the Greek statistical office, the fight against corruption as well as the implementation of the earlier privatization agenda.

After the signing of the third program, there remained no political party in Greece, which could argue credibly that there is another way to stay in the euro-zone. In a new election called for September 2015, Tsipras won again, and barely lost support in comparison to January. This showed that the public accepted the narrative that SYRIZA tried and failed to negotiate a better deal, and there was no alternative to implementing the agreement (Featherstone 2016: 56).

When considering the subsequent rounds of Greek negotiations, the consequences of distrust become clear. Early on Greece was blamed for its own troubles due to doctoring statistics as well as a long history of fiscal profligacy. Making it pay for its past sins was part of the negotiations from the very beginning. The delays in implementing the first program as well as trying to circumvent the conditions increased distrust toward the country, and there was less empathy concerning external factors in the slippages. Increased distrust manifested itself in even tougher and more detailed conditionality. After the third round of negotiations, Greece basically lost its sovereignty in designing public policy and making its own laws.

It is worth to contrast this line of events with the Irish case.

4.3.2 Ireland

Given failing banks, the blanket guarantee on the banking sector and the global recession, confidence toward Ireland was undermined in spite of bold measures to address the crisis. Following the May 2010 rescue program for Greece, bond spread over German bunds rose to 682 basis points by November 2010. Fearing contagion, Ireland was encouraged by European leaders as well to ask for international support. At the end of November the country received a €85 billion program, out of which €17.7 billion came from the EFSF, €22.5 billion from EFSM, €22.5 billion from the IMF, and the remaining amount from bilateral loans and the Irish National Pension Reserve Fund (European Commission 2011: 39).

The support came in a very different package than for Greece. Ireland had a pre-crisis fiscal surplus and no history of doctoring statistics. Unlike in Greece, where even in the midst of crisis populist promises and ridicule of austerity dominated the 2009 election campaign (Visvizi 2012: 21), Ireland took decisive steps from the very beginning to address the crisis. By January 2011 it spent €46.3 billion or 29 percent of GDP on the bank bailout (European Commission 2011: 13). On the fiscal front the authorities focused on front-loaded adjustment and prioritized expenditure-based measures including public sector wage cuts and reductions in entitlement benefits. As a result of these arrangements, when entering the loan program, there were no additional compliance burden for the country, and there were no measures, which were not already planned and in progress (Dellepiane and Hardiman 2012: 11). In other words, Ireland set its own conditions for the program—an achievement later confirmed by IMF head Christine Lagarde (Lagarde 2013).[32]

While there were speculations that Ireland would be forced to raise its low corporate tax rate, which was seen as critical for its ability to draw FDI and is resented in some continental European countries,[33] the country could successfully withstand such pressures. It was also able to achieve a seemingly milder consolidation path than Greece and reach the 3 percent deficit target only by 2015. While a possible reason is the higher level of initial deficit at 32 percent of GDP in 2010, the high number is only technical given the accounting for the bank consolidation. The underlying fiscal deficit was around 13 percent that year (Dellepiane and Hardiman 2012: 13). In turn the government committed itself to a front-loaded expenditure-based adjustment—between 2011 and 2014, a €15 billion fiscal program was proposed with €10 billion expenditure cuts and €5 billion revenue increase (European Commission 2011: 26–27).

From the beginning of the program, Ireland received widespread accolades from Troika authorities and regularly outperformed its carefully chosen targets (Table 4.1). This was the case even when targets were missed on paper. In 2011 the deficit reached 13.4 percent of the GDP instead of the targeted 10.6. However, in 2011 review of the program bank capital injections were excluded from deficit calculations so a 9.9 percent deficit was estimated (European Commission 2012a: 5). There was no similar treatment of capital injections in Greece during the early years of crisis management. With Ireland's commitment to its program, risks were seen essentially in the external environment, which could hinder Ireland's export-based recovery strategy (European Commission 2013: 37).

Overall the Irish negotiations had a very different dynamics than the Greek negotiations. Ireland had a strong pre-crisis record, and its policymakers were more committed to market-friendly policies than most of their negotiating partners. Building on this reputation, they were able to set their own conditions, which were comfortably met. This resulted in a situation when the 9.9 percent deficit in 2011 (13.4 percent with bank support measures) was hailed as widely over-performing the target, while the 9.5 percent deficit in Greece during the same year was seen as a severe breach of conditionality. In 2012—still with a deficit of 7.6 percent and a debt rate approaching 120 percent—the Irish prime minister, Enda Kenny, was presented with a "European of the Year" award by German Magazine Publishers Association[34] and was featured on the cover of *Time* magazine as producer of "The Celtic Comeback." The confidence in Ireland and not in Greece was strongly influenced by domestic political conditions to which I turn in the next section.

4.4 Public Attitudes and the Implementation of the Programs

By some standard measures, there seemed to be no difference in public attitudes toward the crisis in the two countries. As it can be seen from Fig. 4.2, between 2010 and 2013 there was little difference in how the Greek and the Irish public evaluated the national economic situation—steadily over 90 percent of the population believed even in 2013 that the economy was in a poor condition. These numbers certainly did not suggest Ireland as a success story.

There was also little difference in the electoral defeat of parties, which were held responsible for the crisis. The day of reckoning came earlier in Ireland, where the first post-crisis elections were held in February 2011. The ruling party, Fianna Fail, suffered a historic defeat receiving only 17.4 percent of votes down from 41.6 percent in 2007, which meant that it lost 57 seats in Parliament out of 77.[35] The elections were won by Fine Gael, which achieved its best result in history winning 76 seats. A coalition

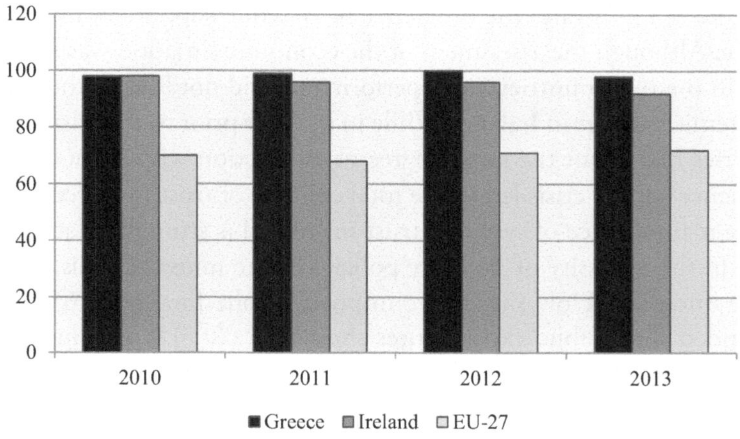

Fig. 4.2 Assessment of national economic situation in Greece and Ireland 2010–2013 (% total bad) (Data: Eurobarometer surveys (Nos. 74, 75, 77, 79) country factsheets. Available: http://ec.europa.eu/public_opinion/archives/eb_arch_en.htm)

government with the Labour Party was formed and headed by the already mentioned Enda Kenny.

Greece also registered historic changes in its traditional party system. While the elections of 2009, which were won by PASOK, did not yet reflect the crisis, the already mentioned elections in 2012 clearly did. However, unlike in Ireland, where the dominant party suffered a historic loss, in Greece basically all mainstream parties became discredited, and new extremist forces gained enormous influence. PASOK, which was considered the most responsible for the crisis, got only 13.2 percent of the votes, down from 44 percent in 2009 and translating to a loss of 119 seats in Parliament out of its 160 in 2009. The elections were narrowly won by New Democracy by 18.85 percent of the votes, which was still considerably lower than its 33 percent performance in 2009. In contrast, SYRIZA and the extreme right party, Golden Dawn, which both opposed the implementation of the Troika agreement, received 16.8 and 7 percent, respectively. While the repeated elections in June could produce a narrow majority for the pro-program forces, the elections already signaled the collapse of systemic support in Greece. By 2015 SYRIZA strengthened significantly and won the snap elections with 36.3 percent of the votes in January and 35.5 percent in September.

Figure 4.3 illustrates the difference in systemic support in Ireland and Greece. Although the assessment of the economic situation was about the same in the two countries, poor performance did not lead to the collapse of systemic support in Ireland. While in the year prior to the crisis the two countries had about the same degree of satisfaction with democracy, the experiences of the crisis led to the total collapse of trust in Greece only.

The maintenance of systemic trust in Ireland is strongly related to the belief in the necessity of austerity policies in the midst of crisis. In 2011 to the question "How should we improve public finances?" 65 percent responded that public expenditures should be cut, 18 percent thought that both tax raises and spending cuts are necessary, while only 7 percent believed that the problem should be handled via tax raises (Millward Brown 2011: 25). Even more striking is the lack of difference along party lines—over 60 percent of the respondents support expenditure cuts, while less than 10 percent believe tax raises to be the solution in every major party from left to right. This remarkable agreement on the course to be followed is probably the primary explanation to why there was almost no resistance to continued austerity in stark contrast to Greece. Left-leaning Irish analysts consider the collective memory of the "Celtic

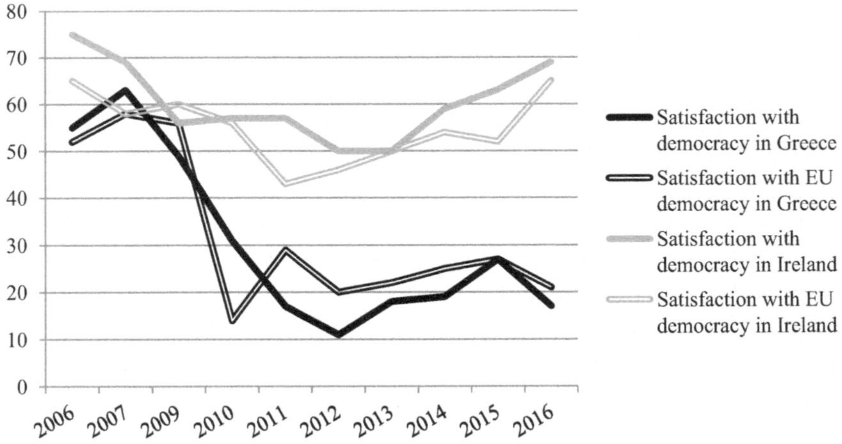

Fig. 4.3 Satisfaction with democracy in Greece and Ireland 2006–2016 (% satisfied) (Data: Eurobarometer surveys (Nos. 65, 68, 72, 73, 76, 78, 80, 82, 84, 85). Available: http://ec.europa.eu/public_opinion/archives/eb_arch_en.htm)

Tiger" years and Ireland as an export-oriented economy as lying at the roots of these beliefs (Mariead and Dukelow 2011; Fraser et al. 2013).

The Irish reaction is in a striking contrast with Greece, where protests have been extremely widespread and strikes as measures to protest are supported by 74 percent of the population (Public Issue 2011). This is also a sign of the collapse of legitimacy, which was based upon an implicit agreement that in return for tolerating poor governance and the prevalence of patronage politics, the private sector can evade taxes. It is hard to escape the conclusion that lacking the memories of success in Ireland as an exporting base, Greeks are much less confident that the collapse of their old system will lead to a better system and there are deep divisions in society about the future.

The differences in public trust were crucial in the implementation of the program conditionality. In Ireland implementation was exceptionally strong, and the country met all performance criteria at each of the reviews (IMF 2015: 14). The banking system was downsized significantly as its balance sheet was reduced by more than 30 percent (European Commission 2015: 58). Prudential oversight was strengthened in order to prevent future real estate bubbles. Beyond reaching the 3 percent deficit target by 2015,[36] Ireland also implemented a new Fiscal Responsibility Law, which made Irish fiscal governance among the strongest in the EU (European Commission 2015: 74). Structural reforms played a moderate role in crisis management given the strong competitive position of the country prior to the crisis (European Commission 2015: 80). Measures on the labor market including increasing the flexibility of wages and active labor market policies had already been planned prior to the crisis.

The Greek record of compliance was much more mixed especially during the early parts of the crisis. Exadaktylos and Zaharidis (2012) provide a strong illustration of the problem by analyzing the "We won't pay" movement. In light of the crisis, the movement declared that they would not accept any new taxes, and they were also protesting against the selling of social goods like roads to private companies. In 2011 they encouraged passengers of the Athens public transport system not to pay their fares, which strongly hurt the already poor finances of these SOEs. In response, the government raised fines for toll evasion leading to a vicious cycle of non-compliance, punishment, and resentment. The episode illustrates the difficulties of fiscal consolidation in a low-trust environment and shows how populist political entrepreneurs can use such situations to build their support base—the movement was strongly entangled with SYRIZA. There were no such obstacles to consolidation in Ireland.

In spite of the extremely difficult conditions for implementing the adjustment program and the mixed reviews of the Troika, after 2013 Greece still made enormous progress. In the annual monitoring of the Euro Plus Pact (Schmieding and Schultz 2014; Schmieding 2015; Schieding and Hense 2016), Greece placed first in front of Ireland in the adjustment indicator in 2013, 2014, and 2016. Ireland ranked first and Greece second in 2015. By 2016 Greece had the largest structural surplus in the EU (Schieding and Hense 2016: 51). However, revenue measures clearly dominated the adjustment as total revenue as percent of GDP rose from the average of 39.3 percent between 2001 and 2010 to 49.7 percent,[37] which signals the reluctance of the Greek political class to reduce the role of the state in the economy. The meager revenues from privatization also point to this reluctance: compared to the 2012 target of €50 billion for the period 2012–2020, in 2015 and 2016 the income from privatization was €0.4 billion and €2.5 billion, respectively (European Commission 2016: 11). Still, due to extensive reforms in the labor and product markets, Greece succeeded to improve its position on the doing business rankings: from place 111 in 2006 to 60 by 2016.[38] There have been wide-ranging reforms of the state administration and the judiciary as well (European Commission 2016: 12).

Regardless of the difference between the attitudes of the public, eventually both countries implemented significant reforms to recover from the financial crisis. However, the relationship with the Troika and the public attitudes toward austerity and structural change were clearly reflected in market reactions, which shows the costs of distrust.

4.5 Market Reactions

Market reaction to the management of the crisis can be traced by looking at the data on ten-year government bond rates. While ECB policies clearly play a role in the fluctuation of interest rates, the comparison of two member states still makes sense and allows inferring country-specific determinants of the rates. As we can see on Fig. 4.4, up until October

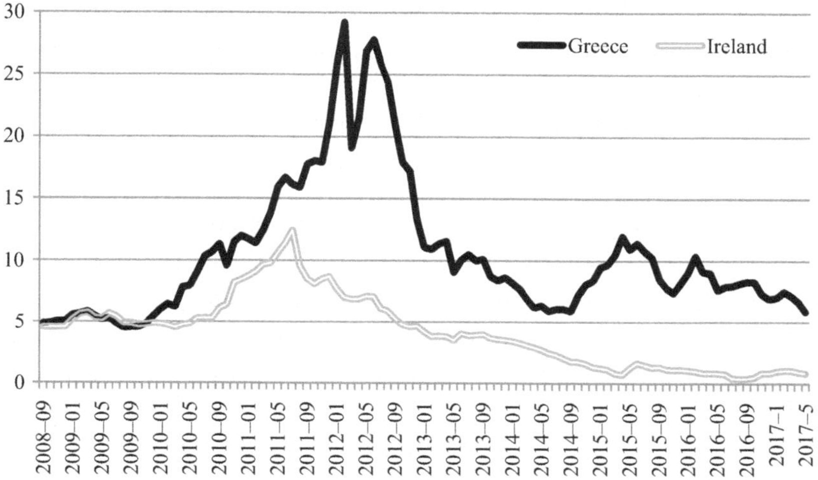

Fig. 4.4 Interest rates on ten-year government bond 2008–2017 (monthly data, %) (Data: ECB Statistical Data Warehouse)

2010 there was basically no difference between Ireland and Greece. When Greece had to ask for a multilateral support program in 2010, rates started to increase. The rise was followed by Ireland a few months later, when the costs of the bank guarantee scheme became evident. The real divide however opened up only in 2011—while markets were clearly calmed by Irish measures, and by 2013 interest rates fell below pre-crisis rates, Greece experienced enormous rate increases as markets feared the exit from the euro-zone. After the second program, markets calmed down, but Greek interest rates were still well over the Irish rates. The victory of SYRIZA and the prolonged negotiation of the third agreement resulted in increasing interest rates again, and at the time of writing, the country still did not reach its pre-crisis rates in spite of the historically low interest rates everywhere in the developed world.

Lack of confidence can also be seen in data on foreign direct investment. While Ireland increased its stock of foreign direct investment from 120.8 to 286 percent of GDP between 2011 and 2016, during the same period the stock of FDI in Greece changed from 10.1 to 14.1 percent of GDP (UNCTAD 2017). While the initial values reflect the different starting positions of the two countries, the Greek number indicates that in spite of the promises of change and the ambitious privatization program, which was part of the second and the third agreements, foreign investors remain skeptical.

The different market reaction had an enormous weight on outcomes.

4.6 Outcomes of Crisis Management

As we could see, both countries have made significant progress in crisis management. While Ireland maintained its competitiveness, Greece implemented long overdue fiscal and structural reforms. Still, the market reception of the two programs was very different, and this showed up in the growth rates of the two countries. Figures 4.5 and 4.6 show the gap between the growth expectations and outcomes based on the IMF World Economic Outlook database.

The difference between the two countries is striking. Greek forecasts turned out to be extremely optimistic in hindsight, while a consistency between targets and outcomes could be observed in Ireland. Given that

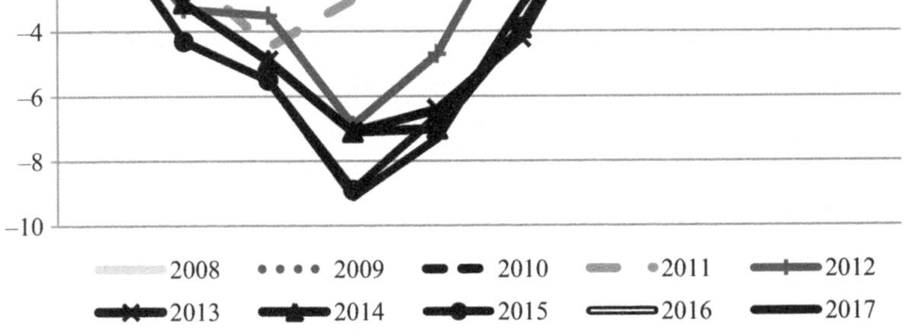

Fig. 4.5 GDP forecasts and reality in Greece 2008–2017 (Data: World Economic Outlook database)

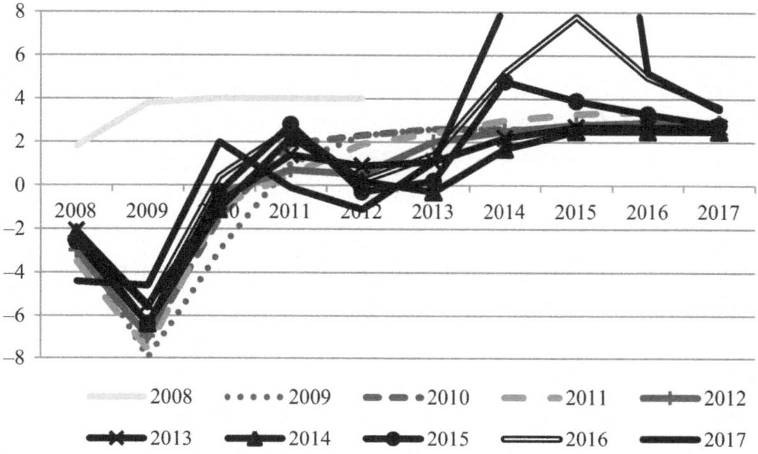

Fig. 4.6 GDP forecasts and reality in Ireland 2008–2017 (Data: World Economic Outlook database. Note: the growth rate in 2015 is an extreme value, 26.3 percent. According to OECD (2016: 1) the reason for the extreme value is the relocation of economic activity by several multinational companies, which includes the relocation of intellectual property and the sales generated by their use)

the two crises took place in parallel, international conditions cannot explain this divergence.

The excessive deviation from targets in the case of Greece raises critical questions regarding program design. In addressing this question, the first IMF ex-post evaluation report emphasizes the underestimation of fiscal multipliers and the "absence of a pick-up in private sector growth," which was expected as a result of structural reforms (IMF 2013: 20–22). In 2014–2015 political uncertainties and renewed fears of Grexit dampened confidence again. The second ex post evaluation report also points to lower than projected confidence effects of reforms and admits that the "political factors may have not been fully exogenous, as the protracted recession and the rapidly falling living standards may have undermined both political support for the program measures and investor confidence" (IMF 2017b: 17).

When we compare the Irish case with Greece, we can speculate about further reasons for the difference between the two countries. Ownership of the program and the presence and utilization of local knowledge probably cannot be dismissed. Given the trust with international partners,

Ireland was basically designing its own program and thus it could utilize local knowledge of its economy. In contrast lack of trust toward Greece was partly driven by a history of doctoring statistics, which also implied that knowledge of the economy was much weaker thus predictions were also more imprecise than in the case of Ireland. Such differences in initial conditions in turn started self-reinforcing cycles, which magnified the difference—while consistency between targets and outcomes ensured confidence for Ireland, regular missing of targets further undermined confidence toward Greece regardless of its underlying efforts. During the prolonged negotiations over the conditionality of the program, the possibility of exit from the euro-zone was never off the table, which implied continued exclusion from markets and deposit flight from banks. The consequences were suffered by the Greek population as the unemployment rate climbed over 20 percent in 2012, and close to half of the population was at risk of poverty by 2014.[39]

* * *

Greece and Ireland represent two archetypes of state intervention into the economy—while the former tries to ensure positive outcomes for selected groups, the latter aims to create an environment, which enables domestic actors to be successful in the global competition. The dominance of partial interests and weak capacities characterize Greece, while high capacities and impartiality describe the Irish state. Although neither was immune from a financial crisis, and neither could avoid the pains of adjustment, the costs differed sharply: while Ireland received international support to design and implement its own focused program to recover from the crisis, Greece practically lost its policy autonomy and suffered significant costs for every single attempt to resist international pressure. Distrust resulted in a vicious cycle of harsh conditions, intense public resistance, and skeptical market reception, which undermined the country's efforts to change. In sum, the country paid an enormous price for its populist politics.[40]

Greece's tragic predicament was not shared by other Mediterranean countries, which also suffered a financial crisis. The next chapter will examine the cases of Cyprus, Portugal, and Spain and ask the question how these countries managed to avoid the fate of Greece.

Notes

1. An earlier version of this chapter was published in Győrffy (2014): 489–501.
2. Data: European Commission (2017), 169.
3. Data: European Commission (2017), 164.
4. Data: Powell (2003) 435 and European Commission (2017), 158.
5. Data: Eurostat GDP per capita in purchasing power standard (PPS).
6. Data: European Commission (2017), 164.
7. While other countries also used creative accounting techniques to enter the euro-zone, Loizides (2013) shows that Greece have reported the least reliable deficit figures and have had the largest dispersion of revisions within the EU between 1991 and 2012.
8. Data: European Commission (2017), 106.
9. Data: European Commission (2017), 140.
10. This was particularly excessive from 2005—monetary social transfers increased from 13.6 to 17.5 percent of GDP, while compensation of employees grew from 11.4 to 13.1 by 2009 (European Commission 2017: 136, 156).
11. In 2010 Greek GDP was €226 billion (European Commission 2017: 16).
12. Data: European Commission (2017), 28.
13. Data: European Commission (2017), 34.
14. Data: European Commission (2017), 80.
15. According to OECD (2010: 9), the efficiency of value-added tax (VAT) collection is by far the lowest in Greece within the euro-zone.
16. The overheating of the Irish economy did not go unnoticed. In 2001 the European Commission publicly reprimanded Ireland for lack of budgetary discipline, while the IMF also noted the dangers associated with labor shortages and easy monetary policy (IMF 2000).
17. Honohan (2010) attributes lack of intervention to the regulatory philosophy of the Irish financial supervisory authorities as well as the separation of banking supervision from the central bank.
18. Data: European Commission (2017), 96.
19. Data: European Commission (2017), 28, 14.
20. Data: European Commission (2017), 160, 164.
21. Areas of misreporting involved the incomplete coverage of public pension funds, state-owned enterprises as well as military outlays (Kopits 2017: 225).

22. As reported by *Economic Policy Journal* on 28 February 2010. Article available: http://www.economicpolicyjournal.com/2010/02/merkel-no-greek-bailout.html. Accessed: 2 July 2017.
23. See European Commission (2010: 13–25) for more details on conditionality.
24. Some of the measures included increases in VAT and excise tax, cuts in public investments, capping 13th and 14th month salaries, freezing recruitment in the central government sector, and raising of the retirement age and penalties for early retirement in the pension system. See Monastiriotis (2013): 5–6.
25. The media coverage of the first program in the two countries was summarized in *The Guardian*, 21 June 2011. Article available: http://www.guardian.co.uk/world/2011/jun/21/german-media-bild-greece-bailout-resentment. Accessed: 2 July 2017.
26. Grexit was first used by Buiter and Rahbari (2012). After their analysis the term spread fast in the financial media.
27. For the details of the program, see IMF (2012c): 45. A detailed, critical analysis of the restructuring is presented by Zettelmeyer et al. (2013), who note the substantial costs the delay caused in the effectiveness of this measure.
28. The sheer volume of conditions is staggering—while the documentation of the first package was 90 pages (European Commission 2010), the second document was 185 pages long (European Commission 2012b).
29. See the report by the *BBC*, http://www.bbc.co.uk/news/world-europe-18564266. Accessed: 2 July 2017.
30. On the specific details of the package, see the Eurogroup statement on 27 November available at: http://www.consilium.europa.eu/uedocs/cms_Data/docs/pressdata/en/ecofin/133857.pdf. Accessed 2 July, 2017.
31. The Memorandum of Understanding for the program is available: https://ec.europa.eu/info/sites/info/files/01_mou_20150811_en1.pdf. Accessed: 2 July 2017.
32. The number of quantitative performance criteria in Irish case was very low not only in comparison to Greece, but also compared to most other financial assistance programs since 2002 (IMF 2015: 11).
33. According to press sources, pressure to increase the corporate tax came from many corners, which include Germany, France, and the European Commission. See reports at http://www.spiegel.de/international/germany/merkel-s-dilemma-chancellor-faces-tough-sell-on-irish-bail-out-a-730578.html or http://www.bloomberg.com/news/2010-11-20/

irish-corporate-tax-rate-increase-isn-t-a-condition-for-aid-sarkozy-says.html. Accessed: 2 July 2017.
34. See report at http://www.independent.ie/irish-news/germans-name-kenny-as-european-of-the-year-28823213.html. Accessed: 2 July 2017.
35. Election results are available at: http://www.electionresources.org.
36. Fiscal deficit was 2 percent in 2015 (European Commission 2017: 160).
37. Data: European Commission (2017): 170.
38. Rankings are available at http://www.doingbusiness.org.
39. The unemployment rate in Greece reached its peak in 2013 with 27.5 percent unemployed. In Ireland the unemployment rate peaked at 16.7 percent in 2010 then fell under 8 percent by 2014 (European Commission 2017: 14). According to the Eurostat's at-risk-of-poverty rate after social transfers, which has a cut-off point at 60 percent of the median income, 48 percent of the Greek population was at risk in 2015, while in Ireland 19.9 percent was at risk.
40. I will return to populism more in depth in Chap. 7.

References

Ardagna, Silvia, and Francesco Caselli. 2012. *The political economy of the Greek debt crisis: A tale of two bailouts.* LSE Center for Economic Performance Special Paper No. 25. Available: http://personal.lse.ac.uk/casellif/papers/greece.pdf. Accessed 2 July 2017.

Barry, Frank. 2006. *Foreign direct investment and institutional co-evolution in Ireland.* Centre for Economic Research Working Paper No. 06/03. Available: http://www.ucd.ie/economics/research/papers/2006/WP06.03.pdf. Accessed 2 July 2017.

———. 2007. Third-level education, foreign direct investment and economic boom in Ireland. *International Journal of Technology Management* 38 (3): 198–219.

Bechtel, Michael M., Jens Hainmueller, and Yotam Margalit. 2012. *Sharing the pain: Explaining public opinion towards international financial bailouts?* MIT Political Science Department Research Paper No. 2012–5. Available at SSRN: http://ssrn.com/abstract=2032147. Accessed 2 July 2017.

Boltho, Andrea. 2000. What matters for economic success? Greece and Ireland compared. In *Small economies adjustment to global tendencies*, ed. Bara Zoltán and László Csaba, 150–169. Budapest: Aula.

Buiter, Willem, and Ebrahim Rahbari. 2012. Rising risks of Greek euro area exit. *Citi Economics, Global Economics View*, February 6. Available: http://willembuiter.com/Citi44.pdf. Accessed 2 July 2017.

Chrysoloras, Nikos. 2013. *Rebuilding eurozone's ground zero: A review of the Greek economic crisis*. GreeSE Paper No. 66. London: London School of Economics.

Dellepiane, Sebastian, and Niamh Hardiman. 2010. Governing the Irish economy: From boom to bust. ECPR Standing Group on Regulatory Governance Biennial Conference, "Regulation in the Age of Crisis", Dublin, 17–19 June 2010. Available: http://regulation.upf.edu/dublin-10-papers/2A2.pdf. Accessed 2 July 2017.

Dellepiane, Sebastian, and Hardiman Niamh. 2012. The politics of tough budgets: The eurozone periphery 2008–2011. 19th International Conference of Europeanists organized by the Council for European Studies, Boston, 22–24 March 2012. Available: http://hdl.handle.net/10197/4224. Accessed 2 July 2017.

European Commission. 2006. *Measuring administrative costs and reducing administrative burdens in the European Union*. Commission Working Document No. 2006(691).

———. 2010. *The economic adjustment program for Greece*. Occasional Papers No. 61. Brussels: Directorate General for Economic and Financial Affairs.

———. 2011. *The economic adjustment program for Ireland*. Occasional Papers No. 76. Brussels: Directorate General for Economic and Financial Affairs.

———. 2012a. *The economic adjustment program for Ireland—Winter 2011 review*. Occasional Papers No. 93. Brussels: Directorate General for Economic and Financial Affairs.

———. 2012b. *The second economic adjustment program for Greece*. Occasional Papers No. 94. Brussels: Commission of the European Communities Directorate General for Economic and Financial Affairs.

———. 2012c. *The second economic adjustment program for Greece first review—December 2012*. Occasional Papers No. 123. Brussels: Directorate General for Economic and Financial Affairs.

———. 2013. *Economic adjustment program for Ireland Spring 2013 review*. Occasional Papers No. 123. Brussels: Directorate General for Economic and Financial Affairs.

———. 2015. *Ex post evaluation of the economic adjustment program Ireland, 2010–2013*. Institutional Paper 04. Brussels: Directorate General for Economic and Financial Affairs.

———. 2016. *The third economic adjustment program for Greece: First review*. Brussels: Directorate General for Economic and Financial Affairs.

———. 2017. *Statistical annex of European Economy, Spring*. Brussels: Commission of the European Communities Directorate General for Economic and Financial Affairs.

Exadaktylos, Theorfanis, and Nikolaos Zahariadis. 2012. *Policy implementation and political trust: Greece in the age of austerity*. GreeSE paper: Hellenic Observatory papers on Greece and Southeast Europe, No. 65. London: London School of Economics.

Featherstone, Kevin. 2016. Conditionality, democracy and institutional weakness: The euro-crisis trilemma. *Journal of Common Market Studies* 54 (S1): 48–64.

Forfás. 2010. *The role of state-owned enterprises: Providing infrastructure and supporting economic recovery*. Dublin: Forfás.

Fraser, Alistair, Enda Murphy, and Sinead Kelly. 2013. Deepening neoliberalism via austerity and 'reform': The case of Ireland. *Human Geography* 6 (2): 38–53.

Gibson, Heather, Stephan Hall, and George Tavlas. 2011. *The Greek financial crisis: Growing imbalances and sovereign spreads*. Working Paper No. 124. Athens: Bank of Greece.

Győrffy, Dóra. 2014. The role of expectations in austerity cycles: The political economy of crisis management in Ireland and Greece. *Acta Oeconomica* 64 (4): 489–509.

Hardiman, Niamh, and Aidan Regan. 2013. The politics of austerity in Ireland. *Intereconomics* 48 (1): 9–14.

Honohan, Patrick. 2009. Resolving Ireland's banking crisis. *The Economic and Social Review* 40 (2): 207–231.

———. 2010. *The Irish banking crisis: Regulatory and financial stability policy 2003–2008*. A Report to the Minister for Finance from the Governor of the Central Bank. Dublin: Central Bank. Available: http://www.bankinginquiry.gov.ie/The%20Irish%20Banking%20Crisis%20Regulatory%20and%20Financial%20Stability%20Policy%202003-2008.pdf. Accessed 2 July 2017.

IMF. 2000. *Ireland: 2000 Article IV consultation*. IMF Country Report No. 00/97.

———. 2012. Implications of a disorderly Greek default and euro exit. *IMF Staff Note*, February 18. Available: http://online.wsj.com/public/resources/documents/ImpactofPossibleGreeceDefault02182012.pdf. Accessed 2 July 2017.

———. 2013. *Greece: Ex post evaluation of exceptional access under the 2010 stand-by agreement*. IMF Country Report No. 13/156.
———. 2015. *Ireland: Ex post evaluation of exceptional access under the 2010 extended arrangement*. IMF Country Report No. 15/20.
———. 2017a. *Greece—2016 Article IV consultation*. IMF Country Report No. 17/40.
———. 2017b. *Greece: Ex post evaluation of exceptional access under the 2012 extended arrangement*. IMF Country Report No. 17/44.
Ioakimidis, P.C. 2001. The Europeanization of Greece: An overall assessment. In *Europeanization and the Southern periphery*, ed. K. Featherstone and G. Kazamias, 73–94. London: Frank Cass.
Jones, Erik. 2012. Future of the euro. In *Great decisions 2013 briefing book*, ed. Foreign Policy Association, 5–18. New York: Foreign Policy Association.
Kopits, George. 2017. The IMF and the euro area crisis: The fiscal dimension. In *The IMF and the crises in Greece, Ireland and Portugal*, ed. Moises Schwartz and Shinji Takagi, 209–253. Washington, DC: IMF Independent Evaluation Office.
Lagarde, Christine. 2013. Ireland and the European Union—Shared determination, shared destiny. *Speech in Dublin*, March 8. Text available: http://www.imf.org/external/np/speeches/2013/030813.htm. Accessed 2 July 2017.
Loizides, John. 2013. Are Greek government deficit and debt statistics reliable? *Journal of Economic and Social Measurement* 38 (1): 79–95.
Mariéad, Considine, and Fiona Dukelow. 2011. Ireland and the impact of economic crisis: Upholding the dominant policy paradigm. In *Social policy in challenging times: Economic crisis and welfare systems*, ed. Kevin Farnsworth and Zoë Irving, 181–198. Bristol: The Policy Press.
MillwardBrown Lansdowne. 2011. *National opinion poll 1st February 2011*. Available: http://www.millwardbrown.com/Libraries/Ireland_Polls_Downloads/Millward_Brown_Irish-Independent_Poll_January_2011.sflb.ashx. Accessed 2 July 2017.
Monastiriotis, Vassilis. 2013. A very Greek crisis. *Intereconomics* 48 (1): 4–9.
NESC [National Economic and Social Council]. 2009. *Ireland's five-part crisis: An integrated national response*. Dublin: NESC.
Ó Riain, Seán. 2000. The flexible developmental state: Globalization, information technology, and the 'Celtic Tiger'. *Politics & Society* 28 (2): 157–193.
OECD. 2010. *Greece at a glance: Policies for sustainable recovery*. Paris: OECD.
———. 2016. *Irish GDP up by 26.3% in 2015?* Press release, October. Available: https://www.oecd.org/std/na/Irish-GDP-up-in-2015-OECD.pdf. Accessed 2 July 2017.

Pappas, Takis. 2010. Macroeconomic policy, strategic leadership, and voter behavior: The disparate tales of socialist reformism in Greece and Spain during the 1980s. *West European Politics* 33 (6): 1241–1260.

Petersen, Thieß, and Michael Böhmer. 2012. *Economic impact of Southern European member states exiting the eurozone.* Bertelsmann Stiftung Policy Brief Series Future Social Market Economy No. 2012/06. Available: http://aei.pitt.edu/73913/1/2012.6.pdf. Accessed 2 July 2017.

Powell, Benjamin. 2003. Economic freedom and growth: The case of the Celtic Tiger. *Cato Journal* 22 (3): 431–448.

Public Issue. 2011. Memorandum and debt: One year after. Available: http://www.publicissue.gr/en/1574/debt-afieroma/#1. Accessed 2 July 2017.

Regling, Klaus, and Max Watson. 2010. *A preliminary report on the sources of Ireland's banking crisis.* Dublin: Government Publications Office. Available: https://www.rte.ie/news/2010/0609/reglingwatson.pdf. Accessed 2 July 2017.

Schmieding, Holger. 2015. *The 2015 Euro Plus monitor—More progress, new risks.* Hamburg/Brussels: Berenberg and the Lisbon Council.

Schmieding, Holger, and Florian Hense. 2016. *The 2016 Euro Plus monitor—Coping with the backlash.* Hamburg/Brussels: Berenberg and the Lisbon Council.

Schmieding, Holger, and Christian Schultz. 2014. *The 2014 Euro Plus monitor—Leaders and laggards.* Hamburg/Brussels: Berenberg and the Lisbon Council.

Tsebelis, George. 2016. Lessons from the Greek crisis. *Journal of European Public Policy* 23 (1): 25–41.

UNCTAD. 2011. Country Factsheet – Ireland. Available: http://unctad.org/Sections/dite_dir/docs/wir11_fs_ie_en.pdf. Accessed 2 July 2017.

———. 2012. Investment Country Profiles – Greece. Available: http://unctad.org/en/PublicationsLibrary/webdiaeia2012d9_en.pdf. Accessed 2 July 2017.

———. 2017. *World investment report 2017.* Annex Table 7. New York/Geneva: UNCTAD. Available: http://unctad.org/en/Pages/DIAE/World%20Investment%20Report/Annex-Tables.aspx. Accessed 2 July 2017.

Visvizi, Anna. 2012. The crisis in Greece and the EU-IMF rescue package: Determinants and pitfalls. *Acta Oeconomica* 62 (1): 15–39.

World Bank. 2007. *Doing business 2007: How to reform?* Washington, DC: World Bank.

Zettelmeyer, Jeromin, Christoph Trebesch, and Mitu Gulati. 2013. The Greek debt restructuring: An autopsy. *Economic Policy* 28 (3): 513–563.

5

The Collapse and Reform of the Mediterranean Social Model in Cyprus, Portugal, and Spain

The experiences of Cyprus, Portugal, and Spain during the crisis stand in sharp contrast to the tragedy in Greece—while all of them needed financial support, they successfully returned to the financial markets within the time frame envisioned in the original program. They have also avoided the collapse of growth and the spiral of austerity that characterized Greece. The question obviously emerges—what made them different?

All four countries are members of the euro-zone, thus devaluation was not a possible path to follow in resolving the crisis. The severity of the original indebtedness cannot be the reason either. As we have already seen in Chap. 1, the net international investment position of the four Mediterranean countries was rather similar—all stood between −80 percent and −90 percent of the GDP in 2008. They have all struggled with similar problems of low productivity and absence of structural reforms prior to the crisis, and all of them can be characterized as low-trust countries. However, only Greece collapsed, while the other three countries weathered the financial crisis.

In order to explain the puzzle, the role of trust is analyzed during the various stages of crisis management. It is argued that although the level of trust was different during the negotiations in the three cases, the commitment and consensus of the elites on implementing the program helped to

D. Győrffy, *Trust and Crisis Management in the European Union*,
https://doi.org/10.1007/978-3-319-69212-8_5

avoid the spiral of distrust, which plagued Greece. Positive reports on the fulfillment of conditionality also contributed to regaining the trust of the financial markets. However, these countries still cannot be considered as unqualified success stories. Public trust in institutions plummeted in all three, and after they exited the program, reforms stalled. Without further reforms, the long-standing problem of low productivity, which would be the key for sustainable growth, cannot be resolved.

The argument proceeds as follows. The first section provides an overview about the Mediterranean model emphasizing the importance of family relations, clientelism, and inefficient public administration. Then the impact of European integration is discussed, especially the inflow of cheap money from abroad. Following an overview about the origins of the financial crisis the role of trust is evaluated during the negotiation, implementation, and market reception of the international financial assistance programs. The last part of the chapter evaluates the outcomes of crisis management in the three countries.

5.1 The Mediterranean Social Model

The existence of a Mediterranean social model is not without controversies. In the classic exposition of Esping-Andersen (1993), there is no Mediterranean model. It is considered as a version of the Continental model with a strong reliance on families for caregiving and the male breadwinner bias in employment protection. However, in his widely cited classification of European social models, Sapir (2006) considers the Mediterranean welfare state as the worst of all worlds—the labor market is highly protected, which reduces efficiency, while the welfare state does not provide services on the scale of Continental or Nordic countries implying a higher incidence of poverty.

Since the publication of Esping-Andersen's classic work, there has been a growing literature on the existence of a Mediterranean model. In his widely cited overview of this model, John Gal (2010) argues that eight countries belong to the "extended family of Mediterranean welfare states": Cyprus, Greece, Israel, Italy, Malta, Spain, Portugal, and Turkey. He names three distinguishing features of the model: an important role for religion, a strong role of the family in caregiving, and the persistence of clientelism in public life. Based on World Values Survey data, he argues that religion plays a more important role in people's life than in Northern Europe (Gal 2010: 290). While there is a significant difference across these countries, separation between Church and state is also more contested, and thus religious authorities have greater influence on public policies. The role of the family in welfare provision is not independent from the role of religion, which places a high degree of responsibility on caring for relatives. Lacking institutionalized child or elderly care, these responsibilities fall on the shoulder of women, who are thus unable to enter and often not even expected to enter into the formal labor market. Family relations are tight, while relations outside of the family are more constrained than in other social models. Finally, personal relations are also dominant in policy-making in the form of clientelism, which "may entail personal relations between a politician and an individual seeking a specific favor, but it may also emerge as reciprocal relations between politicians, political parties or political elites and social groups or social categories that can vary in size and characteristics" (Gal 2010: 293).

The cultural characteristics of the Mediterranean model yield specific welfare and employment arrangements, which are summarized by Ferrara (2000: 168–171). He notes seven major features of the Southern model comprising Greece, Italy, Portugal, and Spain:

1. Generous social protection for those in the formal labor market (mostly male workers), while weak protection for those in the irregular labor market (women, young people and minorities)
2. Unbalanced protections of risks—high protection of pensioners, while family and housing subsidies are underdeveloped
3. Universal health care provision
4. Parallel public and private health care systems, where private provision is much more effective
5. Presence of particularistic and clientelistic norms in welfare provision
6. Uneven distribution of the burden of financing the welfare state
7. High (15–30 percent) incidence of black economy

There have been substantial changes in the Mediterranean welfare model since the 1990s. These include a movement from adversarial labor relations toward a more consensual model and sectoral-level collective agreement. There were also efforts to promote fixed-term contracts and make the labor market regulations more flexible. Still, up until the crisis, strict employment protection remained one of the distinctive features of the model (Karamessini 2007: 24). The most important change in the model however came from greater female participation in the labor force (Fig. 5.1), which in turn increased the need for institutionalized childcare services. These are still inadequate as their opening hours are still not necessarily compatible with working hours for parents. For children below kindergarten age, involvement of grandparents generally provides the solution (Karamessini 2007: 21).

The Mediterranean model is also distinguished by the dominant role of small- and medium-size companies. They provide work for the entire family often outside formal employment structures. The state protects their salience through internal market regulations and the tolerance of their tax evasion (Karamessini 2007: 5). However, they are often resistant to grow, and thus economies of scale cannot take effect, which in turn worsens productivity.[1] As Table 5.1 shows, SMEs have a way higher share

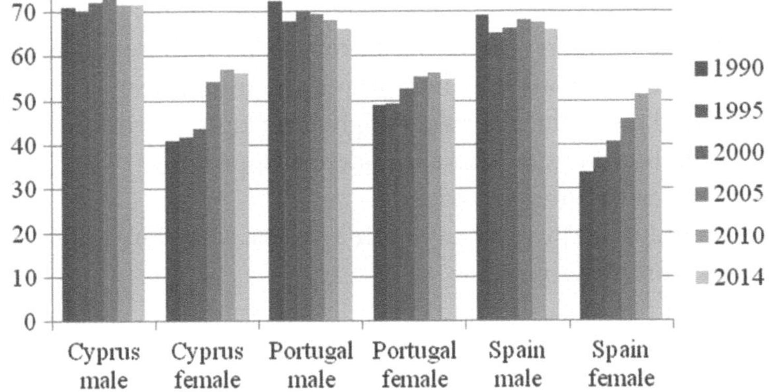

Fig. 5.1 Labor force participation rate in Cyprus, Portugal, and Spain (% of population aged 15+) (Data: World Bank Databank)

Table 5.1 Share of persons (% of labor force) employed by enterprise size class in manufacturing (2013)

	SMEs	Micro	Small	Medium	Large
EU 28	59	13.7	19.8	25.4	41.1
Cyprus	87.4	35.4	30.1	22.1	23.4
Portugal	79.7	19.4	30.1	30.2	20.3
Spain	71.1	20.7	26.7	23.8	28.9
Germany	46.8	6.8	15.8	24.3	53.2

Source: Eurostat

in manufacturing than the EU average, and the difference is particularly strong vis-à-vis Germany.

As many of the welfare services are provided by the family, state redistribution is generally lower than in Northern Europe. Prior to the crisis, even after a decade of convergence, all three countries had lower redistribution rates than the euro-zone average—total government expenditure as percent of GDP in 2007 was 37.4 in Cyprus, 44.5 in Portugal, 39 in Spain while 45.3 in the euro-zone.[2]

Low level of spending has far-reaching consequences for the model. The low coverage of unemployment insurance is often cited as one of the main reasons for having strict employment regulation—the other being the oil crisis in the 1970s and the growing unemployment as a result (Karmessini 2007: 10). Underdeveloped family policies imply that the burden of child and elderly care falls on the shoulders of women. Low spending on education means that the low-skill working population is much higher in these countries than the EU average. Recently vocational training has been promoted almost everywhere, but participation in lifelong learning is very low by EU standards (Karmessini 2007: 14). The problem of an educated workforce continues as shown by the Programme for International Student Assessment (PISA)—most of these countries with the exception of Portugal still underperform the OECD average (OECD 2016: 44). Innovation is also lagging behind Northern Europe—Mediterranean countries mostly belong to the moderate innovator group according to European Innovation Scoreboard.[3]

Low redistribution levels are probably not independent from the perception of corruption surrounding the state. 82 percent of the citizens of Southern EU countries believe that corruption is widespread in their country. They are also the most likely to answer affirmatively to the question whether corruption affects their daily life (ERCAS 2015: 16). Corruption and tolerance for tax evasion imply that the state has difficulties in raising revenues, which in turn has negative effect on the budget balance.

Widespread corruption leads to distrust, but the Mediterranean model in general can be characterized as a low-trust regime. The focus on the family and the lower degree of cooperation with those outside the family is conducive to particularistic trust norms and not conducive to generalized trust. The persistent clientelism at the state level is contributing to corruption, and does not foster institutional trust. Poor educational attainments are also generally associated with distrust.

The Mediterranean model comprises a diverse set of countries, and Cyprus, Portugal, and Spain are among the better performers. As we can see from Fig. 5.2, their governance indicators are much better than those of Greece, although they fall well behind Ireland. In 2007 only Spain had a particularly low score on political stability and the absence of violence due to the Basque ETA terrorist attacks the year before.

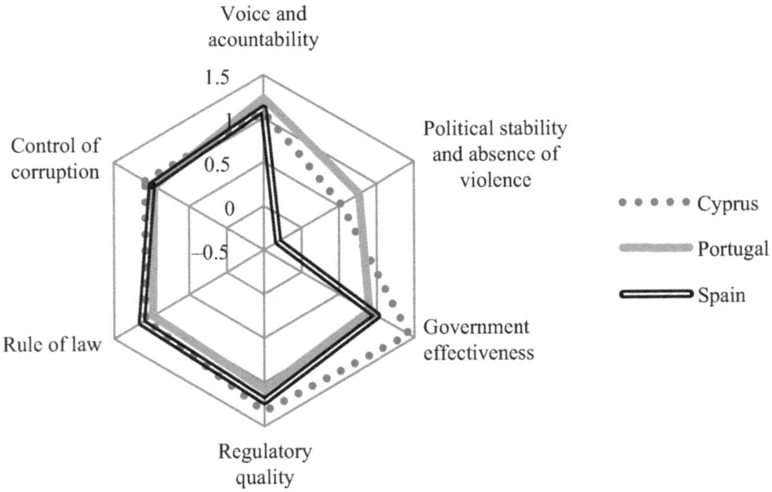

Fig. 5.2 World Governance Indicators in Cyprus, Portugal, and Spain in 2007 (Data: World Governance Indicators at: www.govindicators.org)

Still, given the general characteristics of the Mediterranean model, these countries not competitive with Northwest EU countries—this is evident in its productivity performance. According to Eurostat, in 2004 nominal labor productivity per hour worked was 79.5 percent in Cyprus, 65.8 percent in Portugal, and 95.2 percent in Spain in comparison to the EU average. In the explanation of Dettori et al. (2012), total factor productivity is strongly influenced by human capital, social capital, and technology. The Mediterranean model is lagging behind in all three areas—weak education systems produced lower level of human capital, lack of trust implies low level of social capital, while lack of innovation and lack of attractiveness for FDI imply lags in technological innovation. Indeed, prior to the crisis, FDI stock as percent of GDP was 49.8 in Portugal and 39.8 in Spain significantly below the 75.4 percent rate in Ireland (UNCTAD 2017). Cyprus is an outlier among the three countries as it is on par with Ireland given the large international investments into its financial sector.

5.2 The Road to the Crisis

The road to the crisis was surprisingly similar for the three countries, and their experiences are not very different from those of Ireland. Joining the EU and then introducing the euro opened up the way for cheap capital inflows. These in turn generated a consumption boom and high rates of growth, and thus reduced the incentives for structural reforms, which could improve productivity. Benigno and Fornaro (2014) call this phenomenon the financial resource curse. They argue that similarly to the natural resource curse, the root of the problem is a shift of resources across sectors—in this case from tradable to non-tradable sectors such as construction. In the meantime productivity is stagnant or decreasing, and export competitiveness declines. This problem can be observed in all three countries.

Cyprus joined the EU in 2004. One of the most important changes with accession was the opening up of its tightly restricted banking sector and the liberalization of capital flows (Clerides 2014: 14). Deposits grew sharply, and the size of the banking sector reached over eight times of the

GDP (Charalambous 2014: 13). A large share of this money had Russian origins—estimated at third or half of all deposits by Moodys[4] and attracted by high interest rate offers (Clerides 2014: 17). This money was not lent out for productive investments—in spite of private sector lending almost tripling, gross capital formation remained low (Clerides 2014: 12). Instead, the funds were used for consumption as well as investment into real estate and construction. A huge property bubble developed by 2008, while wages rose over productivity (Clerides 2014: 5). Although public finances seemed to be in order, the budget greatly benefitted from the real estate and consumption boom.

When the new communist government led by Demetris Christofias took over in 2008, it saw the opportunity to expand the budget for social spending and increase debt—it accumulated a cumulative deficit of 30 percent of the GDP between 2009 and 2013 (Phylaktis 2015: 6). The immediate source of vulnerability for the country however came from the heavy exposure to Greece at around 10 percent of assets (Sapir et al. 2014: 47). Eventually the over 50 percent haircut on Greek debt increased the non-performing loans in the banking sector and necessitated the bailout of the two largest banks, the Bank of Cyprus and Laiki. However, given the deteriorating fiscal situation, the government could not afford such bailouts. The former president of the Central Bank of Cyprus, Athanasios Orphanides, strongly blames the Communist government for not attaining better terms for Cyprian banks during the Greek debt restructuring negotiations (Orphanides 2014: 18). Political inaction also became the source of vulnerability—the Communist government was unwilling to heed warnings from economists and the ECB after the crisis in Greece (Orphanides 2014: 7–11). Finally, an unexpected event took place in July 2011—in the village of Mari, confiscated arms originally intended for Syria were stored in the sun for two years and then exploded. The explosion destroyed a power plant, which provides half the electricity on the island. The economy slid into deep recession as it also lost access to the financial markets.

The inflow of cheap money and the misallocation of resources also played a critical role in Portugal's crisis (Reis 2013). The country joined the EU in 1986 following a right-wing dictatorship between 1933 and 1974. The accession to the EU and then the introduction of the euro in the first round brought a substantial inflow of cheap credit, which resulted in high growth rates during the second part of the 1990s. The inflow of money led to overheating of the economy as wages grew faster than productivity—the erosion of competitiveness could be seen in the large current account deficit of the country (Blanchard 2007: 4). The inflow of cheap money also played a role after the introduction of the euro—private sector indebtedness rose from 92.1 percent of GDP to 159.2 percent between 1998 and 2007 (Lane 2012: 52). This went to consumption as gross capital formation continued to decline from 26.5 percent between 1996 and 2000 to 21.9 percent between 2006 and 2010.[5] One difference from other countries however is that the consumption boom did not lead to a real estate bubble—instead employment rose the most in wholesale and retail trade. These sectors also observed the lowest increase in productivity (Reis 2013: 156). This implies that Portugal can also be seen as an example of misallocation of resources from the tradable to the non-tradable sector.

Anemic growth and lack of competitiveness was eminent well before the crisis, but restoration of competitiveness was proving difficult. According to Blanchard (2007: 7–8) Portugal suffered from strict labor market regulations, which precluded unjustified wage cuts as well as lay-offs. High wages in the public sector especially compared to poor performance also factored against wage cuts in the private sector. The increase of productivity was hindered by the dominance of SMEs and the widespread informality in the economy, which cheapens labor and discourages capital investment thus hindering productivity improvements (Blanchard 2007: 14–15). The public sector also had efficiency problems, which could be seen from the large-scale public debt—71.7 percent of GDP in 2008—and regular fiscal deficits averaging 4.5 percent between 2001 and 2008.[6] While Portugal did not accumulate toxic assets, the country was hit during the financial crisis via a fall in export markets. The global credit crunch also endangered the financing of the public debt and the current account as well as ended the credit-led growth of the period.

Similarly to Cyprus and Portugal, the roots of the crisis in Spain are also in the inflow of cheap money. With the accession to the EU in 1986 and then the introduction of the euro, interest rates fell substantially. Given the fast growth similarly to Ireland, real interest rates were negative between 2002 and 2007 (Ahearne et al. 2008: 2). This gave rise to a real estate bubble—as real interest rates were negative, money flew to the real estate sector, where expectations for price rises allowed the making of profits leading to more rise in prices. The increase of housing prices during this period was over 180 percent (Otero-Iglesias et al. 2016: 24). Initially, the rise in prices was rationalized by large-scale immigration, but as shown by Gonzalez and Ortega (2013), it was responsible for about one-quarter of the increase in prices.

Important participants in the real estate bubble were the cajas—regional public savings banks, which accounted half of the financial sector's assets. These regional banks were part of the local elites with strong ties to policy-makers with a distinctive regulatory framework (Quaglia and Royo 2013: 5). As in the other two cases, the government strongly benefitted from the real estate boom and the budget appeared disciplined as a result. Productivity problems could also be spotted—total factor productivity fell by 2 percent during the period 1995–2007 (Benigno and Fornaro 2014: 61). This was a result of a shift in the allocation of resources toward the non-tradable sector, where productivity growth is generally smaller. Santana et al. (2016) also show that industries which are more prone to cronyism—as measured by the Bribe-Payers Index of Transparency International—were also more prone to misallocation of capital than others and registered larger productivity losses. This is further supported by evidence from cajas—Garciano (2012) shows that the political connection of a caja was a "good predictor of trouble brewing." At a deeper level, Royo (2014) explains the entrenched interests by the dominance of proportional representation in which loyalty to party leaders yields a place on party lists. This results in the emergence of an entrenched political class, which feeds on public resources.

In the context of the global financial crisis the real estate boom collapsed in Spain leading to significant problems at several cajas. The lax oversight of these banks implied slow recognition of problems and delayed action, which eventually aggravated the situation.

Overall the three countries show remarkable similarities regarding the roots of the crisis. All three countries struggled with poor productivity performance and the inflow of cheap money associated with their EU and euro-zone accession. The resulting overheating of the economy reduced the incentives for structural reforms. Prior to the crisis, only the current account imbalances, which were discussed in Chap. 1, signaled the problems of competitiveness.

5.3 Negotiation of the Programs

While the three countries showed substantial similarities on their road to the crisis, their negotiations of financial assistance differed considerably yielding very different conditions.

As Cyprus became excluded from the financial markets on 26 May 2011 and its bonds were downgraded, the Christofias government was unwilling to turn to the EU for help and was also unwilling to address the deteriorating fiscal situation. Instead it arranged a bilateral loan with Russia, which was 15 percent of Cyprian GDP in December 2011 (Clerides 2014: 31). However, the mounting fiscal and banking sector problems were not addressed. In June 2012 the ECB stopped accepting Cyprian bonds as collateral,[7] which forced the government to turn to the Troika for assistance.

The Christofides government was unwilling to sign an agreement until the next elections in February 2013. Negotiations were prolonged, and instead of consolidation, the government engaged in an anti-bank campaign. According to Orphanides (2014: 30), this campaign exaggerated the banks' financing needs, which lead to talks about the necessity of bail-in.

On the side of the EU, German elections were looming, and many Germans felt resentment about Greece. Cyprus was a very small country, and there was little fear of contagion in case of collapse. The negotiating positions were thus highly asymmetrical. In this case the small island could be used as a way to show toughness in the negotiations. The Germans did not like the Cyprian business model, and they did not want to bail out Russians especially before elections. Merkel's finance minister, Wolfgang Schauble, went to the negotiations with a clear mandate: without bail-in there would be no bailout.[8]

The program was eventually signed by the new government after the elections in March 2013, when a pro-EU president led by Nicos

Anastasiades took office. It took 271 days to sign the agreement from the start of the negotiations (Phylaktis 2016: 67). However, in spite of the new government's pro-EU stance, the humiliating bail-in had to be accepted—and it took another round to restrict it to deposits over 100 000 euros after the parliament refused the first offer (Phylaktis 2016: 68).

The Troika eventually provided ten billion euros (€9 billion via the ESM and €1 billion from the IMF) or 56 percent of Cyprian GDP. The program was based on three pillars: restructuring and substantial downsizing of the banking sector, consolidation of public finances, and structural reforms to support competitiveness and balanced growth (European Commission 2013: 66). The Memorandum of Understanding listed extremely detailed measures on a variety of areas from banking to energy regulation on 32 pages (European Commission 2013: 67–98).

In the Cyprian case, distrust clearly dominated the negotiations and led to conditions reminiscent of the Greek case. On the side of the EU there was no fear of contagion, thus they could use their leverage to challenge the Cyprian business model.

Concerns over banking stability were the first signs of trouble in Portugal as well. In 2008–2009 two banks (Banco Português de Negócios and Banco Privado Português) needed bailouts financed by taxpayers because of accumulating losses of bad investment and fraud done by people associated with the government (Djankov 2014: 90). At the same time, deposit guarantee was increased from €25 000 to €100 000, a €20 billion fund was created for bank guarantees, and €4 billion was spent on buying shares in troubled banks (Perriera and Williams 2012: 13). These steps however significantly burdened Portugal's already high public debt, which made the country vulnerable to a self-fulfilling financial crisis. As the uncertainty on the financial markets grew in 2011 with the Greek and the Irish crises, Portugal was speculated to be the next in line. Interest rates started to rise, which made the public debt look unsustainable. The minority government failed to pass the necessary fiscal consolidation measures—the rejection of the program in the parliament on 23 March 2011 and the subsequent resignation of the Socrates government led to a subsequent series of downgrades at various credit rating institutions. Interest rates started to rise and the country applied for international financial assistance on 6 April 2011 (Perreira and Williams 2012: 18–19).

The negotiations with the Troika were short—on 11 May, Portugal received a €78 billion package or 36 percent of 2012 GDP. As Perreira and Williamson (2012: 22) recounts: "Although main negotiations were between the Portuguese minority government and the 'Troika' of the IMF, EC and ECB, the main opposition right-wing parties gave their formal agreement to the MoU. Notably, before the Prime Minister stepped down the rightist parties were against any further austerity measures (e.g. tax increases), but once he resigned, and even before general elections, they accepted everything they had opposed and even accepted further austerity measures."

Trust during these negotiations did not appear to be an issue. Portugal's structural problems were well known, and there was a general consensus on their nature—the government and the opposition fought over who is better able to address them. The crisis empowered elite groups interested in implementing reforms, which were decades overdue. The outgoing center-left government started implementing the program, and the incoming center-right government continued it. Consensus across party lines was clearly present as acknowledged by IMF officials (IMF 2011) as well as analysts (Afonoso et al. 2015: 21). Interviews with participants from the negotiations emphasize very intelligent policy discussions, without any policy imposed by the Troika (Moury and Freire 2013: 46). In fact, the government was able to refuse several measures they deemed inappropriate. There was an understanding that the reform measures would be necessary even without the Troika. The strong political commitment of authorities is also noted in the 2016 ex post-evaluation report by the European Commission (2016d: 13).

The terms of the program reflected the consensus—restore competitiveness, jobs, and growth (IMF 2011). This implied a three-pillar strategy: structural reforms focusing on boosting competition and employment, fiscal consolidation on cutting debt, and financial stability focusing on deleveraging and recapitalization (European Commission 2011: 16). The program contained wide-ranging conditionality listed on 34 pages (European Commission 2011: 59–93). It was clearly seen as an opportunity for Portugal to implement long-overdue structural reforms.

In Spain the fall in real estate prices led to the increase in non-performing loans in cajas exposed to the sector. The Bankia bank, the country's largest mortgage lender, was the first to get into trouble, and it had to be nationalized in May 2012 (Quaglia and Royo 2013: 6–7). The cost was estimated at €23 billion. Several other mortgage banks were downgraded to junk status. This meant the inability of the state to finance its public debt, which was shown by rising interest rates. Spain was offered €100 billion assistance on 9 June 2012.[9] It is telling that the official request for support came only on 25 June 2012 when Spain accepted the offer.[10]

Spain's was the opposite of the Cyprian position. The country could not be allowed to fail since its size precluded bailout—it is the problem of too-big-to-fail and too-big-to-bailout. Letting out Spain from the euro was unthinkable even for Germany (Kulish and Minder 2012).

The country traditionally has cohesive and homogenous economics elite with strong ties between academia and public administration, and they speak the same neoliberal language as their international partners (Ban 2016). Prior to the stabilization program, Spain had already implemented harsh fiscal consolidation measures during the previous Zapatero government (Dellapiane and Hardiman 2015: 203), and it did not run deficits before the crisis. As a result, the only conditions given for the loan were financial sector reforms. The package was an 18-month program with front-loaded financing and no regular disbursements tied to reviews. As the Prime Minister Mariano Rajoy put it: it was not a bailout but a loan without conditions. This was also confirmed by Angela Merkel.[11] While this was not exactly true, as there were fiscal targets to be monitored in the Memorandum of Understanding (European Commission 2012: 62), the list of conditions is clearly shorter at nine pages and much more focused on the financial sector than in the other two cases (European Commission 2012: 55–63).

In the case of Spain the importance of trust during the negotiations can clearly be seen. There was a shared sense of being in the same boat as well as a feeling of collegiality, which resulted in much softer conditions in comparison to other programs.

When we consider the three negotiations together, it is striking that the similarities of problems led to such different outcomes: while Cyprus had to sign a humiliating bail-in, Portugal used the opportunity to commit itself to a set of overdue reforms, Spain received financing almost without conditionality. However, the implementation of the programs was again remarkably similar in the three countries.

5.4 Public Attitudes and the Implementation of Conditionality

In comparison to Greece, protests were much less severe in the three countries even though public trust fell greatly during the crisis. In the following I will first document the collapse of public trust then look at the implementation of the program by policy-makers and the reaction of the public to the measures.

5.4.1 An Erosion of Trust

The erosion of trust can be seen in all three countries on Fig. 5.3, which shows the parallel collapse of trust. As we can see, the collapse of trust was particularly notable in Cyprus and Spain, while Portugal had low level of

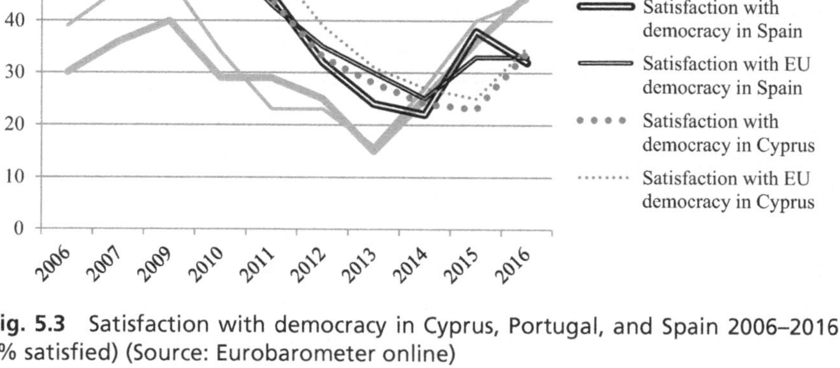

Fig. 5.3 Satisfaction with democracy in Cyprus, Portugal, and Spain 2006–2016 (% satisfied) (Source: Eurobarometer online)

trust prior to the crisis as well. However, in the case of Cyprus the collapse of trust cannot be attributed to the program—as it was discussed earlier, the Christofides government policy mistakes probably played a strong role.

In spite of the collapse of public trust, the government continued to implement the program conditions in all three countries. Elite consensus played a critical role in this outcome.

5.4.2 Elite Consensus on Cooperation with the Troika

While public trust was low, a strong elite consensus over the implementation of the program implied that public dissatisfaction did not become an impediment to comply with the conditions.

In Cyprus the Memorandum of Understanding signed by the Cyprian government and the Troika acted as a catalyst for consensus over fiscal consolidation. Meeting between government and opposition parties even produced a statement for "common front" on the Memorandum of Understanding with the Troika (Charambolous 2014: 71). In fact, most legislation related to the program was passed with opposition support in the Parliament (Charambolous 2014: 73).

Elite consensus over implementing the conditionality of the program was also strong in Portugal. As it has been discussed above, the fiscal consolidation, which was originally proposed by the outgoing Sócrates government, was included into the Memorandum of Understanding, and was eventually implemented by the incoming center-right government led by Passos Coelho. A change of government thus made no difference in implementation. In fact, as Moury and Freire (2013: 44) argue, the new government used the crisis and the Troika to press long overdue structural reforms. The changes to the Memorandum of Understanding show an ever stricter set of conditions. In this case the Troika helped to empower domestic actors aiming at large-scale structural reforms.

Elite consensus over the program characterized Spain as well. The conditions were considered as necessary and well designed. As in the other two countries, a change in government did not reverse policies—the austerity policies of the Zapatero government were continued by the incoming Rahoy government. Both governments pushed the idea of TINA (Léon et al. 2015: 193–195). Pressures from the Troika provided external legitimacy for the government, which largely abandoned a tripartite approach to reforms (Molina and Miguélez 2013).

5.4.3 Public Reactions

There were much fewer protests against the programs than in Greece. Low level of politicization of the society and generally weak civil society probably contributed to this outcome.

In Cyprus there were only three demonstrations against the conditions of the program with around 5000–7000 people participating in them (Charanbolous 2014: 61–62). At the same time, an increase of charity contributions could be observed, which Charanbolous (2014: 73) views as a substitute engagement to protests. In the 2014 European Parliamentary elections, there was no strengthening of alternative political actors, and the four traditional parties dominated. Although Cyprians deeply resented the bail-in and the partial loss of their deposits during the financial crisis, none of the major parties embraced an anti-EU program even though a collapse of trust in the EU could be observed in Eurobarometer surveys (Athanasiadou et al. 2014: 4–5).

Protests were more prevalent in Portugal. At the prospect of the 2011 fiscal consolidation package, large demonstrations were staged across the country. Two thirds of the protests were initiated by trade unions, and in all of them internet-based social activism played a critical role (Accornero and Pinto 2015: 501, 505). As it was discussed earlier, although the Zapatero government collapsed once it was unable to push through its austerity package in 2011, the incoming center-right government was even more committed to consolidation and structural change. While initially the number of demonstrations grew, after a large demonstration against the Troika in March 2013, the protests stopped and the government continued to implement the program (Accornero and Pinto 2015: 504). In the 2014 European elections, they did not seem to have an impact as the center-left Socialist Party and center-right Social Democrats won the majority of votes.

In fact, most people initially blamed the government for the crisis, and the majority did not oppose the conditions. Only the Communists were in opposition, while supporters of mainstream parties agreed with the terms (Moury and Freire 2013: 52). However, two years after the signing of the program, over 80 percent of the population was for the renunciation or renegotiation of the conditions. Portugal exited from the program in 2014. In the 2015 elections, the governing center-right party won, but it failed to get a majority of the votes—losing around 11 percent of their 2011 result. The Socialists, led by Antonio Costa, could eventually form a minority government based on the promise to end austerity with the help of two left-wing parties—the Left Bloc and the Communist-Greens coalition. Satisfaction with democracy increased immediately, and the government stopped a number of contentious structural reforms. Still, with a history of a far-right dictatorship, the country is very hesitant to embrace extremist ideas (Salgado and Zúquete 2016). Anti-EU sentiment is largely absent even though similarly to Cyprus, trust in the EU declined sharply (Fig. 5.3).

Spain saw the largest popular movement against austerity politics. Although in comparison to other Mediterranean countries, it had the least severe conditionality, it was the one that had its political system most transformed by the crisis. Protests and strikes started in 2010, and they continued to increase until 2013 against austerity, corruption, and the bailout of banks (Orriols and Cordero 2016, Medina 2015). In the period of austerity and recession, several scandals oriented attention to the dangers of corruption—from 2012 people viewed corruption as the biggest problem in Spain (Medina 2015: 12). The protests against austerity and corruption gave rise to Indignados or 15M, which defined itself as a left-wing resistance movement to the center-left Socialist government. Over 80 percent of the population agreed with the 15M aims (Medina 2015: 17). While Podemos, which appeared in 2014, does not consider itself as an heir to 15M, there are clear continuities between the two movements in their stance against austerity politics.

In the 2015 general elections, Podemos became the third largest party with 21 percent of the votes. Their results were hailed as the end of two-party system in Spain (Orriols and Cordero 2016). However, it is also notable that the traditional two parties, the Socialists (PSOE) and the center-right People's Party (PP), preserved their standing although jointly they fell to 50.7 percent in the 2015 general elections. Given the difficulties of forming a majority government, a year later new elections were held, where Podemos formed an alliance with smaller left-wing parties and suffered a surprise decline in votes. It also failed to overtake the center-left Socialist party as the main opposition force. As argued by Hedgecoe (2016), moderate voters were turned off by the alliance with extreme left parties. At the same time, the second election was also inconclusive. Though Mariano Rajoy could form a minority government with the help of the new centrist party Ciudadanos—established in opposition to separatist movements—during the investiture vote he needed the abstention of PSOE in order to succeed (Torres 2016).

Similarly to Portugal, with a long history of right-wing dictatorship, the extreme right could not arise in Spain even during the period of austerity. There are no anti-immigration or anti-EU parties in the Spanish parliament. Furthermore, it is also notable that corruption scandals were parallel with the politics of austerity—a mild one in comparison to other countries—thus the transformation of the party system and the resulting political gridlock cannot be blamed solely on austerity.

5.4.4 Implementation of the Programs

The presence of an elite consensus and the relative lack of widespread public protest facilitated the implementation of the program conditionality in all three countries.

Cyprus had the most far-reaching terms, and it duly complied in most cases. As shown by Table 5.2, the country over-performed the original fiscal criteria in most years. The European Commission regular reviews[12] show full compliance with the fiscal criteria and data provision, and register at least partial compliance on the other fields—financial stability policy, fiscal structural measures, labor market, and goods and services market. In cases of partial compliance, administrative delay rather than lack of commitment is cited as a reason for the partiality of compliance. The banking sector was downscaled to half of its size before the crisis, while supervision and regulation have been improved. The program

Table 5.2 Fiscal policy criteria and actual outcome in Cyprus, Portugal, and Spain (general government net lending as % of GDP)

	2011	2012	2013	2014	2015	2016
Cyprus 2012		−6.3	−6.5	−8.4	−6.3	−2.9
Cyprus actual		−5.8	−4.9	**−8.8**	−1.1	−0.3
Portugal 2011	−5.9	−4.5	−3	−2.3	−1.9	
Portugal actual	**−7.4**	**−5.7**	**−4.8**	**−7.2**	**−4.4**	−2.7
Spain		−6.3	−4.5	−2.8		
Spain actual			**−4.8**	**−4**	**−3.5**	**−3.3**

Source: For conditions for Cyprus European Commission (2013: 47), for Portugal European Commission (2011: 18), for Spain European Commission (2012: 62). Actual data on general government net lending: Eurostat. Bold numbers signal the deviation from fiscal conditionality

ended in March 2016, when the country could return to the financial markets. At the same time, once the program was over, structural reforms slowed down significantly especially in the fields of public administration, health care, justice, and privatization (European Commission 2016e: 5–6).

Under the center-right coalition, Portugal also faithfully implemented the measures signaled in the Memorandum of Understanding. While this might not be evident from the significant difference between the fiscal criteria and the actual balance every year (Table 5.2), in the post-program comprehensive review, the Commission called the Portuguese efforts "impressive," and cited a number of acceptable reasons for the missing of the criteria—the negative effect of the cycle, the rise in interest rates, and the demographically induced rise in pension costs. It also noted that expenditure cuts were responsible for 60 percent of the adjustment (European Commission 2014a: 19). The government's efforts at implementation were also shown by the tough measures it took once the Constitutional Court judged certain elements of the program unconstitutional. The review is also positive on the implementation of structural fiscal reforms, stabilization of the financial sector, and structural reforms on the labor and product markets, network industries, services, the judiciary, and public administration.

However, Portugal's early exit from the program, the easing of financing conditions on the markets, and the significant cash buffer the government built implied that pressure for further measures was reduced, and a form of reform fatigue set in. Following the change in the government in 2015, the Costa government tried to implement its anti-austerity agenda, which included minimum wage increase, reduction of working hours for public servants, and cuts in the personal income tax (Gago 2016). In its Macroeconomic Imbalance Report, the European Commission noted that "fiscal consolidation effort up to 2014 has been replaced by a pro-cyclical loosening of the fiscal stance in 2015" (European Commission 2016b: 9). However, a rise in interest rates since the change in government showed the limit of discretion regarding fiscal expansion. The December 2016 visit of the Troika already praised the government for respecting the 3 percent deficit target (IMF 2016). The government thus navigated between preserving market access, avoiding punishment from the EU and maintaining its legitimacy.

Among the three countries Spain had the best record of implementation—in the final conditionality review (European Commission 2014b: 32–34) all conditions were considered observed or no longer relevant. The country used only 40 percent of the rescue funds. The restructuring and recapitalization of the banks went smoothly as well as the setting up of the SAREB to deal with legacy assets. The program is considered highly successful.[13] At the same time, it should also be noted that although Spain did not face fiscal conditionality similar to Cyprus or Portugal, it failed to achieve the 3 percent fiscal deficit target even in 2016 similarly to Portugal.

Overall strong elite commitment and external pressure could overcome the public trust deficit, and the program conditions were duly implemented in all three countries. The commitment of the government was also rewarded by external actors. As both Portugal and Spain continued to break the 3 percent deficit threshold even in 2016, Wolfgang Schauble intervened in order to stop sanctions against them in the Commission stressing "the need for political stability" (Eder 2016). However, it is also interesting that the greatest political upheaval could be observed in Spain, which faced the most lenient conditions among the three countries. This implies that there is no linear relation between severity of conditionality and public protests. This thesis is also supported by the fact that extremist parties did not gain power in any of the countries, while anti-EU parties are also missing from the political scene in spite of a significant decline of trust in the EU.

5.5 Market Reactions

The programs helped the three countries restore market access. Spain exited the program in December 2013, Portugal announced exit ahead of time in June 2014, while Cyprus left the program in March 2016. All three countries regained access to the financial markets and have seen their long-term interest rates fall below pre-crisis levels (Fig. 5.4). While extremely low global interest rates are partly responsible for this outcome, we can also observe that following the signing of the programs, there is a steady downward trend in the rates. The lowest peak and the lowest rate are registered by Spain suggesting the confidence of the markets. Portugal and Cyprus experienced a sharper rise in their interest rate, and even in 2017 they have to pay close to 4 percent interest on the long-term bonds. While this rate is still well below the Greek value, it suggests that the tasks of crisis management are not necessarily over for these countries. A closer look at macroeconomic outcomes explains why.

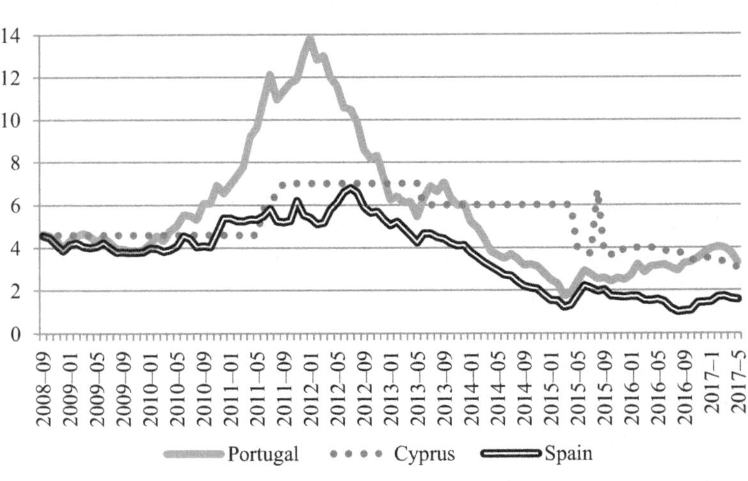

Fig. 5.4 Long-term interest rates (%) in Cyprus, Portugal, and Spain 2008–2017 (Data: European Central Bank) (Note: The graph for Cyprus registers the primary market rate, which has a cutoff yield fixed by the government. The free market rate for long-term Cyprus bonds with maturity 2020 peaked at 16.5 percent in June 2012 (European Commission 2013: 36))

5.6 Economic Outcomes

Although financing conditions improved significantly for all three countries, the usual macroeconomic variables do not suggest a sweeping success story. In 2016 public debt stood at 107.8, 130.4, and 99.4 percent of GDP in Cyprus, Portugal, and Spain, respectively.[14] Unemployment rates were 13.1 percent in Cyprus, 11.2 percent in Portugal, and 19.6 percent in Spain.[15]

An examination between expectations and outcomes in growth rates on Figs. 5.5, 5.6, and 5.7 also suggest a substantial deviation in all three cases. All the three countries experienced a double-dip recession, and forecasts continually worsened up until 2013. However, from 2014 there was a significant improvement as they all managed to recover faster than expectations. Spain surpassed its forecasts the most by registering over 3 percent growth rate in 2014 and 2015. Cyprus also saw at a faster rate than predicted. In the case of Portugal, we can observe a consistency between predictions and reality after 2013, but it should also be noted that the growth rate is still below 2 percent. Still, we can see that the three countries successfully avoided the fate of Greece, where the outcome was almost always worse than the forecast.

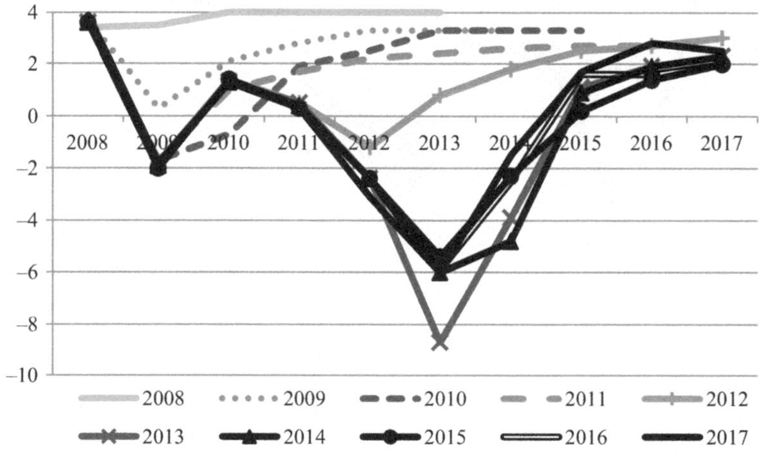

Fig. 5.5 GDP forecasts and reality in Cyprus 2008–2017 (Data: World Economic Outlook database)

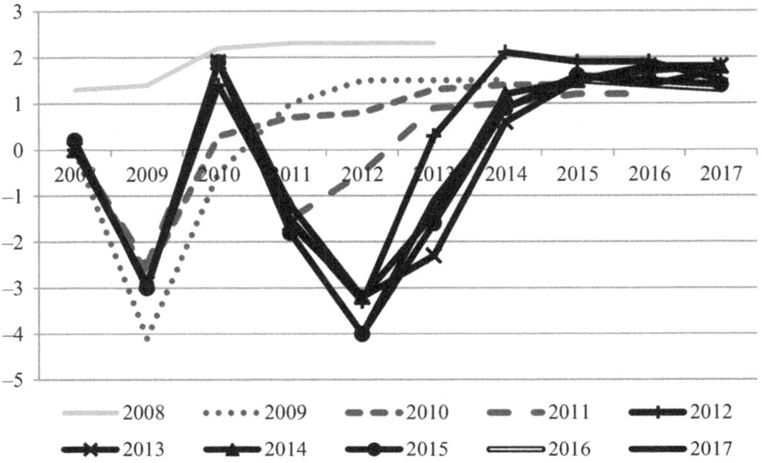

Fig. 5.6 GDP forecasts and reality in Portugal 2008–2017 (Data: World Economic Outlook database)

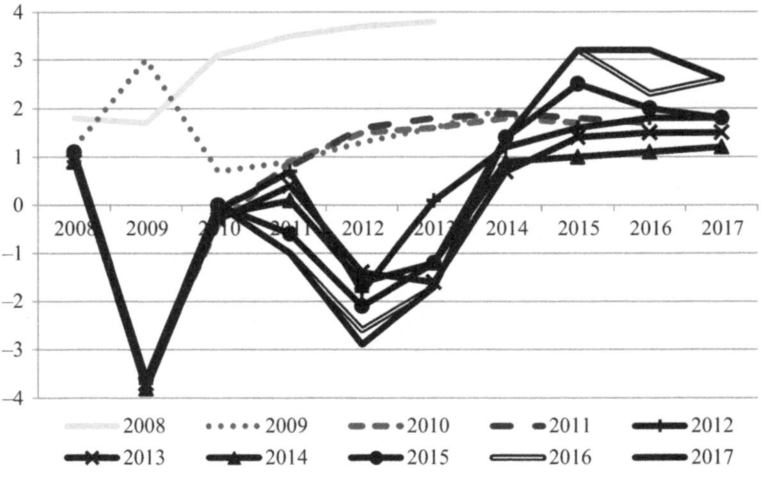

Fig. 5.7 GDP forecasts and reality in Spain 2008–2017 (Data: World Economic Outlook database)

However, even a cursory look at some of the main macroeconomic variables suggests that in spite of the commitment to implement the conditionality of the programs, there is no easy or fast way out of a structural crisis. Detailed analysis from European Commission Macroeconomic Imbalance Procedure indicates very similar problems in the three countries: deleveraging and the still large share of non-performing loans (in Cyprus close to 50 percent) plague investments, especially for SMEs (European Commission 2016a: 54, b: 14, c: 65). While financing problems can be attributed to the crisis, at a deeper level the problems are structural—transforming the economy into a knowledge-based economy proves to be a difficult challenge for countries in the Mediterranean model. The dominance of SMEs in the economy is one reason for this outcome—the productivity and innovation gap vis-à-vis large firms is particularly emphasized in the report on Spain (European Commission 2016c: 14). As pointed out by Blanchard (2007: 14), the dominance of informality allows "small inefficient firms to survive... preventing economies of scale from being exploited." Reducing informality however is dependent upon reducing regulations, which are still mentioned as important factors in discouraging businesses in all three countries (European Commission 2016a: 53, b: 50, c: 49). However, low-trust environments are generally characterized by high level of regulations—as agreements are not trusted, more control thus more regulation is necessary for monitoring and enforcement (Aghion et al. 2010). The loss of trust during the crisis management period thus probably made the program of deregulation more difficult. Besides acting as a disincentive for small companies to grow, the resulting poor business environment also discourages foreign direct investment, which plays a critical role in technology transfer and the increase in productivity.

The structural problems of the economy have been also worsened by the focus on fiscal consolidation. Innovation and productivity is inherently dependent on education—in all three countries, spending on education decreased since 2010.[16] Finally, the consolidation also made it difficult to develop the welfare state further—Léon and Pavolini (2014) call the process "back to familism." The underdeveloped family support scheme makes it difficult for women to continue entering into the labor market, and thus their talents are not utilized fully. Since the beginning of the crisis, the growth of female participation in the labor force stagnated or reversed in all three countries according to World Bank data.[17]

Increasing trust in public administration and improving education systems and family policies are more complicated tasks than cutting wages and relaxing labor market regulations. While the latter requires political will to overcome resistance, the former requires governance capacity as well as funds to accomplish the objectives. Neither is presented by the window of opportunity opened by the crisis.

* * *

The cases of Cyprus, Portugal, and Spain indicate that there was nothing predetermined about the collapse of Greece. The three countries shared many of the problems Greece faced including stagnant productivity, international indebtedness, and current account deficits. Still, they avoided the austerity spiral Greece suffered.

Elite commitment to the implementation of the financial support programs played an important role in avoiding the fate of Greece. This commitment was present in the three countries in spite of very different conditionality—while conditions for Cyprus can be considered punitive, Spain received a loan with very lenient conditions. Still, neither the government nor the main opposition party questioned the importance of implementing the program.

The commitment by the major parties survived the collapse of public trust, which accompanied the reforms. As a result, market confidence recovered; the three countries could return to the financial markets and exit the program. While extremely loose monetary policies around the world are partly responsible for this outcome, the case of Greece shows that a return to market financing still cannot be taken for granted.

The fulfillment of program conditionality and the renewed access to financial markets however does not imply unqualified success for these countries. While the crisis was used as a window of opportunity to implement long-due structural reforms, many of the original problems persist.

This includes the dominance of SMEs in the economy, widespread informality, and stagnant productivity. These problems require the continuation of structural reforms. However, all three countries saw a form of reform fatigue following their exit from the program. This is especially true in Portugal, where the new government is supported by extreme left forces. However, in the face of plummeting public trust, continuation of long-term reforms proves to be a difficult task in all three countries.

Overall the three cases show how the crisis can be used as a window of opportunity for implementing long overdue reforms. They also show that cooperation with the Troika does not necessarily imply the rise of extremist or anti-EU movements—although trust in the EU fell sharply in all three countries, no parties emerged, which would ask for a referendum on membership. At the same time, the three cases indicate the limits of crisis-induced reforms, and the need for building policies rather than just retrench them. This implies that eventually building public trust is an unavoidable task—strengthening government capacity and the belief that it works for the common good rather than particular interests. The corruption scandals engulfing Spain are particularly damaging to such objectives. However, the prevalence of clientelism presents considerable obstacles in all three countries.

Low level of public trust and widespread corruption perceptions are shared features of the Mediterranean and the Eastern countries of the EU. In the following chapter I will consider how these shaped the crisis management in Hungary, Latvia, and Romania. The cases can also provide insight into how and when crisis management leads to the dominance of EU-skeptic parties.

Notes

1. The size of these companies is not necessarily the cause for their low level of productivity. As shown by Farkas (2016: 211), there is significant heterogeneity in the EU about the difference in productivity between large companies and SMEs. For example, in Denmark or the United Kingdom, there is barely any difference in productivity across small, medium and large enterprises. However, in countries, which are characterized by a large number of

foreign multinationals and/or the presence of a large black economy, the difference in productivity between SMEs and large companies is sizable. A more extensive discussion of SMEs is outside the scope of the chapter. ILO (2015) provides a comprehensive overview about the sector's role in job creation and productivity.

2. These values are considerably lower than the Greek 47.1 percent—as it was discussed in the previous chapter, the state expanded there rapidly in the 1980s. Data: European Commission (2017): 158.
3. The European Innovation Scoreboard aims to provide a comprehensive assessment of innovation performance by EU member states. Its rankings are available: http://ec.europa.eu/growth/industry/innovation/facts-figures/scoreboards_en. Accessed: 2 July 2017.
4. The precise share of Russian money varies by source—while Moody's estimates €31 billion out of 88, the Bank of Cyprus estimate is just €6.5–13 billion (Kalotay 2013).
5. Data: European Commission (2017) 48.
6. Data: European Commission (2017) 164 and 160.
7. Orphanides (2014: 19–22) provides an extensive discussion about the communication between the ECB and the Cyprian authorities about consolidation measures and the possibility of waiving collateral eligibility rules.
8. See the Reuters report at: http://www.reuters.com/article/us-eurozone-cyprus-stumbled-insight-idUSBRE92H0RH20130318. Accessed: 2 July 2017.
9. Eurogroup statement on Spain. Available: http://www.consilium.europa.eu/uedocs/cms_data/docs/pressdata/en/ecofin/130778.pdf. Accessed: 2 July 2017.
10. See the report by cnn.com at http://money.cnn.com/2012/06/25/investing/spain-banks/. Accessed: 2 July 2017.
11. See the report on *Euractiv.com*: http://www.euractiv.com/section/euro-finance/news/spain-joins-the-group-of-debt/. Accessed: 2 July 2017.
12. There were eight reviews in total for the Cyprus bailout program. These reports are available at the website of the DG Economic and Financial Affairs: http://ec.europa.eu/economy_finance/assistance_eu_ms/cyprus/index_en.htm. All the reviews have a one-page summary of compliance performance.
13. See the interview with Klaus Regling (EMS Managing Director) at https://www.esm.europa.eu/interviews/klaus-regling-interview-el-mundo-spain. Accessed: 2 July 2017.

14. Data: European Commission (2017): 164.
15. Data: European Commission (2017): 14.
16. According to COFOG data between 2010 and 2014 education spending decreased in Cyprus from 6.2 percent to 5.8 percent, in Portugal from 7.6 percent to 6.2 percent, in Spain from 4.5 percent to 4.1 percent of GDP.
17. According to World Bank Databank, woman participation in the labor force declined between 2010 and 2014 from 57.1 percent to 56.2 percent in Cyprus and from 56.3 percent to 54.9 percent in Portugal, and grew from 51.4 percent to 52.5 percent in Spain—still a very low number. While male labor force participation also decreased, it is over 65 percent in all three countries.

References

Accornero, Guya, and Pedro Ramos Pinto. 2015. 'Mild-mannered?' Protest and mobilization in Portugal under austerity 2010–2013. *West European Politics* 38 (3): 491–515.

Afonoso, Alexandre, Sotirios Zartaloudis, and Yannis Papadopoulus. 2015. How party linkages shape austerity politics: Clientelism and fiscal adjustment in Greece and Portugal during the eurozone crisis. *Journal of European Public Policy* 22 (3): 315–334.

Aghion, Phillippe, Yann Algan, Pierre Cahuc, and Andrei Shleifer. 2010. Regulation and distrust. *Quarterly Journal of Economics* 125 (3): 1015–1049.

Ahearne, Alan, Juan Delgado, and Jakob von Weizsäcker. 2008. *A tale of two countries*, Bruegel Policy Brief No. 2008/04. Brussels: Bruegel.

Athanasiadou, Nicoleta, Costas Melakopides, and Christos Xenophontos. 2014. Cyprus. *EU-28 Watch* 10: 3–5.

Ban, Cornel. 2016. *Ruling ideas: How global neoliberalism goes local.* Oxford: Oxford University Press.

Benigno, Gianluca, and Luca Fornaro. 2014. The financial resource curse. *The Scandinavian Journal of Economics* 116 (1): 58–86.

Blanchard, Oliver. 2007. Adjustment within the euro: The difficult case of Portugal. *Portuguese Economic Journal* 6 (1): 1–21.

Charalambous, Giorgos. 2014. *Political culture and behavior in the Republic of Cyprus during the crisis*, PCC Report 2/2014. Oslo: Peace Research Institute Oslo.

Clerides, Sofronis. 2014. The collapse of the Cypriot banking system: A bird's eye view. *Cyprus Economic Policy Review* 8 (2): 3–35.

Dellapiane-Avellaneda, Sebastian, and Niamh Hardiman. 2015. The politics of fiscal effort in Ireland and Spain: Market credibility vs political legitimacy. In *The politics of extreme austerity: Greece in the eurozone crisis*, ed. Georgios Karyotis and Roman Gerodimos, 222–239. Houndmills/New York: Palgrave Macmillan.

Dettori, Barbara, Emanuela Marrocu, and Raffaele Paci. 2012. Total factor productivity, intangible assets and spatial dependence in the European regions. *Regional Studies* 46 (10): 1401–1416.

Djankov, Simeon. 2014. *Inside the euro crisis: An eyewitness account*. Washington, DC: Peterson Institute for International Economics.

Eder, Florian. 2016. Wolfgang Schäuble bails out Spain, Portugal. *Politico.eu*, July 27. Available: http://www.politico.eu/article/wolfgang-schauble-bails-out-spain-portugal-sanctions-juncker-german-finance-minister/. Accessed 2 July 2017.

ERCAS. 2015. *Public Integrity and Trust in Europe*, Report Prepared for the Dutch Ministry of the Interior and Kingdom Relations. Berlin: European Research Center for Anti-Corruption and State-Building. Available: http://www.eupan.eu/files/repository/20160202135959_2016-01-21_-_Public_integrity_and_trust_in_Europe_-_final.pdf. Accessed 2 July 2017.

Esping-Andersen, Gosta. 1993. *The three worlds of welfare capitalism*. Cambridge, UK: Polity Press.

European Commission. 2011. *The economic adjustment program for Portugal*, Occasional Papers No. 79. Brussels: Directorate General for Economic and Financial Affairs.

———. 2012. *The financial sector adjustment program for Spain*, Occasional Papers No. 118. Brussels: Directorate General for Economic and Financial Affairs.

———. 2013. *The economic adjustment program for Cyprus*, Occasional Papers No. 149. Brussels: Directorate General for Economic and Financial Affairs.

———. 2014a. *The economic adjustment Program for Portugal 2011–2014*, Occasional Papers No. 202. Brussels: Directorate General for Economic and Financial Affairs.

———. 2014b. *Financial assistance program for the recapitalization of financial institutions in Spain fifth review – Winter 2014*, Occasional Papers No. 170. Brussels: Directorate General for Economic and Financial Affairs.

——— 2016a. *Country report Cyprus 2016*, Commission Staff Working Document No. SWD(2016)120. Brussels: Directorate General for Economic and Financial Affairs.

———. 2016b. *Country report Portugal 2016*, Commission Staff Working Document No. SWD(2016)90. Brussels: Directorate General for Economic and Financial Affairs.

———. 2016c. *Country report Spain 2016*, Commission Staff Working Document No. SWD(2016)78. Brussels: Directorate General for Economic and Financial Affairs.

———. 2016d. *Ex post evaluation of the economic adjustment program Portugal, 2011–2014*, Institutional Paper 040. Brussels: Directorate General for Economic and Financial Affairs.

———. 2016e. *Post-program surveillance report – Cyprus Autumn 2016*, Institutional Paper 042. Brussels: Directorate General for Economic and Financial Affairs.

———. 2017. *Statistical annex of European economy, Spring*. Brussels: Commission of the European Communities Directorate General for Economic and Financial Affairs.

Farkas, Beáta. 2016. *Models of capitalism in the European Union: Post-crisis perspectives*. London: Palgrave Macmillan.

Ferrera, Maurizio. 2000. Reconstructing the welfare state in Southern Europe. In *Survival of the European welfare state*, ed. Stein Kuhnle, 166–181. London: Routledge.

Gago, Angie. 2016. Is austerity reversible? The Portuguese government receives the visit of the Troika. *EUvisions.eu*, February 15, 2016. Available: http://www.euvisions.eu/is-austerity-reversible-the-portuguese-left-government-receives-the-visit-of-the-troika/. Accessed 2 July 2017.

Gal, John. 2010. Is there an extended family of Mediterranean welfare states? *Journal of European Social Policy* 20 (4): 283–300.

Garciano, Luis. 2012. Five lessons from the Spanish caja debacle for a new euro-wide supervisor. *Voxeu.org*, October 16. Available: http://voxeu.org/article/five-lessons-spanish-cajas-debacle-new-euro-wide-supervisor. Accessed 2 July 2017.

Gonzalez, Libertad, and Francesco Ortega. 2013. Immigration and housing booms: Evidence from Spain. *Journal of Regional Science* 53 (1): 37–59.

Hedgecoe, Guy. 2016. 5 takeaways from Spain's repeat elections. *Politico.eu*, June 27. Available: http://www.politico.eu/article/5-takeaways-spain-elections-podemos-rajoy-news/. Accessed 2 July 2017.

ILO. 2015. *Small and medium-sized enterprises and decent and productive employment creation*, Report no. 4. International Labor Conference, 104th Session. Geneva: International Labor Office. Available: http://www.ilo.org/ilc/ILCSessions/104/reports/reports-to-the-conference/WCMS_358294/lang--en/index.htm. Accessed 2 July 2017.

IMF. 2011. Interview on Portugal with Paul Thomsen. *IMF Survey online*, May 6. Available: https://www.imf.org/en/News/Articles/2015/09/28/04/53/soint050611a. Accessed 2 July 2017.

———. 2016. *Portugal: Staff Concluding Statement of the Fifth Post-Program Monitoring Mission*. Washington: IMF. Available: http://www.imf.org/en/News/Articles/2016/12/08/MS120816-Portugal-Staff-Concluding-Statement-of-the-Fifth-Post-Program-Monitoring-Mission. Accessed 2 July 2017.

Kalotay, Kálmán. 2013. The 2013 Cyprus bailout and the Russian foreign direct investment platform. *Baltic Rim Economies* 3: 58–59.

Karamessini, Maria. 2007. *The Mediterranean welfare state: Changes and continuities in recent decades*, Discussion Paper No. 174. Geneva: International Institute for Labor Studies.

Kulish, Nicholas, and Raphael Minder. 2012. Spain holds the trump card in bailout negotiations. *The New York Times*, June 6. Available: http://www.nytimes.com/2012/06/07/world/europe/spain-holds-a-trump-card-in-bank-bailout-talks.html. Accessed 2 July 2017.

Lane, Philip. 2012. The European sovereign debt crisis. *Journal of Economic Perspectives* 26 (3): 49–68.

Léon, Margarita, and Emmanuele Pavolini. 2014. 'Social investment' or back to 'familism': The impact of the economic crisis on family and care policies in Italy and Spain. *South European Society and Politics* 19 (3): 353–369.

Léon, Margarita, Emmanuele Pavolini, and Ana M. Guillén. 2015. Welfare rescaling in Italy and Spain: Political strategies to deal with harsh austerity. *European Journal of Social Security* 17 (2): 182–201.

Medina, Lucia. 2015. *From recession to long-lasting political crisis? Continuities and changes in Spanish politics in times of crisis and austerity*, Working Paper No. 334. Barcelona: Institut de Ciències Polítiques i Socials.

Molina, Oscar, and Fausto Miguélez. 2013. *From negotiation to imposition: Social dialogue in austerity times in Spain*, Working Paper No. 51. Governance and Tripartism Department. Geneva: International Labor Office.

Moury, Catherine, and André Freire. 2013. Austerity policies and politics: The case of Portugal. *Pôle Sud* 39: 35–56.

OECD. 2016. *PISA 2015 results*. Paris: OECD.

Orphanides, Athanasios. 2014. *What happened in Cyprus? The economic consequences of the last communist government in Europe*, MIT Sloan Research Paper No. 5089–14. Cambridge, MA: Massachusetts Institute of Technology – Sloan School of Management.

Orriols, Lluis, and Guillermo Cordero. 2016. The breakdown of the Spanish two-party system: The upsurge of Podemos and Ciudadanos in the 2015 general election. *South European Society and Politics* 21 (4): 469–492.

Otero-Iglesias, Miguel, Sebastian Royo, and Federico Stainberg. 2016. *The Spanish financial crisis: Lessons for the European banking union*, Informe 20. Madrid: Elcano Royal Institute.

Pereira, Paolo T., and Laura Wemans. 2012. *Portugal and the global financial crisis – short-sighted politics, deteriorating public finances and the bailout imperative*. Department of Economics, ISEG – School of Economics and Management, University of Lisbon. Working Paper No. 26/2012/DE/UECE. Available: http://pascal.iseg.utl.pt/~depeco/wp/wp262012.pdf. Accessed 2 July 2017.

Phylaktis, Kate. 2016. The Cyprus debacle: Implications for the European Banking Union. In *European Banking Union: Prospects and challenges*, ed. Juan Castaneda, David Mayes, and Geoffrey Wood, 67–77. London: Routledge.

Quaglia, Lucia, and Sebastian Royo. 2013. *Banks and the political economy of the sovereign debt crisis in Italy and Spain*, Open Forum CES Paper Series No. 18. Cambridge, MA: Harvard University Center for European Studies.

Reis, Ricardo. 2013. The Portuguese slump and crash and the euro crisis. *Brookings Papers on Economic Activity* 1: 143–193.

Royo, Sebastián. 2014. Institutional degeneration and the economic crisis in Spain. *American Behavioral Scientist* 58 (12): 1568–1591.

Salgado, Susana, and Jose Zúquete. 2016. Portugal. Discreet populisms amid unfavorable contexts and stigmatization. In *Populist political communication in Europe*, ed. Toril Aalberg, Frank Esser, Carsten Reinemann, Jesper Strömbäck, and Claes H. de Vreese, 236–248. London: Routledge.

Santana, Manuel García, Josep Pijoan-Mas, Enrique Moral-Benito, and Roberto Ramos. 2016. Growing like Spain 1995–2007. *Voxeu.org*, May 23. Available: http://voxeu.org/article/growing-spain-1995-2007. Accessed 2 July 2017.

Sapir, André. 2006. Globalization and the reform of European social models. *Journal of Common Market Studies* 44 (2): 369–390.

Sapir, André, Guntram B. Wolff, Carlos de Sousa, and Alessio Terzi. 2014. *The Troika and financial assistance in the euro area: Successes and failures*. Study on the request of the Economic and Monetary Affairs Committee. Available: http://www.bruegel.org/publications/publication-detail/publication/815-the-troika-and-financial-assistance-in-the-euro-area-successes-and-failures/. Accessed 2 July 2017.

Torres, Diego. 2016. 5 takeaways from Mariano Rajoy's second term. *Politico.eu*, October 30. Available: http://www.politico.eu/article/5-takeaways-from-mariano-rajoys-second-term/. Accessed 2 July 2017.

UNCTAD. 2017. *World investment report 2017*. Annex Table 7. New York and Geneva: UNCTAD. Available: http://unctad.org/en/Pages/DIAE/World%20Investment%20Report/Annex-Tables.aspx. Accessed 2 July 2017.

6

Crisis Management Outside the Euro-Zone: The Cases of Hungary, Latvia, and Romania

Weak institutions and low trust are not just the characteristics of Mediterranean states but also of Central and Eastern Europe, where persistent distrust is one of the legacies of communism (Bjornskov 2007). The crisis hit the region before countries in the euro-zone were affected. The three countries, which needed international financial support (Hungary, Latvia, and Romania), have shown healthy recovery since 2014, and their strong growth seems to stand in contrast to the performance of Mediterranean countries. What explains their relative success?

In order to understand these cases, a historical narrative is warranted. While scholars often classify the Eastern member states of the EU as a separate model of capitalism, where modernization is based on FDI (Farkas 2016), these countries have very different trajectories going back to communism. A historical approach allows us to understand the different choices these countries made. Based on such analysis, the chapter will show that the three countries represent three different models of crisis management: Latvia resembles the Irish model, Romania, the Mediterranean countries, while Hungary represents the case of a seemingly successful populist adjustment. However, while the coping mechanisms with lack of trust were not dissimilar to the cases discussed earlier,

D. Győrffy, *Trust and Crisis Management in the European Union*,
https://doi.org/10.1007/978-3-319-69212-8_6

the chapter confirms the importance of trans-nationalization as a factor in recovery.

The chapter proceeds as follows. First it provides an overview about the transition experiences of the three countries and then traces the roots of the financial crisis. The third section examines the relationship with the IMF and other institutions during the negotiations of financial support, followed by an analysis of the public reception of the programs during the implementation phase. The fifth section discusses market reception, and the sixth assesses the outcomes of crisis management in terms of growth, social costs, and institutions. The final section concludes the chapter.[1]

6.1 Divergent Transitions

Following the end of the Cold War, Hungary, Latvia, and Romania all faced the tasks of building a democracy and market economy. They started the transition with very different inheritance concerning their relationship to the communist past and the level of public debt. Still, they faced the same task of implementing the so-called SLIP agenda, which stands for stabilization, liberalization, institution-building, and privatization (Farkas 2016: 204–205). The seal of approval on the completion of these tasks was the accession to the EU, which also marked the end of transition. Neither the SLIP agenda nor the EU accession process prescribed the size of the state or a particular social model for these countries—instead inherited factors strongly shaped the choices on the welfare system.

6.1.1 Hungary

Due to the revolution in 1956, under the leadership of János Kádár, Hungary became the country of goulash communism, where market reforms started as early as 1968, and in spite of periodic reversals, they were continued up until the transition.[2] As a consequence of the reforms, the standard of living was somewhat higher than in other countries of the Soviet block, and by retreating into their private sphere, people could find a sense of security. While this was an undisputed benefit for the generations in the Kádár regime, for the transition it implied a heavy burden: the relatively high standard of living was financed by debt, and following the unavoidable difficulties of the transition, people became nostalgic about the old regime. Furthermore a number of inherited features of the previous system survived, most importantly the expectation of the population for welfare benefits and the weak culture of rule of law, which was mainly the result of the extensive second economy under Socialism.

During the early years of transition the inheritance was not considered as particularly difficult. There was a widespread consensus among the major political actors over the main tasks of transformation—the establishment of democracy and market economy that would eventually lead the country into the EU. The last Socialist government from 1988 took radical steps on stabilization and liberalization: it abolished import restrictions without compensation for domestic producers; it liberalized all prices except energy, and it also proceeded with privatization via sale to the highest bidder (Csaba 1998: 1381). The inherited debt from the Socialist past, 73 percent of the GDP in 1989, also facilitated adjustment as it made privatization to foreigners politically feasible and thus paradoxically helped the country to step on the path of export-led growth (Mihályi 2001). Hungary quickly became a leader in attracting FDI—already by 1995 its stock of FDI was 24.4 percent of GDP, which was almost double of the stock in the Czech Republic and well over the 5.6 percent in Poland and the 6.5 percent in Slovakia.[3]

At the same time, the favorable initial conditions and the commitment to market reforms had their costs. The transformational recession between 1989 and 1993 led to an 18 percent loss of output.[4] Given the strict rules of bankruptcy, over 30,000 companies went through some forms of bankruptcy leading to a drop in employment by 30 percent and a rise in non-performing loans in the banking sector to 32 percent (Ábel and Szakadát 1997: 643). The loss of employment opportunities and rising popular dissatisfaction placed increasing demands on the welfare system of the country. In response to these pressures, the government considerably eased the regulations regarding disability pensions, early retirement, and maternity benefits, which contributed to low employment rates for decades.

The increasing welfare expenditures and the costs of bank consolidation led to enormous deficits, and in March 1995, in the shadow of the Mexican crisis, major fiscal adjustment became unavoidable. By relying on monetary, fiscal, and incomes policy, the economy was stabilized, and Hungary avoided a financial crisis without entering into a recession or suffering further employment losses. However, the favorable external assessments came with enormous political costs. The reduction of entitlements, such as introducing needs-based family allowances or tuition fee in higher education, aimed to signal the importance of individual responsibility in the new regime, but their main result was the triggering of serious resistance to the package. The opposition denied that such harsh measures were necessary and the finance minister, Lajos Bokros, soon became the least popular figure in the country. After the crisis was over he was forced to resign from his post in 1996. While the three-pillar pension reform was introduced by his successor in 1997, no major reforms took place for a decade after his leave. The unpopularity of the package and the loss of the following elections in 1998 made policy-makers extremely reluctant to introduce fiscal restrictions. Promising material benefits to buy support became the norm for all parties before the subsequent elections.

The early start of the SLIP agenda, the reliance on FDI for modernizing the economy, and the strong consensus over European integration made Hungary a leader during the transition and in the accession negotiations. Together with Poland, Hungary was the first country to sign the association agreement with the EU and apply for membership in 1994. During the process of negotiations it was never a question that the country belonged into the first round of enlargement, which took place in 2004. At the time it had the highest standards of governance among the three countries examined in this chapter (Fig. 6.1). However, the reception of the Bokros package, the extensive welfare state, and the nostalgia for the security of the Kádár regime signaled the difficulties ahead.

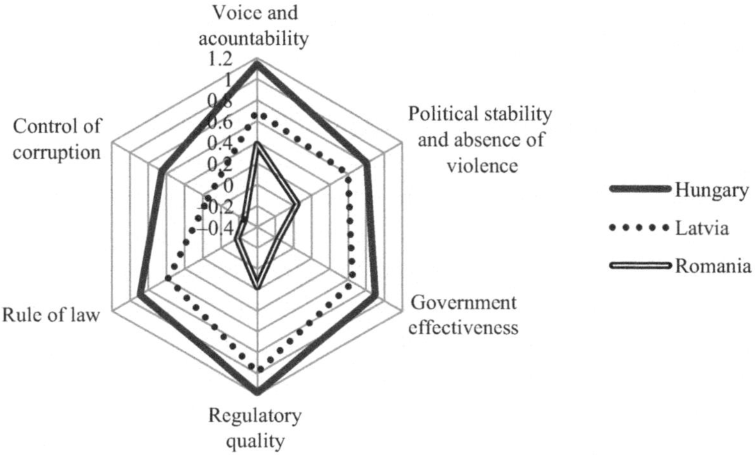

Fig. 6.1 World Governance Indicators in Hungary, Latvia, and Romania in 2004 (Data: World Governance Indicators at: http://www.govindicators.org)

6.1.2 Latvia

Latvia started transition from a very different point than Hungary. Following independence in 1991, it faced the triple task of political and economic transition as well as state-building. Unlike in Hungary, there was no desire to preserve elements of the old system and there was no inherited debt either. The total rejection of the Soviet past guided the transition, which meant a strong commitment to market economy and European integration.

The rejection of the past was symbolized by the exit from the rouble zone and the setting up of an independent central bank modeled on the German Bundesbank (Bohle and Greskovits 2012: 108). Its major aim was to bring down the inflation rate from triple digits and ensure the credibility of the new currency, the lats. While the country did not introduce an official currency board arrangement, the peg to the IMF special drawing rights then to the euro essentially functioned that way (Bohle and Greskovits 2012: 109). Beyond the strict exchange rate arrangement, Latvia followed the example of Estonia in introducing wide-ranging market reforms during the early 1990s. This included strict fiscal policy, a flat-tax system, and complete trade liberalization (Aslund and Dombrovskis 2011: 9–10). However, as the process of privatization was dominated by concerns for national ownership, FDI played a less significant role in the economy—even by 2007 the stock of FDI stood at 35.5 percent of GDP, considerably lower than in Estonia at 70.4 percent or Hungary at 68.6 percent.[5] The absence of FDI implied the slow modernization of the economy—in terms of R&D the country ranked last among EU member states even in 2011 (Farkas 2016: 181). The reforms of the state were also less successful compared to the frontrunner countries, which is shown by Fig. 6.1—in 2004 Latvia's quality of governance was way behind Hungary's especially on the field of control of corruption.

From the start of the transition, joining the EU was a major objective. Disputes surrounded the restrictive citizenship laws, which required language tests and were meant to limit access to career opportunities in the government and certain professions for the Russian minority (Bohle and Greskovits 2012: 121). During the accession process these laws were eased but the number of people without citizenship is still high—around 13 percent of the population in 2017.[6] In the 1997 opinion of the Commission on Latvia's request for accession to the EU, this issue featured prominently along with concerns about restructuring state-owned enterprises (SOEs), foreign investment, and the quality of governance (European Commission 1997). As a result, Latvia was to be included only into the second round of accession. The country finally started the negotiations in 1999, finished them by 2002, and joined the EU in 2004. During the negotiations the EU paid particular attention to the restructuring, privatization, and regulation of network industries such as energy, telecommunications, and the financial sector (Bohle and Greskovits 2012: 133).

The economic performance of Latvia did not reflect the early doubts of the Commission. Between 1997 and 2007, output grew by over 7 percent on average.[7] During this period the budget deficit mostly remained below 3 percent of GDP, public debt hovered between 10–15 percent of GDP, and by 2001 the inflation rate decreased to 2.3 percent.[8] However, the excellent performance had an important dark side. Between 1999 and 2007, social benefits other than in kind were reduced from 14.5

percent to 7 percent of the GDP, which is way below the euro-area average of 15–16 percent.[9] Cutting social expenditures was a major element of fiscal discipline, which contributed to social dissatisfaction (Bohle and Greskovits 2012: 116). This played an important role in the buildup of private debt prior to the financial crisis.

6.1.3 Romania

Romania had always been considered as a laggard during the transition, and it implemented the transition agenda significantly later than Hungary or Latvia. An important reason for the Romanian style gradualism is that early during the transition there seemed to be no need for radical reforms. The country started out with no public debt, which was a legacy from Ceausescu's drive to repay all public debt even at the cost of unimaginable suffering for the population. After the fall of Ceausescu, human capital was lacking for building a market economy—Romanians had no experience with enterprise during communism, and there was not even a sizable diaspora to help like in the Baltics (Papadimitriou 2006: 219).

The postponement of the transition agenda could be seen in the difficulties to lower the inflation rate and the slow privatization of SOEs. The average rate of inflation was 98.5 percent between 1991 and 2000, and single digit inflation was registered only in 2005.[10] Privatization was also postponed, as there was a strong belief that by keeping large companies in state hands, the population can be shielded from the pains of transition (Papadimitriou 2006: 220). During the early period of transition, privatization was mostly limited to small and medium enterprises (Farkas 2016: 199). As Papadimitriou (2006: 220–221) explains, inflation and the postponement of privatization are related: subsidies given to SOEs to cover their losses and make up for their tax arrears increase quasi-fiscal deficits and fuel both consumption and investment.

Lack of progress with the tasks of transition meant significant disadvantage in attracting FDI flows. Privatization to foreign investors started a decade later than in Hungary as the government tried to avoid sales to strategic investors and experimented with voucher and insider methods (Kalotay 2008: 17). As a result of the gradualist program, by the end of the 1990s, Romania had the worst privatization record in the region, and FDI inflows averaged 1 percent of GDP (Papadimitriou 2006: 221).

Although in 1996 there was a change in power, and the new center-right coalition was committed to accelerating structural reforms, initially these efforts resulted in high inflation and a large-scale recession similar to the transformational recession in other countries. Price liberalization in agricultural and energy sectors pushed back the inflation rate to 150 percent, and the economy shrank by an average of 4.4 percent between 1997 and 1999 (Farkas 2016: 199).

Given the delays in the major tasks of transition, it is unsurprising that in 1997 the European Commission decided to exclude Romania from accession negotiations, and only changed its position in 1999 (Papadimitriou and Gateva 2009: 11). Although after the 2000 elections the Social Democrats came back to power led by Adrian Nastase, the country was under increasing pressure to finish accession negotiations with the EU or otherwise risk international isolation (Papadimitriou 2006: 224). Compliance with the *aquis communitaire* provided a roadmap of reforms for the government. While providing such anchor was the main benefit from EU accession for all countries (Csaba 2006: 88–89), for Romania this was particularly relevant as it faced significantly stricter conditionality than countries joining in 2004 (Papadimitriou and Gateva 2009: 14–15).

A clear roadmap and strong monitoring led to remarkable progress—by 2003 inflation came close to 10 percent, the rate of growth surged over 5 percent, and fiscal deficits was reduced below 3 percent of GDP.[11] However, by 2003 only 40 percent of large state enterprises were privatized (Papadimitriou 2006: 225). In the following years, a number of high-profile privatizations were concluded in the banking and energy sectors easing fiscal pressures and attracting FDI (Kalotay 2008: 18). Nastase still lost in 2004 as the public resented the clientelism and corruption of his administration (Papadimitriou 2006: 226).

Following the defeat of the social democratic government, the new center-right Tariceanu government pushed the country into the Baltic direction. Romania introduced a flat tax of 16 percent for personal income tax and corporate tax as well as established an inflation-targeting regime for monetary policy. However, at the same time the IMF (2006: 14) also called attention to increased wage and pension expenditures by the government. Ban (2016: 94) considers this regime as neoliberal populism, when "the deregulation of consumer credit, lax zoning regulation, and the light-touch taxation of real estate transactions fueled a consumer and real estate bubble fueled by massive capital flows." Essentially the Romanian regime developed in a very similar manner to the Baltics, which Csaba (2009: 107) considers as cases of a new variety of macroeconomic populism, where "financing and sustainability considerations, the smoothing of the business cycle and entering the eurozone are not among the priorities of the governments and central banks."

Although Romania transformed itself from a laggard to a neoliberal model during the process of the transition, the weakness of the state was evident all along. As we can see in Fig. 6.1, in 2004 the quality of governance in Romania was well below the quality in Hungary and Latvia. As Bohle and Greskovits (2012: 208) argue a "weak state is unable to devise and enforce clear and stable rules of the game." This also implies difficulties in designing and enforcing complex regulations and collecting taxes. For such countries the flat-tax system reduces "public agencies' enforcement activities to a minimum at which they could appear efficient" (Bohle and Greskovits 2012: 221). As in Latvia, the low level of redistribution strongly contributed to increasing private indebtedness prior to the crisis.

6.2 The Road to the Crisis

With the completion of transition and joining the EU, all three countries were able to access the international financial markets. They all took advantage of this access, and public and/or private sector indebtedness grew sharply.

In *Hungary* the period after 2000 can be characterized by the permanent election campaign and the lack of any major reform even in the midterm of government. Government debt increased steadily—from 51.7 percent of GDP in 2001 to 71.6 percent by 2008 (Fig. 6.2). Politically motivated spending[12] was the major reason behind this increase

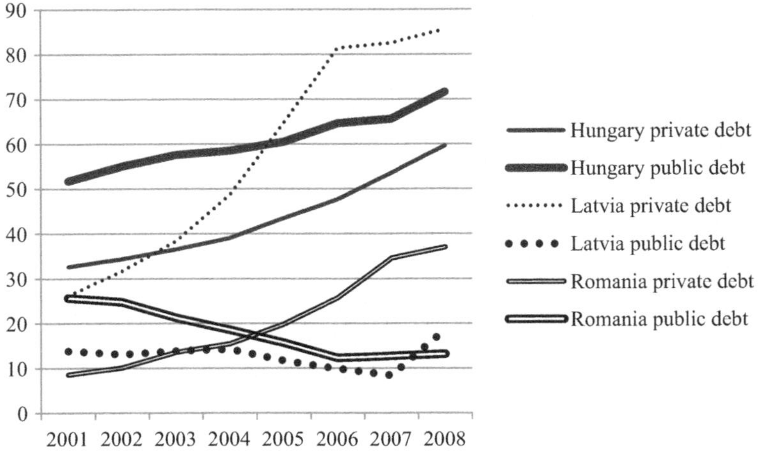

Fig. 6.2 Public and private debt in Hungary, Latvia, and Romania 2001–2008 (% of GDP) (Data: Public debt, European Commission 2017 164, 165; Private debt, World Databank domestic credit to private sector indicator)

as well documented by Ohnsorge-Szabó and Romhányi (2007).[13] Efforts to reduce the imbalances took place during midterm through suboptimal revenue-increasing measures, which led to a worsening business environment. The increase in taxes and the administrative measures to fight the informal economy substantially increased administrative costs and created an unfavorable environment for investment. Hungary continued to have one of the lowest employment rates in the EU ranging around 61.2 percent and 62.6 percent between 2000 and 2008 for persons aged 20–64.[14] Low employment implied low contribution to the budget, and entrenched demand for welfare services, which in turn had to be financed by high taxes on those who work.

The situation was further worsened by rapid credit growth in the private sector. The parallel growth of public and private indebtedness makes Hungary an outlier among the three countries examined in the chapter (Fig. 6.2). Credit growth mostly took place in foreign currency.[15] The major reason for foreign indebtedness was the large interest rate differential between loans in domestic currency and in euro. Given the weak credibility of Hungarian economic policy due to the above reasons, domestic interest rates remained steadily high—as a result between 2004 and 2007, euro loans were cheaper by 6.5 percentage points for housing and 15.5 percentage points for consumption goods (Darvas and Szapáry 2008: 40). The high interest rate influenced foreign currency lending through the exchange rate channel as well—the forint remained strong and stable in relation to the euro, which contributed to the underestimation of exchange rate risk by borrowers. As the credit boom created the illusion of prosperity, it is unsurprising that the sharp increase in foreign currency borrowing was not countered by effective policy measures.[16] The growing indebtedness in foreign currency made the country extremely vulnerable to any change in market sentiment and the volatility of the currency.

Given the above circumstances, it is unsurprising that following the collapse of Lehman Brothers in September 2008, the subsequent freeze of the global financial markets and the sharp devaluation of its currency, Hungary was the first EU country, which had to turn to the IMF for help in October 2008 in order to maintain financing for the government and the financial sector.

In *Latvia* strengthening EU integration and improving access to credit were the major methods to address the dissatisfaction of the public (Bohle 2010: 8–9). As shown by Fig. 6.2, Latvia experienced the most dynamic increase in private sector credit growth among the three countries. The credit boom resulted in the highest rate of inflation in the EU (11.7 percent in 2007) and enormous current account deficits reaching over 21 percent in 2006 and 2007.[17] The overheating of the economy was also signed by real estate prices—between 2004 and 2007, square meter prices increased from €400 to €1700 (Blanchard et al. 2013: 332–334). In spite of the obvious signs of overheating, there were no serious efforts to rein in the credit boom given its enormous popularity (Aslund and Dombrovskis 2011: 29).

The slowdown of the economy started before the crisis given the overvaluation of the currency as well as the tightening credit conditions due to the reaction of primarily Scandinavian banks to the obvious signs of overheating. Following the last quarter of 2007, exports, domestic consumption, and investments started falling. Until the third quarter of 2009, GDP fell by 25 percent (Blanchard et al. 2013: 338). The global financial crisis contributed to the fall affecting Latvia via two channels:

the fall in international demand and the freeze of the global financial markets. While the first resulted in a 5 percent decline in external demand, the credit crunch led to a fall of 43 percent in domestic demand (Blanchard et al. 2013: 339).

The immediate trigger for the financial crisis in Latvia was the fall of the largest domestic bank, Parex, which owned 14 percent of Latvian bank assets. Its resources were domestic and external deposits in roughly equal share. During the crisis this became problematic given the possibility of self-fulfilling run by depositors—who were aware that there is no lender of last resort in a currency board arrangement. The panic started following the collapse of Lehman Brothers, when international financial markets froze and Parex' loans were not rolled over (Blanchard et al. 2013: 340–341). The bank lost 25 percent of its deposits, and the panic was not mitigated even by government interventions, which included the reduction of reserve requirements.

The collapse of external and domestic demand, the credit crunch, and the instability of the banking system raised questions regarding the commitment of Latvia to maintain its fixed exchange rate system. In order to support financial stability, the country turned to the IMF and the EU for assistance.

Private sector credit growth was the main source of the crisis in *Romania* as well although it was more moderate than in Latvia (Fig. 6.2). With the anticipation and eventual accession to the EU, the country gained access to the international financial markets. Capital inflows were channeled by the banking sector, where foreign banks accounted for 90 percent of assets (Farkas 2016: 441). The inflow of funds led to a boom in consumer and real estate spending, which resulted in a sharp increase of wages—nominal unit labor costs compared to 2010 levels grew from 68.7 percent to 113.9 percent between 2002 and 2008.[18] As a result imports grew far more quickly than exports, which in turn led to an increasing current account deficit. However, these imbalances were hidden behind favorable GDP performance—between 2001 and 2008, growth averaged 6.55 percent.[19]

The sharp increase in capital inflows led to the development of vulnerabilities in the banking sector. As Hudecz (2013: 268) shows the share of foreign currency denominated loans rose from 10 percent to over 90 percent between 2001 and 2004. Bakker and Klingen (2012: 147) also point to the vulnerabilities in the public sector, where employment rose by 24 percent between 2004 and 2008, while there were also several rounds of pension increase, especially prior to elections. In 2008 spending on wages and pensions increased by 35 percent and 46 percent respectively compared to the previous year (IMF 2012: 6).

The collapse of Lehman Brothers hit Romania during the run-up to the November 2008 general election campaign. Even though borrowing became difficult, the government financed its pre-election campaign by dangerous, short-term loans (Bakker and Klingen 2012: 148), which increased vulnerabilities. By October 2008 the country experienced a sudden stop in capital inflows, which led to the contraction in credit and a severe weakening of the exchange rate resulting in a significant increase of the debt burden for households with foreign currency loans.

In order to stabilize its finances and regain market confidence, the newly elected government led by Emil Boc turned to the IMF and the EU for financial assistance.

6.3 The Negotiations of Programs

Unlike in the case of euro-zone member states, there was no delay or difficulty for countries outside the euro-zone to turn to the IMF. Hungary, Latvia, and Romania were the first EU member states to ask for financial assistance, and the joint involvement of the EU and the IMF established the lines of cooperation for euro-zone countries as well. The signing of the negotiations occurred rapidly in all three cases although the circumstances varied significantly.

Hungary completed the negotiations very fast during 2008 Fall. The authorities asked for assistance on 9 October, after a failed government bond auction, weakening exchange rate and falling stock market price for the largest domestic bank, OTP (Bakker and Klingen 2012: 93). An IMF team flew to Budapest two days later, and a stand-by agreement was signed on 6 November. Aslund (2010: 26) alludes to the triumph IMF officials felt that after years of functioning without clients finally they became relevant again. In retrospect, the reason for the short duration of the program (18 months) and the streamlined conditionality was the belief that the problem was a "short-term liquidity crisis" (IMF 2011: 7).

The negotiations were smooth, and there were no differences of opinion between the IMF and the European Commission, which was also involved (Lütz and Kranke 2014: 319). In return for the €20 billion support package, Hungary had to implement a front-loaded expenditure-based consolidation, which involved a nominal wage freeze and the elimination of the 13th month salary for all public sector employees, the elimination of 13th month pensions, raising the statutory retirement age, and reductions in universal welfare programs. On the revenue side, the already announced tax cuts were postponed, and authorities committed themselves not to make any tax changes, which leads to loss of revenues (IMF 2008: 10). Minor cuts in personal income tax and social security contributions took place in parallel to the increase in VAT and corporation tax. Following a decade of resistance by the political elite, in the context of the program, the parliament also adopted strict fiscal rules constraining the growth of debt and established a fiscal council to provide independent assessment of budgetary policy and evaluate legislative proposals based on their budgetary impact. As emphasized by the IMF ex post program review (IMF 2011: 12), the program was based on a blueprint presented by the Hungarian authorities at the beginning of the negotiations.

The strong cooperation of the Hungarian government in designing and implementing the program was signaled not only by the fast completion of the agreement, but also in its modification—as it became clear that the 2009 recession would be greater than expected, the lenders showed flexibility in adjusting the deficit target from 2.6 percent to 2.9 percent in May 2009 (IMF 2009a: 11).

The 2010 elections changed the relationship between the Hungarian government, the IMF, and the European Commission. Viktor Orbán was handed a two-thirds majority in the Hungarian parliament by voters based on the promise to end austerity, cut taxes, and implement an unorthodox adjustment program. The early elements of the program such as the special taxes on multinationals, the de facto nationalization of private pensions, or the possibility to repay mortgages early at preferential rates[20] were not taken well by the markets, especially during a period of turbulence within the euro-zone. Given the weakening of exchange rate, the country had to turn to the IMF again in November 2011. A second stand-by agreement however was never signed—the government negotiated for over a year before stating in December 2013 that it does not want to sign a new program.

Ex post it appears that the Orbán government had no serious intention to enter into a stand-by agreement as the negotiations in themselves were sufficient to stop speculations against the forint. As the financial markets calmed and the current account was in surplus, by the end of 2013 it became clear that there would be no new agreement. During the extended negotiations the government was able to conduct a public campaign listing all the measures presumably asked by the IMF, which it was not willing to introduce such as the introduction of property tax and the cutting of pensions. Although the IMF continuously denied the presence of such list of mandatory conditions, the government could sustain its image of fighting against austerity (Farkas 2014: 255–259). Naturally, such techniques were not conducive to fruitful exchange of views for a new program. Still, the government succeeded both in stopping the speculation against the forint and avoiding the potentially harsh conditionality of a new agreement.

Negotiations with *Latvia* were concluded as rapidly as with Hungary during the first round—the country invited the IMF in mid-November 2008, and on 19 December, the rescue package was announced (Bakker and Klingen 2012: 115). The negotiations were characterized by high level of cooperation where open discussion and persuasion were the main methods, which shaped the outcome (Dahan 2012)—in spite of several contentious issues among participants. There were much more actors than usual at the table. Besides the IMF and the EU, representatives of the Scandinavian countries were also there given their 60 percent stake in the country's banking system. Out of the €7.5 billion package, the IMF gave 1.7 billion, the EU 3.1 billion, and 1.8 billion came from the Scandinavians. Furthermore, Latvia received bilateral loans from the Czech Republic, Estonia, and Poland (Aslund and Dombrovskis 2011: 45–46).

One of the most critical questions of the program was whether to give up the peg. Latvians insisted to the peg because over 90 percent of their loans were in euro, and they considered accession to the euro-zone as an exit from this situation (Bakker and Klingen 2012: 115). In order to maintain the peg, they were aware of the need for internal devaluation and severe fiscal consolidation. During the negotiations the European participants supported the Latvian strategy given the fear of losses from the banking system as well as the possible regional spillover effects. On the other hand, the IMF was not convinced that Latvia can execute the tough measures needed to maintain the peg, and they even suggested the unilateral adoption of the euro, which was strongly opposed by the EU (Lütz and Kranke 2014: 320). Seeing the firm stance of the Europeans, the IMF was finally willing to agree to the Latvian strategy and signed the package without devaluation.[21]

Fiscal consolidation was another contentious issue during the negotiations. An important element of the program was the reduction of fiscal deficit below 3 percent of GDP by 2011. During the negotiations the giving up of flat tax and the low corporate tax came up, but Latvians refused these requests although they agreed to raising the VAT from 18 percent to 21 percent (Aslund and Dombrovskis 2011: 44). The main problem for the adjustment was however the difficulties of forecasting the fall in GDP. In the original package, 5 percent loss of GDP was forecasted for 2009, which soon proved overly optimistic and the output loss was close to 18 percent. The conditions of the package needed to be renegotiated and the idea of devaluation came up again from the IMF (Aslund and Dombrovskis 2011: 85). The IMF also suggested a more gradual path of adjustment with a deficit target of 13 percent for 2009 and the reach of the 3 percent threshold only by 2014 (Lütz and Kranke 2014: 320). However, Latvia went with the recommendation of the EU, and committed itself to the EU target of a more ambitious adjustment (Table 6.1). In support of the Latvian strategy the European Commission sent the next tranche of the package. In July 2009 the other creditors also agreed to prolong the deadline for the 3 percent deficit by one year. The time was used by the Latvian government to implement further austerity measures, which included a further 20 percent wage cut in the public sector as well as cuts in pensions (Aslund and Dombrovskis 2011: 85–88).

During the negotiations the IMF expressed continued skepticism about the ability of Latvia to sustain the peg and implement internal

Table 6.1 Fiscal conditionality and outcomes in Hungary, Latvia, and Romania (budget balance as % of GDP)

	2008	2009	2010	2011	2012	2013	2014	2015	2016
Hungary 2008	−3.4	−2.6							
Revised target		*−2.9*							
Hungary actual	**−3.6**	**−4.6**	**−4.5**	**−5.5**	−2.3	−2.6	−2.1	−1.6	−1.8
Latvia 2009		−5.3		−3.0					
Revised target			*−8.5*	*−6*	*−3*				
Latvia actual		**−9.1**	**−8.7**	**−3.3**	−1	−1	−1.6	−1.3	0
Romania 2009		−5.1	−4.1	−3.0					
Revised target			*−6.8*						
Romania actual		**−9.5**	**−6.9**	**−5.4**	**−3.7**	−2.1	−1.4	−0.8	−3

Data: For Hungary Memorandum of Understanding (2008) and IMF (2009a), for Latvia Memorandum of Understanding (2009a) and IMF (2009b), for Romania Memorandum of Understanding (2009b) and IMF (2010). Data on actual outcomes is from European Commission (2017: 160–161). Bold numbers indicate the years when the 3 percent deficit threshold were breached

devaluations. Such skepticism was probably the reason for the relatively high number of structural conditions in the program (IMF 2013: 16). However, with the support of the EU, the country succeeded in preserving its priorities and negotiated the conditions in good faith. In this case debates about the specifics of the package did not undermine trust among the negotiators.

Romania approached the IMF for financial assistance on 29 March 2009, and by 6 May the country received a €20 billion package—out of which 12.95 billion came from the IMF, 5 billion from the EU, 1 billion from the World Bank, and 1 billion from the European Bank for Reconstruction and Development (EBRD) and the European Investment Bank (EIB). The rapid approval of the program suggests smooth negotiations in this case as well.

The fast negotiations reflected the government's willingness to implement serious measures to fight the crisis. The radical approach of the government seemed to take even the IMF by surprise. As Ban (2016: 210) describes: "It is not everyday that one hears the managing director of the IMF charged with being an ideologue of the left and a proponent of 'state capitalism' whose fondness for it was deemed traceable to his communist youth. Yet this is exactly what happened in Romania in 2010 when Dominique Strauss Kahn asked the Romanian government to spread the costs of austerity more equitably."

The conditionality for the program resembled other stand-by agreements. The leading item was fiscal consolidation, in order to reverse pre-crisis overspending and restore confidence. For the longer term, in order to improve transparency and predictability, fiscal governance reforms were expected including the establishment of a fiscal council. The third part of the agreement concerned achieving price stability, strengthening the bank resolution framework, and improving banking supervision. Finally, structural conditions included measures to improve the efficiency of public administration, the business environment, and the absorption of EU funds.[22]

As the economic recession was significantly deeper than expected, in 2010 a supplemental memorandum of understanding was signed, which contained further conditionality (Supplemental of Memorandum of Understanding 2010). Among other measures it proposed a VAT increase from 19 percent to 24 percent, a cut in public sector wages by 25 percent and social assistance programs by 15 percent. It also included conditions of arrears, and steps toward privatization or closure of two SOEs. These commitments allowed the easing of the fiscal target similarly to the cases of Hungary and Latvia (Table 6.1).

In order to curb fiscal imbalances the government used simple and radical measures—not unlike during the pre-crisis period (Ban 2016: 213). They aimed to signal their commitment to an expenditure-based consolidation. In an interview, the IMF mission chief, Jeffrey Franks, emphasized that these measures were not their idea. When asked about the 25 percent wage cut in the public sector and whether this could have been avoided, he replied that "there were a number of possibilities that policymakers could have chosen——different mixes of revenue and expenditure measures——but their decision was to rely almost entirely on public expenditure cuts." He also emphasized that it was the IMF, which called attention to the importance of defending the most vulnerable members of the population from the impact of austerity: "given that the authorities wanted to rely on heavy expenditure cuts in adjusting their budget, we asked that they put in place some protection for the most vulnerable" (Andersen 2010). According to Lütz and Kranke (2014: 321) the Romanian authorities were strongly encouraged in these positions by the representatives of the European Commission, who were more radical than the IMF.

After the expiration of the program, Romania could return to the financial markets. However, the government realized that further structural reforms were necessary and there were still considerable uncertainties on the global financial markets (IMF 2014: 6). On 24 March 2011, a second stand-by agreement was signed in order to provide precautionary support against external shocks. The conditionality of the program was similar to the first program emphasizing fiscal consolidation and financial stability. However, structural conditionality became more extensive and included the energy sector and transport, the governance of SOEs and labor market reforms, and changing policies for the R&D sector.[23]

The cooperation with the IMF continued even after a change in government in 2012. Although in opposition the Social Democrats were against the severe austerity of the Boc government, eventually the slogan became "high-quality fiscal consolidation." While the new appointees to key economic posts were less committed to neoliberalism than Boc's people, they recognized the external constraints, and advised the prime minister to respect the agreement with the Troika (Ban 2016: 238). Their continued adherence to the program was also signaled by the fact that in June 2012 the new Ponta government signed a supplemental memorandum of understanding with the Troika, and in 2013 a third balance of payment program was agreed for precautionary assistance. Similarly to the previous program, the objective was to continue fiscal consolidation and structural reforms. While funds were drawn only from the first program, the second and the third programs provided some leverage on economic policy for the Troika.

6.4 Public Trust and the Implementation of Program Conditionality

While the atmosphere of negotiations differed, Hungary, Latvia, and Romania are rather similar in terms of the political difficulties associated with the implementation of the program. As Fig. 6.3 shows, in all three countries, with over 50 percent satisfaction rate, EU democracy is judged

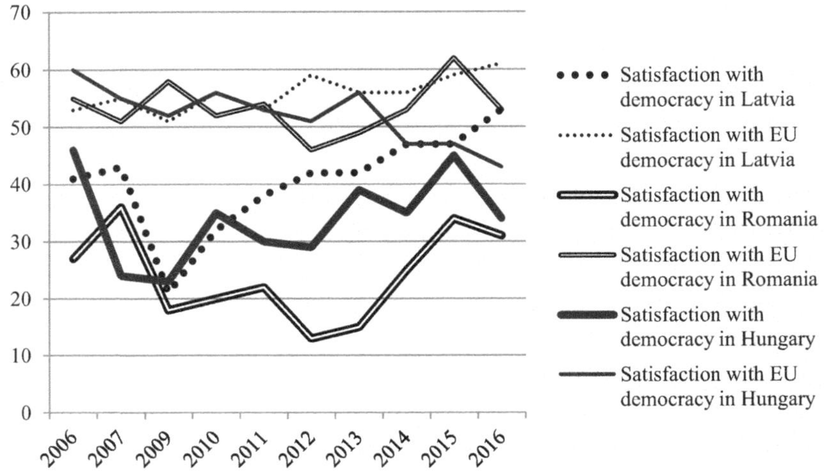

Fig. 6.3 Satisfaction with democracy in Hungary, Latvia, and Romania 2006–2016 (% satisfied) (Data: Eurobarometer online)

much more favorably than national democracy. Satisfaction with the latter was well below 50 percent in 2006, and it fell close to 20 percent by 2009 signaling considerable disillusionment with the system. The collapse of systemic confidence was paralleled with political turmoil in all three countries causing substantial difficulties in implementing the terms of the program. The various performances of the three countries are signaled by the differences in the recovery of trust in the system.

In *Hungary* the political difficulties started well before the crisis: following reelection in 2006, the center-left government was forced to implement substantial fiscal consolidation due to high fiscal deficits and growing debt (Fig. 6.2). This became especially difficult after the so-called Őszöd speech, when prime minister Ferenc Gyurcsány admitted following irresponsible policies and lying day and night in order to win the 2006 elections. After a leaked tape about his admission, protests against the government became widespread and efforts at fiscal adjustment faced strong resistance. The level of dissatisfaction increased even further after Hungary had to turn to the IMF in October 2008. Gyurcsány finally resigned in March 2009, and it was left to his successor, Gordon Bajnai, to implement the IMF program.

The technocratic government led by Bajnai implemented the conditions to the letter. As emphasized by the IMF (2011: 16) "despite difficult and evolving circumstances, program conditionality was met throughout the program – all the quantitative performance criteria were met at each review." During the program an implicit grand coalition took shape as the main opposition party, Fidesz, was criticizing only certain elements of the program such as family leave policies and the wealth tax. Even during the campaign it did not promise any further change to the adjustment; there was no promise of the reintroduction of the 13th month pension, for example. After he came to power, Viktor Orbán praised the performance of the Bajnai government—although more during negotiations with foreign partners than in the election campaign (Farkas 2014: 154). However, all this did not change the fact that the electorate was furious with the Socialists. In 2009 austerity was paralleled with a significant, 6.6 percent drop in GDP, and the public blamed Gyurcsány and the center-left government for both. This atmosphere opened the way for a two-third Fidesz majority led by Viktor Orbán.

Orbán's original plan for the new government was to implement tax cuts to stimulate the economy and negotiate higher deficit target for 2010. In the context of the Greek crisis, however, Brussels was unwilling to allow the 6.8 percent deficit hoped by the new government (Farkas 2014: 148–149). However, this failure did not lead to the reconsideration of Orbán's plans to cut taxes. As one of the first measures of the new government, a 16 percent flat-tax system was introduced with substantial benefits to families. Further tax cuts included a 10 percent corporate tax for small- and medium-size enterprises. The total costs of these measures were HUF 444bn or about 1.5 percent of GDP annually (Tóth and Virovácz 2013). Since expenditures were not cut in a parallel manner, countermeasures were necessary to reach the deficit target. Such measures included the raising of the VAT to 27 percent and the levying of special taxes on the financial sector, energy suppliers, telecommunication, and retail companies (Government 2011: 66–67). Although these were announced as temporary crisis taxes, they were made permanent once it became evident that the reduction in income taxes did not have the expected impact on growth.[24] The government also gained substantial revenue by the de facto nationalization of the second pillar of the pension system in November 2010. It amounted to around HUF 3000bn or 10 percent of GDP as well as the reorientation of pension contributions to the budget amounting to around 1.5 percent of GDP (Government of the Republic of Hungary 2011: 47).

The agreement with the IMF expired in October 2010. However, the program lapsed even before that time—Orbán's approach to fiscal consolidation raised substantial doubts in the IMF as they viewed them as risks to growth and sustainability (IMF 2011: 23). The IMF was in a precarious position as it was an active coordinator in the so-called Vienna Initiative, which was signed in May 2009 ensuring that Western banks do not leave the Central and Eastern European region in response to the crisis. There was an implicit expectation in the agreement that the IMF and EU protect the interests of foreign banks in the financial assistance programs (Mabbett and Schelke 2015: 516). Orbán's bank levy clearly went against this agreement.

The continuing crisis in the EU and Orbán's attempt to make multinationals pay for the costs of the crisis management led a fall in market confidence and the substantial weakening of the forint—from HUF/€263 in April 2010 to 316 by November 2011. This development was not against the wishes of the government as they strongly believed in the role of exchange rate policy to stimulate exports. However, the weakening of the forint also meant that the problem of foreign currency loans had to be addressed as non-performing loans accumulated in the banking sector.[25] This was done through a long moratorium on evictions as well as the possibility to repay the foreign currency loans at an exchange rate well below the market rate through an early repayment scheme between September and December 2011. These measures implied substantial further costs for the banks amounting to a net loss of 1 percent of GDP (European Commission 2014: 32).

Throughout the crisis the government acted in an ad hoc manner without consultations or impact studies. Impromptu decision-making became a defining feature of policy (Csaba 2012: 303). The unconcealed desire of the government for increasing its discretion over policy-making was signaled by the systematic cut down on institutional checks and balances. In retrospect, it is probably more precise to state that the crisis management was used as an excuse to centralize power and build an illiberal democracy.[26] Steps toward this objective included the nomination of party members to head independent institutions such as the posts of the President, the head of the State Audit Office, and from 2013 the National Bank of Hungary. The independent fiscal council, which was established in 2009, was abolished in 2010. The power of the Constitutional Court was also curbed following its resistance to a retroactive law on severance payments. While in the new Constitution, apparently strict fiscal rules and a powerful fiscal council were included, the formally strict rules have little constraining influence on the Orbán government but might become debilitating on a future government.[27] These steps fit well with other measures for cementing Orbán's power including the restrictive media law in 2010 and the new electoral law in 2011,[28] which allowed Fidesz to gain another two-thirds supermajority in 2014 even though it received almost 8 percentage points less votes, which means it lost close to 500,000 voters.

The reelection of the Orbán government, however, was not only due to the change in the electoral law. As Fig. 6.3 shows, satisfaction with democracy steadily improved after 2009, and it surpassed 40 percent by 2015. The continued popularity of the government was not necessarily due to its aggressive stance against the IMF or the EU—the latter's support remained over 50 percent until 2014 (Fig. 6.3). Instead, the main factors contributing to Orbán's reelection were probably the 3.2 percent real increase in old age pensions in 2013 and the administrative cut in utilities' prices from the second part of 2012, which brought down the inflation rate and provided tangible fall in costs for Hungarian households at the expense of foreign multinationals. Benczes (2016) aptly notes that through these steps Hungary made the journey from goulash communism to "goulash populism." As a result, the government was successful in presenting itself as the lesser evil during the 2014 elections, and won again against the opposition, which included the exact same leaders, who were held responsible for the crisis. However, the example of Latvia shows that Fidesz' unorthodox approach to crisis management was not the only way to rebalance the economy and preserve political power.

Similarly to Hungary, in *Latvia* the crisis started before the collapse of Lehman Brothers. At the end of 2007, the slowdown of the economy coincided with the fall of the prime minister, Aigar Kalvitis, after the dismissal of the head of the anti-corruption bureau. His follower, Ivars

Godmanis, had considerable reputation as the first prime minister of Latvia. However, even during the Fall 2008, there was sizeable opposition to the plans for fiscal stabilization. Support for radical measures started increasing as the collapse of the economy became evident, and the maintenance of the peg came to be questioned (Aslund and Dombrovskis 2011: 33–34). The budget for 2009 was harshly criticized by the opposition for not being radical enough and trying to protect certain interest groups from the effect of cuts (Aslund and Dombrovskis 2011: 38–40). In response to widespread protests, Godmanis resigned in February 2009, and the president nominated the former minister of finance, Valdis Dombrovskis. as the new prime minister.

Dombrovskis implemented radical fiscal adjustment even by the standards of the IMF, which continued to raise doubt about the "quality, composition and sustainability of the adjustment measures" as well as their adverse social impact (IMF 2013: 23). On the revenue side, consumption taxes were increased substantially,[29] although as noted by Comite et al. (2012: 82) compliance dropped sharply afterwards thus overall taxes as share of GDP did not rise. The increase in consumption taxes were partially offset by a 2 percent cut in personal income taxes. On the expenditure side, major savings came from cuts in public sector wages as well as reforms in health care, education, and public administration. The measures included the closure of half of the 75 state agencies, the decrease of territorial units from 548 to 119, cuts in the health and education budget by 26 percent and 27 percent, respectively. In discussing these steps, Comite et al. (2012: 82–83) emphasize that in these sectors, reforms had been long overdue, plans were available, and the financial crisis provided the window of opportunity to implement them. It is also important that social protection and social assistance programs were enhanced during the crisis including the extended duration of unemployment insurance benefits, the expansion of the guaranteed minimum income program and the introduction of a public works program (Harrold et al. 2012: 123–126). The scale of adjustment reached 8 percent of GDP in 2009, a further 5.4 percent in 2010, and 2.3 percent in 2011 (Blanchard et al. 2013: 345).

In parallel to fiscal consolidation, structural reforms also took place in order to improve the ease of doing business and productivity. As a result of changes, by early 2010 wages fell by 27 percent in the public sector and 6 percent in the private sector along with a steep rise in unemployment (IMF 2013: 19). The adjustment contributed to sharp reversal of the current account balance, which improved from −21.1 percent in 2007 to −0.8 percent by 2015.[30] This way the currency board system could be maintained, thus Latvia averted the problem of debt explosion, which would have occurred in the case of devaluation given the level of foreign currency loans. This problem in Latvia was handled through the introduction of the euro in January 2014.

The harsh measures did not lead to a collapse of government popularity, and in October 2010 Dombrovskis was reelected with an even greater majority. The anti-austerity campaign of the opposition failed. The government continued to implement the program, and by 2012 Latvia achieved the 3 percent deficit target of the Maastricht criteria (Table 6.1). Throughout the effort confidence in the system continued to improve (Fig. 6.3) showing people's willingness to accept considerable economic hardship for the sake of euro-zone accession.

The population was less understanding of radical reformers in *Romania*. The 2008 elections were won by the Democrat-Liberal Party (PDL) led by Emil Boc. In order to form a majority for the handling of the economic crisis, the Social Democrats (PDS) gave them temporary support, while a convincing conservative majority could be formed only in 2009. The changes in the composition of the government however did not influence the commitment to implement the program, which had the full support of the president and the central bank as well. The commitment to the program from the government came from a deeply held commitment to free market and an aversion to state redistribution. Ban (2016: 232) cites an interview with Emil Boc saying that "if we want to redistribute more than we do, we should wait until we reach German output levels and civil service quality."

The radicalism was reflected in the policies of the government. Fiscal consolidation was expenditure-based and front-loaded—the structural deficit narrowed by 6 percentage points during the 2009–2011 program (IMF 2012: 11). When it became clear that the initial actions will not be sufficient to achieve the program objectives, aggressive actions were taken in June 2010 including the already mentioned 25 percent cut in public sector wages, 15 percent cuts in social transfer, and 5 percent increase in the VAT rate.

The government also took a radical approach on structural reforms.[31] In 2010 a new fiscal responsibility framework was introduced with medium-term budgetary planning, fiscal rules, and the establishment of a fiscal council. The new institution became a strong voice for enforcing the agreements with the Troika (Ban 2016: 225). The labor market was also liberalized in 2011: hiring and firing labor became easier and the scope of collective bargaining was narrowed resulting in a reduced influence of trade unions (Trif 2013).

The Boc government eventually collapsed after the violent protests during the winter in 2011–2012 in response to a new health care legislation, which tried to reduce health care services, privatize hospitals, and insurance. Emil Boc resigned, and his successor also failed to survive a motion of non-confidence in the Romanian Parliament. The government was taken over by the opposition led by Victor Ponta. The December elections that year yielded an absolute majority to Ponta's Social Liberal Union. However, the low turnout of around 40 percent reflected the apathy of the population in the middle of austerity.

During the Ponta governments some reversals took place on the margins, such as increasing public sector wages and reducing VAT for food, but the repeal of the labor code or the introduction of progressive tax system did not take place (Ban 2016: 239). Still, the IMF (2014: 7) notes that "political turmoil and local and parliamentary elections held in the second half of 2012 complicated the implementation of the reform agenda."

Although even the Ponta government respected fiscal conditionality, and the country achieved the 3 percent deficit threshold, deeper structural reforms, such as the governance of SOEs, were less successful. Initially the IMF did not ask for the privatization of SOEs but instead called for governance reforms to avoid losses and reduce arrears (IMF 2012: 15). In a 2014 review of the Romanian program, it was noted that political interference into selecting board members was still taking place, and only two companies were privatized out of the 13 promised (IMF 2014: 22).

The reduction of unpaid bills was also a major objective of reforming the health care sector. These measures were only partially successful—while they reduced existing arrears, they could not prevent the emergence of new ones because of the underfinancing of the sector (IMF 2014: 19).

EU fund absorption is a third area, where progress was insufficient as absorption rate remained the lowest in the EU—the IMF estimated that the country could lose a total of 10 percent of GDP because of their inefficiency (IMF 2014: 21). For the 2007–2013 period, Romania ended up with a 52 percent absorption rate, which "reflects weak project management capacity in the government and in beneficiaries and a preference for initiating projects funded through the state budget" (IMF 2015: 4). The latter type of projects "do not carry the level of monitoring and evaluation that accompanies in EU-funded projects" (IMF 2015: 8).

The evaluation of the third assistance program also notes that even previously adopted laws are not implemented in a proper manner. The review of the European Commission mentions the effectiveness of application of the Fiscal Responsibility Law as well as the new laws on the governance of SOEs (European Commission 2015: 2). Problems with the latter include personnel selection, the openness of financial statements, and privatization (European Commission 2015: 3).

One key concept coming up in implementation reports is the issue of capacity. Initially Romanian authorities had no problems with commitment, and even the IMF program report applauded "strong program ownership by the authorities" (IMF 2012: 21). At the same time, the report also highlighted implementation capacity both in the discussion of reducing arrears and EU funds absorption. While the program report is written in a highly diplomatic language, Romanian authors drew the following conclusion (Ciobanu and Toarna 2014: 42): "Eradicating state management inefficiency and corruption has slipped once more of the agenda of the Romanian reforms, making it to cause difficulties in the absorption of the EU funds, in solving the arrears issues related to the SOEs companies and their privatization and in improving the health care system for Romanian citizens."

Following the change in government in 2012, problems of ownership and capacity worsened. The 2014 IMF review already notes the weak ownership of the government to structural reforms, especially the "institutional resistance to surrendering political control of key SOEs" (IMF 2014: 23). They conclude that detailed conditionality cannot replace strong ownership (IMF 2014: 28). Ownership was especially questionable during the third program, when not even a single review could be concluded. "No review could be finalized during the EU programme, despite progress in several policy areas. The reasons preventing the completion of the reviews included fiscal policy measures threatening sustainability, sluggish progress with the SOEs restructuring and governance reforms, and the undoing of former program achievements" (European Commission 2015: 6). The European Commission concludes that program compliance was mixed. "After consolidating public finances between 2009 and 2014, the government decided to significantly cut various taxes outside the budget process, posing risks for breaching both the national fiscal framework and SGP requirements" (European Commission 2015: 4).

Overall Romania shows a mixed record in terms of compliance. While simple tasks such as fiscal consolidation and the adoption of new legislation were implemented vigorously, progress on more complex tasks was limited given the capacity constraints of the government. As the programs included ever more detailed structural reforms, compliance performance worsened. Essentially Romania's overall performance reflects a pragmatic recognition of realities—they implemented the reforms, which were necessary to regain access to the financial markets, but other considerations became dominant once they achieved this objective.

6.5 Market Reactions to the Programs

As shown by Fig. 6.4, market reception was mostly favorable for all three countries. All of them benefitted from the confidence generated by the already mentioned Vienna Initiative, which ensured that foreign banks maintain their exposure and recapitalize their subsidiaries in the region (Mabbett and Schelke 2015: 516). Besides this factor, the steady fall in interest rates also reflected the commitment for macroeconomic stabilization as well as the impact of loose monetary conditions worldwide.

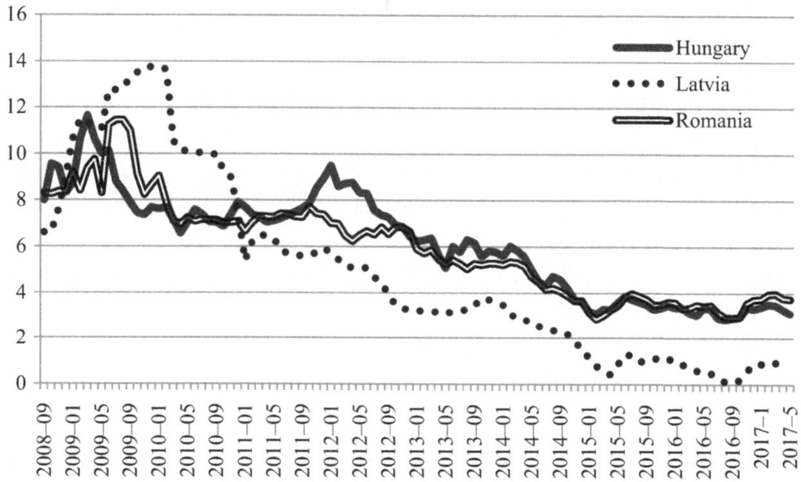

Fig. 6.4 Long-term interest rates (%) in Hungary, Latvia, and Romania 2008–2017 (Data: ECB Statistical Data Warehouse)

As we can see, interest rates rose sharply for all three countries from Fall 2008 with Latvia reaching the highest rates during 2009. However, once it became evident to market actors that Latvia was able to preserve its currency board and implement the consolidation measures, interest rates fell steadily. With the introduction of the euro by 2014, rates are well below their pre-crisis level. Romania shows a very similar path, although a flattening of the curve can be observed until March 2015 and there remains an almost 2-percentage-point difference compared to Latvia. Interest rates fell the fastest in Hungary after the 2009 agreement, and they were below Latvian and Romanian rates up until Fall 2010. However, following the unorthodox measures they rose again and approached 10 percent by 2012. From this peak they slowly decreased in parallel with the Latvian rates, but we can see from the figure that similarly to Romania, a steady 2-percentage-point difference persists compared to Latvia even as markets calmed down after 2014. Still, in light of the highly unorthodox measures taken by the Orbán government, this is a rather surprising reaction from the financial markets. Johnson and Barnes (2015: 559) explains this by pointing out the declining debt rates and low fiscal deficit of the country—the reaching of orthodox objectives via unorthodox means.

6.6 Crisis Management Outcomes

The favorable market reception of the programs implied that all three countries achieved the basic goal of regaining market access following adjustment. However, growth performance, social costs and changes in the quality of governance differed considerably as well as the amount of support received from the EU.

Figures 6.5, 6.7, and 6.8 show GDP projections and outcomes based on the IMF World Economic Outlook database. As we can see, the most consistent performance is shown by Latvia (Fig. 6.6), which experienced a sharp fall in GDP in 2009 then grew faster than projected. Since 2013 its growth has been steadily between 2 percent and 3 percent. Romania also recovered strongly (Fig. 6.7) although its performance until 2012 was below expectations. From 2013 however, its growth surpassed expectations, and in 2016 and 2017 it registered growth rates over 4 percent, among the fastest in the EU. In contrast to Latvia and Romania, Hungary

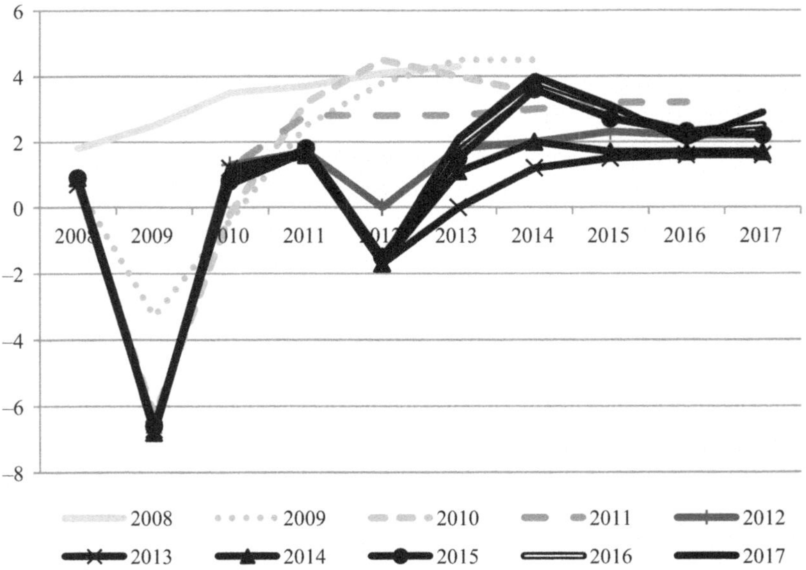

Fig. 6.5 GDP forecasts and reality in Hungary 2008–2017 (Data: World Economic Outlook database)

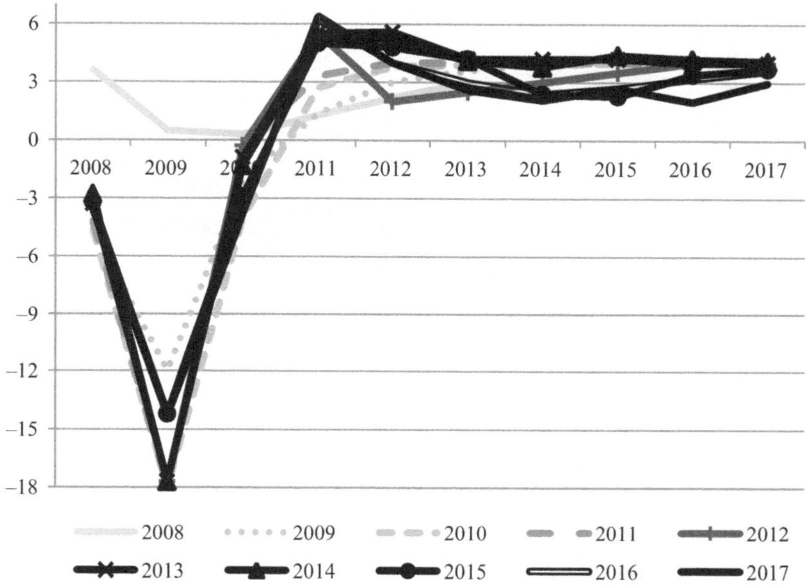

Fig. 6.6 GDP forecasts and reality in Latvia 2008–2017 (Data: World Economic Outlook database)

experienced an unexpected double-dip recession with negative growth rate in both 2009 and 2012. From 2013 we see an acceleration of growth reaching 4 percent in 2014, then a slowdown below 3 percent from 2015.

When evaluating the growth rates in these three countries, we cannot forget that they are among the poorest countries of the EU, and thus they receive substantial transfers from the EU. Table 6.2 shows their net balance with the EU budget as percent of GNI.

As we can see from Table 6.2, there is considerable difference among the three countries in their support from the EU budget. Between 2008 and 2015, Hungary succeeded in drawing the most funds from the EU averaging almost 3.8 percent of the GNI. In 2013 and 2014, the figure surpassed 5 percent of the GNI, which gave a boost to the economy and contributed strongly to Orbán's reelection. Latvia also received substantial transfers from the EU averaging 3.22 percent of the GNI, but it is still almost half a percentage below the Hungarian average. Among the three countries, Romania is the poorest and had the most difficulties in

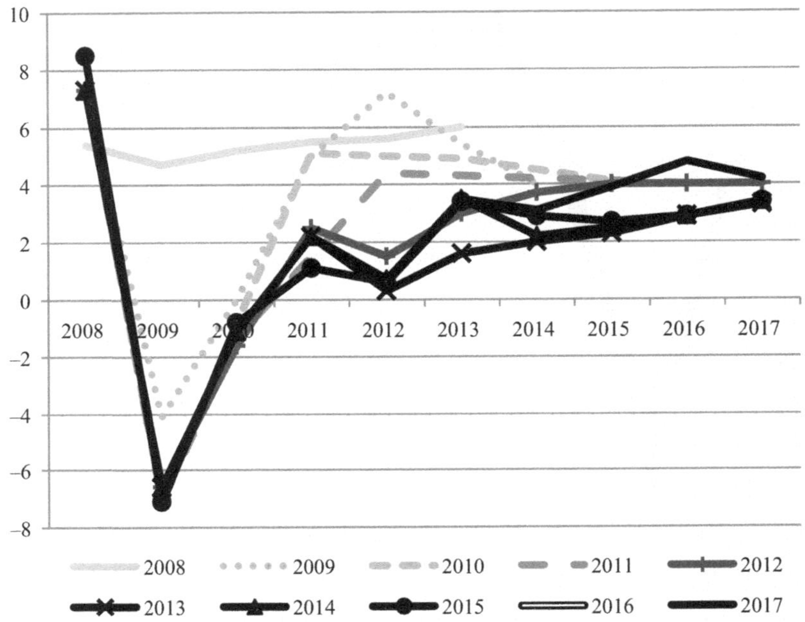

Fig. 6.7 GDP forecasts and reality in Romania 2008–2017 (Data: World Economic Outlook database)

Table 6.2 EU budget operating balance in Hungary, Latvia, and Romania 2008–2015 (% of GNI)

	Hungary	Latvia	Romania
2008	1.11	1.69	1.14
2009	3.05	2.49	1.42
2010	2.95	3.7	0.99
2011	4.62	3.62	1.1
2012	3.47	4.33	1.55
2013	5.08	3.46	2.94
2014	5.64	3.35	3.09
2015	4.38	3.12	3.27
Average	3.7875	3.22	1.9375

Data: European Commission at http://ec.europa.eu/budget/figures/interactive/index_en.cfm

tapping on EU funding as shown by the less than 2 percent annual transfers on average. However, its performance has improved considerably since 2012, and the funds probably contribute to its strong growth performance since then. Still, the numbers show that the unorthodox approach to crisis management taken by Orbán was still harmful for the country's growth as Hungary registered lower growth rates than Latvia and Romania even with much more funding from the EU. The institutional changes played an important role in this performance.

Figure 6.8 compares the quality of governance in 2004 and in 2015 in the three countries. The largest change took place in Hungary—while in 2004 it performed far better than Latvia or Romania, by 2015 Latvia performs better in every dimension with the exception of political stability. The deterioration of performance is particularly notable on the control of corruption as well as voice and accountability. Significant

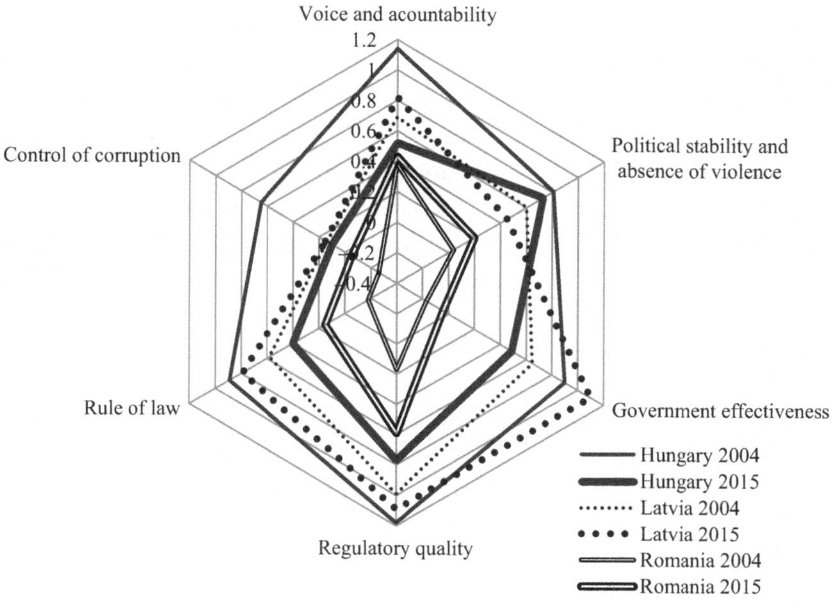

Fig. 6.8 World Governance Indicators in Hungary, Latvia, and Romania 2004 vs. 2015 (Data: World Governance Indicators at: http://www.govindicators.org)

drop can be seen in the rule of law and regulatory quality as well. All these indicate the impact of institutional changes to sustain power and increase the discretion of the government in decision-making. In contrast, Latvia and Romania saw improvements in most dimensions. Romania registered a highly impressive performance, which is probably related not only to the surveillance during the financial assistance program, but also to the accession process to the Schengen area. Prior to accession the EU expected the strengthening of the judiciary and the fight against corruption. Progress has been monitored by regular reports related to the so-called Cooperation and Verification Mechanism (CVM). As Spendzharova and Vachudova (2012: 55) argue, making Schengen entry conditional on CVM benchmarks strongly helped the reform process. Regardless of the reason for change, the dynamic improvement in Romania's institutional quality is probably an important reason for the impressive growth performance of the country.

When evaluating the growth performance of the three countries, we cannot forget about the social costs of crisis management. Table 6.3 shows the changes in the Gini index, poverty and employment rates as well as unemployment in the three countries. In terms of absolute numbers, Hungary shows the best performance on inequality, poverty, and unemployment. This is however not the consequence of crisis management, but rather relates to the differential transition paths of the three countries—while Hungary mostly preserved its inherited welfare state from Socialism, Latvia and Romania opted for a neoliberal state during

Table 6.3 The social consequences of crisis management in Hungary, Latvia, and Romania

	Gini index	People at risk of poverty (% of population)	Employment rate (20–64 years)	Unemployment rate (15–74 years)
Hungary 2009	24.7	29.6	60.1	10
Hungary 2016	28.2	26.3	71.5	5.1
Latvia 2009	37.5	37.9	66.6	17.5
Latvia 2016	34.5	28.5	73.2	9.6
Romania 2009	34.5	43	63.5	6.5
Romania 2016	34.7	38.8	66.3	5.9

Data: Eurostat

the transition. As a consequence, social indicators were much more favorable in Hungary prior to the crisis.

When we consider the changes during crisis management, we can see that inequality worsened considerably in Hungary, stagnated in Romania, and fell in Latvia between 2009 and 2016. In all three countries, the share of people at risk of poverty fell considerably by 2016, but it fell almost 10 percentage points in Latvia, 5 percentage points in Romania, and just 3 percentage points in Hungary although the former two countries clearly had a higher starting point. However, it should be also noted that this performance was achieved with a redistribution rate of 36.3 percent in Latvia, 34.7 percent in Romania, and 47.5 percent in Hungary.[32]

Compared to 2009 all three countries show substantial improvement in employment and unemployment indicators. Hungary performs well in both dimensions, while unemployment is still close to 10 percent in Latvia and the employment rate is below 70 percent in Romania. Similarly to other aggregate indicators, the Hungarian performance is partly the result of a mix of orthodox and unorthodox policies. While there were considerable cuts to unemployment insurance and strong moves toward the liberalization of the labor markets, a significant element in the improvement comes from the extensive public works program, which provides employment to an annual average of 200,000 people, or about 5 percent of total employment (Sharle 2016: 55). If they were counted as unemployed, the unemployment rate would be over 10 percent. Migration also represents an important source of improvement for the labor markets. Latvia and Romania are among the countries which have lost the highest percentage of their population since EU accession. While the exact numbers are very difficult to obtain, according to the calculations of Hárs (2016: 44), over 12 percent of Romanians and 8 percent of Latvians live in the EU-15 in contrast to only 3 percent of Hungarians. However, migration has been increasing steadily in Hungary as well since the crisis—according to Gödri (2014) while prior to the crisis the number of emigrants were below 30,000 annually, their number reached 60,000 in 2011 and 80,000 in 2012. Even more striking is the fact that in 2013, 33 percent of the 18- to 40-year-old population considered migration with 47 percent of those aged 18–24. These plans indicate considerable pessimism toward remaining in the country—not dissimilar to the pessimism of people living in Latvia or Romania. As in the case of other indicators, reality seems to be less rosy than the numbers would indicate.

* * *

Hungary, Latvia, and Romania were not members of the euro-zone at the outset of the crisis, and their successful recovery after the crisis might indicate that it was easier to manage the crisis without the euro than within the euro-zone. However, a deeper examination of their cases shows the simplicity of this argument. The most important difference these countries show in comparison to the Mediterranean countries is the greater trans-nationalization of their economies, including their banking sectors. The commitment of foreign banks to support their subsidiaries in these countries prevented a run on banks as experienced by Greece (Mabbett and Schelke 2015). Finally, all three countries received substantial transfers from the EU, which helped their recovery.

In terms of managing the crisis, they struggled with the same problem of low trust as the Mediterranean countries. The problem was overcome in Latvia by a shared commitment between the elite and the public to neoliberal ideas of the state, which was the result of the rejection of their Soviet past. This makes Latvia's crisis management very similar to that of Ireland. In Romania, policy-makers were committed to change similarly to the cases of Cyprus, Portugal, and Spain. For them capacity constraints represented the greatest obstacles to complex reforms. Hungary is the most interesting case among the three—while it followed the orthodox path of Ireland and Latvia in 2009, the level of distrust approached the Greek levels in a second round of negotiation with the Troika in 2012. Hungary successfully avoided the fate of Greece after it became able to finance itself from the international financial markets. This allowed Orbán's government to continue his unorthodox policies of adjustment. While Hungary's recovery from the crisis is not dissimilar to that of Latvia and Romania in terms of aggregate indicators, the collapse of institutions represents a lasting change compared to the pre-crisis period.

The institutional changes and their impact on the emergence of populist politics will be examined in the next chapter.

Notes

1. An earlier version of this chapter discussing the cases of Hungary and Latvia appeared as Győrffy (2015).
2. The following discussion on the path to crisis relies on Győrffy (2013): 128–137.
3. Data: UNCTAD (2017).
4. Data: UN ECE (2003): 112. The concept of transformational recession originates from Kornai (1994), who argues that the shift from communism to a market economy initially triggers a recession for a number of reasons including the disturbances to the coordination mechanisms, the consequences of hardening the budget constraint and the weakness of the financial system. All these factors contribute to a collapse in investment and consumption.
5. Data: UNCTAD (2017).
6. Data: Institute on Statelessness and Inclusion (2017) 75.
7. Data: European Commission (2017) 28.
8. Data: European Commission (2017) 58, 160, 164.
9. Social benefits other than in kind imply social benefits in cash as well as social insurance in cash or kind. Data: European Commission (2017) 136.
10. Data: European Commission (2017) 59.
11. Data: European Commission (2017) 59, 29, 161.
12. This includes subsidized credit for housing, increase in the public sector wage bill, increase in pensions, and other social security benefits.
13. Writing in 2007 they showed that in the absence of politically motivated spending since 2000, public debt would have been 36.9 percent of the GDP in 2006 instead of the 66 percent.
14. Data is from Eurostat.
15. By 2008 the share of foreign currency lending approached 70 percent of total household loans. For a detailed overview about the buildup of these loans, see Hudecz (2013): 273–275. I rely primarily on his assessment in the following discussion of the main causes of foreign currency lending in Hungary.
16. The complete lack of response to the growth of foreign currency lending is unique in the Central and Eastern European (CEE) region as shown by Bethlendi (2011: 211). Based on interviews with the participants, the reluctance of the government to constrain the credit boom is docu-

mented by Szentkirályi (2011). This was especially important, since financial supervision in Hungary is separate from the independent central bank, and the supervisory body (PSZAF) is under the authority of the Ministry of Finance.

17. Data: European Commission (2017) 58, 96.
18. Data: European Commission (2017): 79.
19. Data: European Commission (2017) 29.
20. These steps will be discussed in greater detail in the next section on the implementation of the program.
21. This was harshly criticized during and after the negotiations. On the debate and the establishment of the IMF position, see Rosenberg (2009).
22. The detailed conditionality is available in the Memorandum of Understanding (2009b).
23. For a more extensive overview, see the Memorandum of Understanding (2011).
24. As Erdős (2012: 121–122) explains, the absence of a stimulation effect of the tax cut is due to the fact that it favored primarily those with high incomes, who are most likely to either increase their savings or spend it on imported goods, which means that there is no demand growth in the domestic economy.
25. The ratio of non-performing foreign currency loans increased from 7.5 percent in 2010 to 18 percent by 2013 (European Commission 2014: 32).
26. The explicit objective to build an illiberal democracy instead of a liberal one reversed the trend of liberalization and decentralization, which started in 1968. János Kornai (2015) calls it a "dramatic U-turn" in the history of Hungary.
27. Under the debt rule, public debt cannot be higher than 50 percent of GDP, and above this threshold the Parliament has to adopt a budget, which contributes to the decline of the debt rate. The task of the new fiscal council is to evaluate the conformity of the budget plan to this rule with veto power over its adoption if it does not conform to the rule. However, the council has no ex post power over the budget, and there are also no rules about financing the debt reduction, which made the nationalization of private pension funds an acceptable method. Even more importantly, the debt rule was postponed to 2016 by the Law on Financial Stability in 2011. It is also important that out of the three members of the fiscal council, two are clearly political appointees as the Head of the National Bank of Hungary and the Head of the State Audit Office. For a comparison between the old and the new fiscal council, see Curristine et al. (2013): 20–23.

28. The new law cut the number of parliamentary representatives from 399 to 199 with 100 elected from single-member districts and 99 through proportional party lists. The second round of voting was abolished in the districts, which was extremely advantageous for Fidesz as it was facing a highly fragmented opposition.
29. Based on the Memorandum of Understanding (2009a), the standard and reduced rates of VAT were raised from 18 percent to 21 percent and 5 percent to 10 percent, respectively, along with increases in excise taxes on alcohol, tobacco, petrol, and coffee.
30. Data: European Commission (2017) 96.
31. For a full list of structural reform measures, see the review by Boc (2011).
32. Data: European Commission (2017) 158–159.

References

Ábel, Isván, and László Szakadát. 1997. A bankrendszer átalakulása Magyarországon 1987–1996 között (The transformation of the banking system in Hungary between 1987 and 1996). *Közgazdasági Szemle* 44 (7–8): 635–552.

Andersen, Camilla. 2010. IMF survey: Romania: Delayed recovery now expected. *IMF Survey Online*, May 11. Available: http://www.imf.org/external/pubs/ft/survey/so/2010/int051110a.htm. Accessed 2 July 2017.

Aslund, Anders. 2010. *The last shall be the first: The East European financial crisis.* Washington, DC: Peterson Institute for International Economics.

Aslund, Anders, and Valdis Dombrovskis. 2011. *How Latvia came through the financial crisis.* Washington, DC: Peterson Institute for International Economics.

Bakker, Bas, and Christopher Klingen. 2012. *How emerging Europe came through the 2008/2009 crisis.* Washington, DC: IMF.

Ban, Cornel. 2016. *Ruling ideas: How global neoliberalism goes local.* Oxford: Oxford University Press.

Benczes, István. 2016. From goulash communism to goulash populism: The unwanted legacy of Hungarian reform socialism. *Post-Communist Economies* 28 (2): 1–21.

Bethlendi, András. 2011. Policy measures and failures on foreign currency household lending in Central and Eastern Europe. *Acta Oeconomica* 61 (2): 193–223.

Bjornskov, Christian. 2007. Determinants of generalized trust: A cross-country comparison. *Public Choice* 130 (1): 1–21.

Blanchard, Olivier, Mark Griffits, and Bertrand Gruss. 2013. Boom, bust, recovery: Forensics of the Latvia crisis. *Brookings Papers on Economic Activity* 44 (2): 325–388.

Boc, Emil. 2011. The reform of the state in Romania (2009–2011). *Transylvanian Review of Administrative Sciences* 34: 5–21.

Bohle, Dorothee. 2010. *East European transformations and the paradoxes of transnationalization*. EUI Working Paper SPS 2010/01. Badia Fiasolana: European University Institute.

Bohle, Dorothee, and Béla Greskovits. 2012. *Capitalist diversity on Europe's periphery*. Ithaca: Cornall University Press.

Ciobanu, Andreea, and Alina Toarna. 2014. The IMF program and Romanian compliance. *Revista Tinerior Economisti (The Young Economists Journal)* 1 (22): 35–42.

Comite, Francesco Di, Gabriele Guidice, Júlia Lendvai, and Ingrid Toming. 2012. Fiscal consolidation in the midst of crisis. In *EU balance-of-payments assistance for Latvia: Foundations of success*, European Economy Occasional Papers No. 120, ed. European Commission, 77–99. Brussels: Directorate General for Economic and Financial Affairs.

Csaba, László. 1998. A decade of transformation in Hungarian economic policy: Dynamics, constraints and prospects. *Europe-Asia Studies* 50 (8): 1381–1391.

———. 2006. *The new political economy of emerging Europe*. Budapest: Akadémiai Kiadó.

———. 2009. *Crisis in economics?* Budapest: Akadémiai Kiadó.

———. 2012. Haladás vagy hanyatlás? Avagy miért marad le Magyarország? [Progress or decline? or why Hungary is falling behind?]. In *Földobott kő? Tények és tendenciák a 21. században*, ed. Muraközy Lászó, 282–303. Budapest: Akadémiai Kiadó.

Curristine, Teresa, Jason Harris, and Johann Seiwald. 2013. *Case studies of fiscal councils – Functions and impact*. Washington: IMF. Available: https://www.imf.org/external/np/pp/eng/2013/071613a.pdf. Accessed 2 July 2017.

Dahan, Samuel. 2012. Conceptualising the EU/IMF financial assistance process. In *EU balance-of-payments assistance for Latvia: Foundations of success*, ed. European Commission, 182–212. Brussels: Directorate General for Economic and Financial Affairs.

Darvas, Zsolt, and György Szapáry. 2008. *Euro area enlargement and euro adoption strategies*. Economic Papers No. 304. Brussels: Directorate General for Economic and Financial Affairs.

Erdős, Tibor. 2012. Egykulcsos jövedelemadó és gazdasági növekedés [Flat tax and growth]. *Közgazdasági Szemle* 59 (2): 109–138.

European Commission. 1997. *Agenda 2000 – Commission opinion on Latvia's application for membership of the European Union*. DOC/97/14. Brussels: European Commission.

———. 2014. *Macroeconomic imbalances – Hungary 2014*. European Economy Occasional Papers No. 180. Brussels: Commission of the European Communities Directorate General for Economic and Financial Affairs.

———. 2015. *Balance of payments assistance program Romania, 2013–2015*. Institutional Paper No 012. Brussels: Directorate General for Economic and Financial Affairs.

———. 2017. *Statistical annex of European Economy, Spring*. Brussels: Commission of the European Communities Directorate General for Economic and Financial Affairs.

Farkas, Zoltán. 2014. *Hét szűk esztendő* [Seven meager years]. Budapest: Napvilág Kiadó.

Farkas, Beáta. 2016. *Models of capitalism in the European Union: Post-crisis perspectives*. London: Palgrave Macmillan.

Gödri, Irén. 2014. *Out-migration from Hungary: On the rise, but still low*. V4 Revue, April 6. Available: http://visegradrevue.eu/?p=2428. Accessed 2 July 2017.

Government of the Republic of Hungary. 2011. *Convergence program of Hungary 2011–2015*. Available: http://ec.europa.eu/europe2020/making-it-happen/country-specific-recommendations/2011/index_en.htm. Accessed 2 July 2017.

Győrffy, Dóra. 2013. *Institutional trust and economic policy: Lessons from the history of the euro*. Budapest/New York: CEU Press.

———. 2015. Austerity and growth in Central and Eastern Europe: Understanding the link through contrasting crisis management in Hungary and Latvia. *Post-Communnist Economies* 26 (2): 129–152.

Harrold, Peter, Indhira Santos, and Emily Sinnot. 2012. Fiscal sustainability, demographic change and inequality: Social sectors from crisis to growth in Latvia. In *EU balance-of-payments assistance for Latvia: Foundations of success*, ed. European Commission, 100–133. European Economy Occasional Papers No. 120. Brussels: Directorate General for Economic and Financial Affairs.

Hárs, Ágnes. 2016. Elvándorlás és bevándorlás Magyarországon a rendszerváltás után – nemzetközi összehasonlításban [Emigration and immigration in Hungary after the transition – An international comparative perspective]. In

Munkaerőpiaci tükör 2016 [Labor market review 2016], ed. Zsuzsa Blaskó and Károly Fazekas, 39–53. Budapest: MTA KRTK.

Hudecz, András. 2013. Parallel stories: FX lending to households in Poland, Romania and Hungary, 1997–2011. *Acta Oeconomica* 63 (3): 257–286.

IMF. 2006. *Romania: Article IV consultation staff report*. IMF Country Report No. 06/168.

———. 2008. *Hungary: Request for stand-by arrangement – Staff report*. IMF Country Report No. 08/361.

———. 2009a. *Hungary: First review under the stand-by arrangement and request for modification of performance criteria – Staff report*. IMF Country Report No. 09/105.

———. 2009b. *Republic of Latvia: First review and financing assurances review under the stand-by arrangement*. IMF Country Report No. 09/297.

———. 2010. *Romania – Staff report for the 2010 Article IV consultation, fourth review under the stand-by arrangement, and requests for modification and waiver of nonobservance of performance criteria – Staff report*. IMF Country Report No. 10/227.

———. 2011. *Hungary: Ex post evaluation of exceptional access under the 2008 stand-by arrangement*. IMF Country Report No. 11/145.

———. 2012. *Romania: Ex post evaluation of exceptional access under the 2009 stand-by arrangement*. IMF Country Report No. 12/64.

———. 2013. *Republic of Latvia: Ex post evaluation of exceptional access under the 2008 stand-by arrangement*. IMF Country Report No. 13/30.

———. 2014. *Romania: Ex post evaluation of exceptional access under the 2011 stand-by arrangement*. IMF Country Report No. 14/88.

———. 2015. *Romania: Selected issues*. IMF Country Report No. 15/80.

Institute for Statelessness and Inclusion. 2017. *The world's stateless children*. Oisterwijk: Wolf Legal Publishers.

Johnson, Juliet, and Andrew Barnes. 2015. Financial nationalism and its international enablers: The Hungarian experience. *Review of International Political Economy* 22 (3): 535–569.

Kalotay, Kálmán. 2008. FDI in Bulgaria and Romania in the wake of EU accession. *Journal of East-West Business* 14 (1): 5–40.

Kornai, János. 1994. Transformational recession: The main causes. *Journal of Comparative Economics* 19 (1): 37–52.

———. 2015. Hungary's U-Turn: Retreating from democracy. *Journal of Democracy* 26 (3): 34–48.

Lütz, Susanne, and Matthias Kranke. 2014. The European rescue of the Washington consensus? EU and IMF lending to Central and Eastern

European countries. *Review of International Political Economy* 21 (2): 310–338.

Mabbett, Deborah, and Waltraud Schelkle. 2015. What difference does euro membership make to stabilization? The political economy of international monetary systems revisited. *Review of International Political Economy* 22 (3): 508–534.

Memorandum of Understanding. 2008. *Memorandum of understanding between the European Community and the Republic of Hungary*. Available: http://ec.europa.eu/economy_finance/publications/publication13495_en.pdf. Accessed 2 July 2017.

———. 2009a. *Memorandum of understanding between the European Community and the Republic of Latvia*. Available: http://ec.europa.eu/economy_finance/eu_borrower/balance_of_payments/pdf/mou_bop_latvia_en.pdf. Accessed 2 July 2017.

———. 2009b. *Memorandum of understanding between the European Community and Romania*. Available: http://ec.europa.eu/economy_finance/publications/publication15409_en.pdf. Accessed 2 July 2017.

Memorandum of Understanding between the European Union and Romania. 2011. Available: http://ec.europa.eu/economy_finance/eu_borrower/mou/20110629-mou-romania_en.pdf. Accessed 2 July 2017.

Mihályi, Péter. 2001. The evolution of Hungary's approach to FDI in post-communist privatization. *Transnational Corporations* 10 (3): 61–74.

Ohnsorge-Szabó, László, and Balázs Romhányi. 2007. Hogy jutottunk ide: magyar költségvetés, 2000–2006 [How we got here: Hungarian fiscal policy 2000–2006]. *Pénzügyi Szemle* 52 (2): 239–285.

Papadimitriou, Dimitris. 2006. Persistent laggard: Romania as Eastern Europe's sysphus. In *Enlarging the euro area: External empowerment and domestic transformation in East Central Europe*, ed. Kenneth Dyson, 215–233. Oxford: Oxford University Press.

Papadimitriou, Dimitris, and Eli Gateva. 2009. *Between enlargement-led Europeanisation and Balkan exceptionalism: An appraisal of Bulgaria's and Romania's entry into the European Union*. Hellenic Observatory Papers on Greece and Southeast Europe No. 25. London: LSE.

Rosenberg, Christoph. 2009. Why the IMF supports the Latvian currency peg. *Economonitor*, January 6. Available: http://www.economonitor.com/blog/2009/01/why-the-imf-supports-the-latvian-currency-peg/. Accessed 2 July 2017.

Scharle, Ágota. 2016. Mennyit nőtt a foglalkoztatás 2008 óta Magyarországon? [How much have employment rates grown in Hungary since 2008?]. In *Társadalmi Riport 2016* [Social report 2016], ed. Tamás Kolosi and György Tóth-István, 54–71. Budapest: Tárki.

Spendzharova, Aneta, and Milada Vachudova. 2012. Catching up? Consolidating liberal democracy in Bulgaria and Romania after EU accession. *West European Politics* 35 (1): 39–58.

Supplemental Memorandum of Understanding between the European Union and Romania. 2010. Available: https://ec.europa.eu/info/sites/info/files/ecfin_2010-07-20-mou-romania_en.pdf. Accessed 2 July 2017.

Szentkirályi, Balázs. 2011. Ki a felelős a devizahitelezésért? [Who is responsible for foreign currency lending?]. *Index.hu*, October 18. Available: http://index.hu/gazdasag/magyar/2011/10/18/ki_a_felelos_a_devizahitelezesert/. Accessed 2 July 2017.

Tóth, G. Csaba, and Péter Virovácz. 2013. Nyertesek és vesztesek. A magyar egykulcsos adóreform vizsgálata mikroszimulációs módszerrel [Winners and losers. The examination of the Hungarian flat tax reform through microsimulation method]. *Pénzügyi Szemle* 58 (4): 385–400.

Trif, Aurora. 2013. Romania: Collective bargaining institutions under attack. *Transfer* 19 (2): 227–237.

UN ECE. 2003. *Economic survey of Europe 2003 no. 2.* Geneva: United Nations Economic Commission for Europe.

UNCTAD. 2017. *World investment report 2017.* Annex table 7. New York/Geneva: UNCTAD. Available: http://unctad.org/en/Pages/DIAE/World%20Investment%20Report/Annex-Tables.aspx. Accessed 2 July 2017.

7

The Politics of Crisis Management: The Role of Limited Government

An important narrative on trust and crisis management is that economic hardship fuels populist movements, or the rise of forces claiming to represent the people against out-of-touch elites.[1] In the words of Kriesi and Pappas (2015: 1):

> As austerity became the new policy norm, economic and social inequalities grew larger, and as European integration appeared to many constituencies as a hopeless project, newly emergent populist leaders rose in some countries to defend the powerless people against sinister elites including politicians (both at the national and EU levels), bankers and industrialists – in short the powerful and the wealthy.

The eight cases examined in this book provide a useful sample to address this issue. Does austerity lead to populism? Why does it become dominant in certain countries and why not in others? In order to answer these questions the chapter explores the institutional roots of trust and relates the ability of the government for credible commitment to the capacity for self-constraint. It is argued that adherence to the idea of limited government—a complex system of checks and balances on state power—is key both for economic success and the avoidance of the

D. Győrffy, *Trust and Crisis Management in the European Union*,
https://doi.org/10.1007/978-3-319-69212-8_7

populist threat. Lacking such commitment by the political elites leads to economic failures and the rise of populists. The eight cases examined in the previous chapter provide some empirical support for this claim.

The structure of the chapter is the following. First, a summary assessment is given on the role of trust in crisis management with particular attention paid to those findings, which are unexpected from the theoretical perspective. The next section explores the roots of trust focusing on the concept of limited government and describing its main indicators. The third section provides a categorization of the eight cases showing how the adherence to the idea of limited government influences economic and political outcomes.

7.1 Trust and Managing the Financial Crisis: A Summary

The eight case studies have shown the relevance of trust during the negotiation, implementation, and the reception of the financial assistance programs.

During the negotiations, higher level of trust was associated with more autonomy in setting the conditionality of the program. This was most clearly the case with Ireland, but the Hungarian, Latvian, Portuguese, Romanian, and Spanish programs were also mostly designed at the national level. In contrast, the absence of trust during the negotiations led to extremely detailed and severe conditionality in the cases of Greece and Cyprus. This would have been probably the fate of Hungary as well if a second program were needed in 2012.

Trust during the negotiations was determined by two main factors: a shared knowledge of economics, which means an agreement on the roots and remedies of the crisis, and pre-program measures to address the financial imbalances.

Speaking the same language of mainstream economics proved to be decisive during the negotiations of the conditionality. Negotiators from Ireland, Latvia, Spain, or Romania came from countries, where mainstream economics is in a dominant position. They understood the problems of their country along the same terms as the IMF or the EU. There were no ideological debates during the negotiations with Portugal either. In contrast, the communist government of Cyprus, or the populist governments of Greece and Hungary, negotiated with a very different economic model in mind than their partners. These differences were not conducive for trust.

While evidence on such claims can only be implied, pre-program policies certainly played an important role during the negotiations. Ireland, Spain, Romania, or Latvia all took decisive steps toward managing the crisis before turning to the Troika. In contrast, the falsification of statistics in Greece prior to the crisis or the strongly expansionary fiscal policy in Cyprus was certainly not conducive to trust.

The role of trust on the severity of conditionality was mitigated by three factors based on the empirical analysis. In the Latvian or the Portuguese cases, harsh conditionality was adopted for domestic reasons—reformer groups wanted to use the crisis as a window of opportunity to implement long-due structural changes. Negotiating power also mattered in the Cyprian and the Spanish case—while the former was used as an experiment for bail-in, the latter was treated in a very lenient manner, given the threat its collapse would have posed to the EU. Finally, the Troika could also be tricked—when Hungary needed a second agreement, Viktor Orbán could prolong the negotiations long enough to wait for the calming of the markets. The feigned negotiations helped to end speculations against the forint without any conditionality.

Public trust for implementation was missing everywhere as trust in government fell in all eight countries (Fig. 7.1). Some recovery in this measure can be observed following a change of government. Hungary entered the financial crisis with very low level of trust in government, and the election of Viktor Orbán led to some increase in trust. The level of trust in government in Hungary is in fact the highest among the program countries during 2011–2015. The refusal to sign another agreement and the standing as the enemy of the Troika probably contributed to this result. Trust in government also improved in other countries following elections: this can be seen in the case of Cyprus in 2013, Portugal and Greece in 2015. However trust hovering around 30 percent or below is hardly a desirable state of affairs.

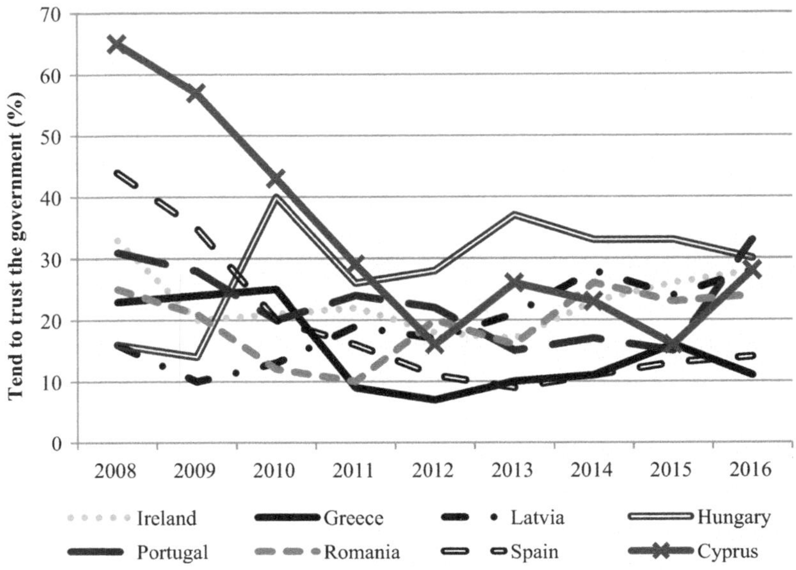

Fig. 7.1 Trust in government in EU program countries 2008–2016 (% of population) (Data: Eurobarometer online)

Although trust in government fell in all eight countries, and mostly remained below 30 percent, the extent to which it hindered implementation differed. While there was considerable patience with austerity measures in Ireland or Latvia due to the widespread public acceptance of neoliberal principles, harsh protests broke out in Greece and Spain. In Greece, distrust strongly hindered the implementation of the program. At the same time declining level of trust did not hinder implementation in Cyprus, Portugal, Spain, or Romania as elite commitment to the program substituted for public support. In these countries low level of trust manifested itself in the form of reform fatigue—following the exit from the program, structural reforms slowed down or reversed in certain cases. In Romania, the lack of trust also reflects weak capacity—while elite commitment worked in the implementation of harsh but simple measures such as cuts in public sector wages, it was insufficient to push through more complex reforms such as health care or the governance of SOEs.

Market trust proved to be essential to recover from the crisis. With the exception of Greece, all countries under examination were able to return to market financing, and due to the loose monetary policy of the ECB, all faced lower rates in 2016 than prior to the crisis. The reactions of the markets were generally hardly surprising in light of the Troika reports on the progress of program implementation. There were few exceptions from this rule. Greece can be considered one—the markets seemed extremely prone to panic and the possibility of Grexit, which implied that even when the country made substantial progress on the conditions, its interest rates did not go down accordingly. The other exception is Hungary, when the markets were more than willing to overlook the details of the adjustment and the skeptical assessment of the Troika.

Overall in the most successful cases—Ireland and Latvia—trust with Troika, the public, and the market reinforced one another and lead to a fast recovery. In the case of Greece there was no trust in any of the relationships, which resulted in a vicious spiral of austerity. Cyprus, Portugal, Spain, and Romania are cases, when collapsing public trust was replaced by an elite commitment of fulfilling the program conditions. However, from this group only Romania can be considered as a success story. Finally, Hungary opted for a different path by giving up cooperation with the Troika, embracing a curious mix of neoliberalism and economic populism, which still allowed it to keep access to the financial markets.

Trust thus matters in crisis management although with the qualifications listed above. The next section analyzes the institutional basis for trust.

7.2 Trust and Limited Government

At its core, every trust relationship entails a belief in the other party's self-constraint from taking advantage of a vulnerable partner. This is even truer for the government given its monopoly on violence and the possibilities to abuse its power. Consequently in order to be trusted, it needs to bind itself through various mechanisms, which preclude the abuse of power. Such mechanisms ensure the credibility of commitments and generate trust.

Without them the government remains trapped in the problem of time inconsistency: as other actors know that the government has a different incentive structure in the future, they do not believe its promises and do not cooperate. While Kydland and Prescott (1977) applied this framework to the problem of inflationary expectations, it is relevant to a far wider range of government commitments, which require sacrifices from other actors in the present and promise rewards later—from paying taxes to buying government bonds. In the following a brief overview is presented on some of the main mechanisms ensuring the limits on government, which will be assessed in the context of individual countries in the next section.

7.2.1 Rule of Law

The idea of limited government has been around since the Antiquity. Chesterman (2008: 334) points to Aristotele who argued that "the rule of law was preferable to that of any individual." According to Tamahana (2004: 115), the most important thread in any definition of rule of law is the "restraint of government tyranny." This understanding evolved considerably later starting from the Magna Charta in England in 1215. Based on the overview of the rule of law tradition, Tamahana (2004: 114–126) argues that over the centuries rule of law essentially implied the three elements, which have been already mentioned in Chap. 1. First, the government must respect the law, and it is also restricted in changing the law: while in the Middle Ages the restraints came from the natural law or customary law, in modern times human or civil rights set the boundaries for discretionary change. A second important theme in the rule of law discourse is formal legality, which means public, prospective laws, with the qualities of generality, equality of application, and certainty. Finally, the "rule of law, not men" underlines the importance of an independent judiciary as guardian of the law.

Throughout history, there were considerable debates about the substantive elements in the rule of law tradition. In the twentieth century, after the horrors of World War II, the rule of law could not remain a simple procedural term (Weiler 2016: 317–318). The Nazi regime conducted its purge and dispossession of the Jews following the existing law.

In light of these experiences, democracy and human rights became integral parts of the rule of law concept. While democratic decision-making is necessary for the legitimacy of the law, human rights ensure that the minority is protected from the tyranny of the majority. Modern concepts of the rule of law take such substantive elements for granted.

The rejection of a dichotomy between procedural and substantial understanding of the rule of law is especially pronounced in countries of the EU. In his overview about the major legal traditions in Europe, Pech (2009: 35) underlines that the procedural components of the rule of law are supposed to protect substantial principles such as human dignity, individual autonomy, and social justice. He also argues that in the English rule of law, the German Rechtsstaat, and the French Etat de droit concepts, there is an underlying common theme, even though it is not spelled out precisely in any of these traditions: essentially they are "'meta-principles' which provide the foundation for an independent and effective judiciary and essentially describe and justify subjection of public power to formal and substantive legal constraints with a view to guaranteeing the primacy of individual and its protection against the arbitrary and unlawful use of public power" (Pech 2009: 34–35).

The debates and difficulties of defining the rule of law naturally make measurement very difficult. This is especially true for the cross-country comparisons and time series data. In the next section I will rely on the rule of law dimension of the World Governance Indicators, where the concept is defined as follows: "capturing perceptions of the extent to which agents have confidence in and abide by the rules of society, and in particular the quality of contract enforcement, property rights, the police, and the courts, as well as the likelihood of crime and violence" (Kaufmann et al. 2010: 4). This understanding is somewhat different from the previously mentioned definitions of the rule of law. It is based on agent perceptions rather than judicial assessment, and it also includes law abidance by citizens. This is justifiable since for everyday decision-making people's perception on the relevance and enforcement of laws is crucial. The annual survey of over 200 countries provides significant scope for comparison over time and across countries, which makes the index highly useful.

7.2.2 International Rule of Law

While the idea of rule of law generally concerns to the national level, the concept has received growing attention at the international level as well. International rule of law requires governments to comply with international law, the rules of regional organizations such as the EU, as well as various international agreements. Enforcement of these agreements is usually less strict than national rules—while there are international tribunals, and even military intervention is possible, the majority of international rules are based on voluntary compliance. As Tamahana (2004: 129) puts it: "the legal regimes that apply to a given sovereign state are only those the state chooses to accept as applicable."

In the case of crisis management, agreements with the Troika represent the requirements of the international rule of law. Whether countries are willing to abide by that can be assessed by performance reviews and also by the relevant discourse—for example, presenting the agreement as a breach on democracy is an often-applied strategy to justify resistance to conditionality.

7.2.3 Size of Government

National and international rule of law are not the only constraints on government discretion. The size of government also shapes the possibilities for autonomy. The optimal size of the government is one of the evergreen subjects of economics, and there is a strong argument that high rates of redistribution can become a hindrance to growth.[2] Still, one cannot forget that quality often matters more than size—the examples of Scandinavian countries show that high-capacity administrations can assume more tasks, and in providing more extensive social services, they are able to generate trust.[3] This is in line with the argument made by Fukuyama (2004) about the need to distinguish between scope and strength of government.

The relationship between trust and the size of government is thus complex—while a larger government can be the source of more corruption and abuse of power, with more services it can also generate higher level of trust. Consequently in the following section, the changes in the size of government will be assessed together with changes in the rule of law. It is assumed that deterioration in the rule of law together with an increasing share of redistribution is a sign of rejection for the idea of limited government.

7.2.4 Other Limits on Government Power

Beyond the rule of law and the size of government there are other limits on government power. Opposition parties, non-governmental organizations, and the media provide monitoring and information over the activities of government. Professional organizations in the academia or the arts set their own standards of performance, which should be independent from political inference. Respecting the freedom and autonomy of these organizations, even when they are presenting uncomfortable feedback to the government, is essential for the proper functioning of a democratic system.

The Charter of Fundamental Rights of the EU[4] guarantees extensive political and civil liberties. Freedom of expression, freedom of association, and academic freedom are generally taken for granted in the EU. However, in certain cases there is a serious breach of these freedoms, which have to be noted in individual cases. Reports by Freedom House are used as a starting point for assessment.

7.3 Limited Government and the Political and Economic Outcomes of Crisis Management

The various dimensions of limited government are summarized in Table 7.1. Essentially we can see three groups of countries: neoliberal countries, with a strong belief in limited government; Mediterranean reformers, which try to preserve their nascent welfare state while increasing their competitiveness; and populist countries, where the idea of limited government is scorned upon. Their experiences can also provide us

Table 7.1 Summary: limited government, economic, and political outcomes

	Neoliberal countries: Ireland, Latvia, and Romania	Mediterranean reformers: Cyprus, Portugal, and Spain	Populist democracies: Greece, Hungary
Rule of law	High level and/or improving	Fluctuation	Significant deterioration
External rule of law	Compliance with the Troika	Compliance with the Troika—strong elite commitment	Rejection of the Troika or forced compliance
Size of government	Small and decreasing	Mostly stable	Stable or growing
Economic outcome	Strong recovery	Slow recovery	Economic collapse (Greece), moderate recovery (Hungary)
The rise of populism	No	Slight—no role in government	Yes, governing

with an insight about what explains economic and political outcomes, and where populism can be expected to emerge.

Ireland, Latvia, and Romania belong to the first group as committed neoliberals, with a strong belief in limited government. As we can see from Fig. 7.2, Ireland has the highest ranking in various dimensions of the rule of law, while as post-communist countries, Latvia and Romania fare considerably worse. At the same time all three countries show a steady improvement of their scores. They are also similar in the evolution of their redistribution rate—while total primary expenditures as percent of GDP increased during the crisis, especially in Ireland, in all three countries, they fell back to around 35 percent by 2012. The Irish rate fell below 30 percent in 2015, but this is probably the consequence of the exceptional 26 percent growth registered that year, which was mentioned in Chap. 4. In any case, improving the rule of law and low level of redistribution signals the adherence to the idea of limited government. From this perspective it is not surprising that these countries had no difficulty in signing a financial assistance agreement with the Troika and they were also committed to implementation—although Romania clearly hit the limits of bureaucratic capacity with implementing structural reforms. Still, the three countries showed the most impressive growth rates following the crisis.

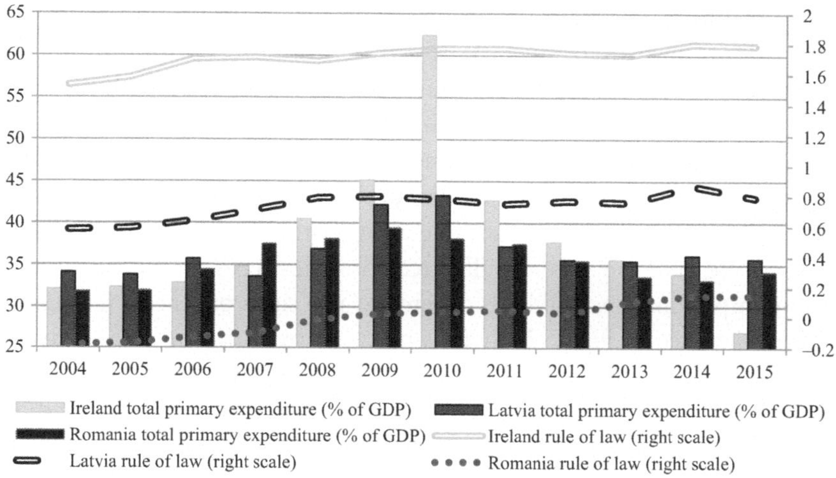

Fig. 7.2 Rule of law and total primary expenditures (% of GDP) in Ireland, Latvia, and Romania 2004–2015 (Data: Rule of law: World Governance Indicators at: www.govindicators.org, Total primary expenditures: European Commission's AMECO Database)

Although they implemented severe fiscal consolidation, and they have limited welfare provisions, none of the three countries saw a populist emergence. While mainstream parties have suffered in Ireland, and a strengthening of Sinn Fein and independents could be observed, "the populism has been mild, and most parties, when they reach government tend towards responsibility rather than responsiveness" (O'Malley and FitzGibbon 2015: 294). Populism did not emerge in Latvia either—as Balcere (2014) explains, although there have been efforts at devising populist messages, these have been electorally unsuccessful. A similar narrative can be said of Romania, where Corbu et al. (2017: 331) argue that although populism has been a constant presence in Romania since the transition, populist parties have been in decline—partly because some elements of their programs such as anti-corruption has been picked up by mainstream parties.

Overall, the three countries show how the adherence to limited government, economic success, and low level of populism can form a virtuous cycle in crisis management.

The second group of countries with Cyprus, Portugal, and Spain are the Mediterranean reformers. As it was discussed in Chap. 5, due to a strong elite commitment, these countries mostly complied with the conditionality of the Troika. Given the importance of the family in the provision of welfare, these states had traditionally lower redistribution rates than the EU average. As women entered the labor force in growing numbers, building a welfare state became an important priority implying the effort to preserve the state. In all three countries recovery has been slow, and unemployment is still high. There are also signs of reform fatigue.

As we can see in Fig. 7.3, there is no clean trend in the rule of law—prior to the crisis it deteriorated in Portugal, stagnated in Spain, and improved in Cyprus. During the crisis management, it improved in Portugal and deteriorated in Cyprus and Spain. The overall quality of rule of law in these countries is above the level of Latvia but well below the level of Ireland. In all three countries we can observe a higher level of redistribution than prior to the crisis, but it is still just around 44 percent in Portugal and below 42 percent in Spain and Cyprus. There is no indication of a deviation from the idea of limited government—apart from

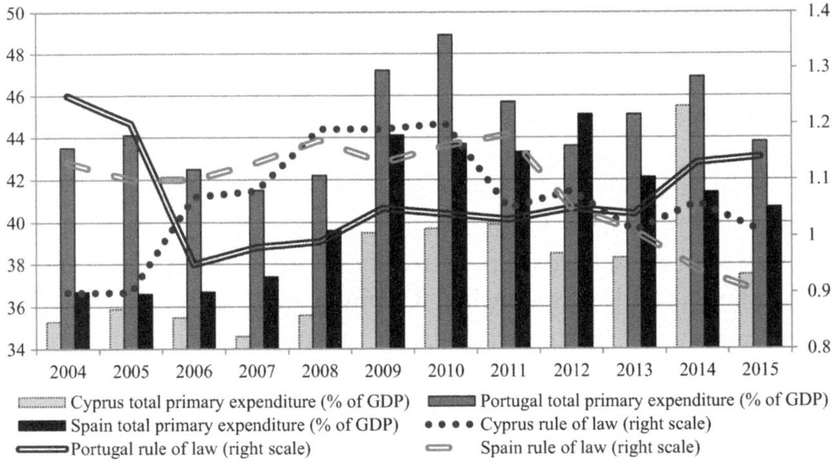

Fig. 7.3 Rule of law and total primary expenditures (% of GDP) in Cyprus, Portugal, and Spain 2004–2015 (Data: Rule of law: World Governance Indicators at: www.govindicators.org, Total primary expenditures: European Commission's AMECO Database)

their commitment to respect the conditionality of the programs, they are also among the best performers in the Freedom in the World rankings even at a time when freedom is threatened in many countries around the world (Freedom House 2017: 20–24).

Populist parties could not break through in these countries. As shown in Chap. 5, after long periods of dictatorships in Spain and Portugal, right-wing, exclusionary populism is largely absent from these countries (Sanders et al. 2017: 257). In Portugal, "it is common for political actors ... to delegitimize each other's policies or proposals by labeling them populist and thus simplistic and unworthy of serious debate" (Salgado and Zúquete 2017: 242). In Spain, Podemos represented a serious challenge to the establishment, but it emphasized more the issue of corruption and participatory politics than anti-austerity (Sanders et al. 2017: 252). Finally, while the far right exists in Cyprus, electorally it is still negligible (Charalambous 2015: 13).

Among the countries, which needed a financial assistance program, populist parties achieved a breakthrough only in Greece and Hungary. As we can see from Fig. 7.4, the two cases are similar along a number of dimensions. Rule of law has been steadily weakening since 2004, well before Tsipras formed his first and Orbán his second government. Both countries have a large redistribution rate, which is relatively constant in

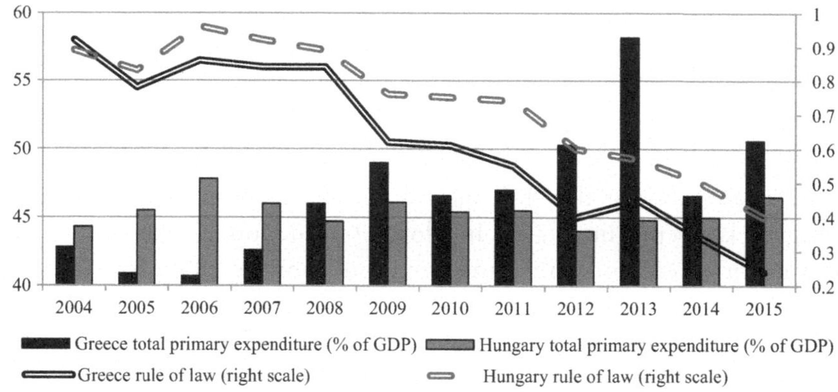

Fig. 7.4 Rule of law and total primary expenditures (% of GDP) in Greece and Hungary 2004–2015 (Data: Rule of law: World Governance Indicators at: www.govindicators.org, Total primary expenditures: European Commission's AMECO Database)

Hungary at around 45 percent for primary expenditures, and steadily growing in Greece. While slightly higher than in other Mediterranean states, Greece had around 40–42 percent redistribution rate prior to the crisis, but since 2008, it has been steadily over 45 percent. The collapse of GDP is clearly part of the explanation, but as we could see in Chap. 4, there is a general preference in Greece to fight tax evasion rather than reduce the redistribution rate.

Hungary and Greece also share the similarity of a significant worsening of the freedom of the press. In both cases the takeover of the state media by government cronies as well as the distribution of state advertisement to various media outlets impacted press freedom negatively (Freedom House 2016a, b). In Hungary academic freedom and the liberties of civic associations are also in danger: as the government started its campaign for the 2018 general elections, organizations associated with George Soros such as Central European University (CEU) and various non-governmental organizations came under attack.[5] These steps indicate that the government is unwilling to accept any restriction on its power. While there are no parallel developments in Greece,[6] the leaders of both countries emphasized their fight for democracy and self-determination in their negotiations with the Troika. However, once we consider the deterioration in rule of law in both countries and the high level of state redistribution, we can see that references to democracy are mostly instrumental, and there is an ongoing effort to fight any constraint on government power.

The similarities in the absence of commitment to limited government however led to rather different economic performance in the two countries: while Hungary was able to weather the financial crisis without a second agreement with the Troika, Greece entered a vicious spiral of austerity. The reason for this difference was elaborated in Chap. 6—while Hungary is deeply integrated in global production chains due to an outward-oriented economic transformation from the 1990s, this cannot be said of Greece. According to UNCTAD data in 2015, inward FDI stock in Greece was 9.1 percent of GDP, while in Hungary it was 76.4 percent (UNCTAD 2017). Significant foreign ownership of banks also helped in Hungary after the Vienna Initiative was negotiated, and foreign banks supported their subsidiaries. Hungary also received considerably more funding from EU transfers, which could be used for investments

—in contrast to its average of 3.79 percent of GDP between 2008 and 2015, Greece averaged only 2.36 percent.[7] At the same time, while Hungary clearly weathered the crisis better than Greece, it also has to be noted that its performance seems much weaker if we compare it to the performance of regional peers, Latvia and Romania (Fig. 7.5).

While there is a marked difference between Greece and Hungary's economic recovery from the financial crisis, they share the tradition of populism. Pappas (2014) uses the two cases to show how countries can slide from populism into illiberal democracy. He characterizes the two cases as populist democracies, which share the following characteristics: there is a single cleavage in society "dividing the good 'people' from some evil establishment," "the promotion of adversarial and polarizing politics," and the "adherence to the majority principle" (Pappas 2014: 3–4). He also shows the parallels between the two countries in bringing populism to power through increasing polarization and the defeat of nascent liberal forces by the populists led by a charismatic leader. In both cases, the history of

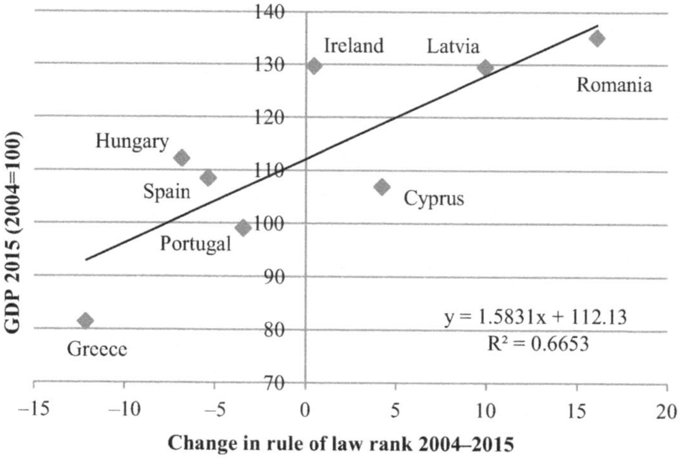

Fig. 7.5 Rule of law and economic growth 2004–2015 in EU program countries (Note: Rule of law ranking goes from 0 to 100 implying the percentage of countries, which are below the level of a given country. Thus 100 means that all other countries have lower performance on the indicator, while 0 means that no country fares worse. Change in rule of law rank means a change in this 0–100 scale. Data: GDP: European Commission's AMECO database, rule of law: World Governance Indicators)

populism goes back decades, and it is not the product of the financial crisis. As argued by Papathanassopoulos et al. (2017: 203), "populism is the bedrock ideology of the Greek political system since it affects both the left and right wings of the political spectrum." In the case of Hungary, Enyedi (2015: 243) argues that "there has been no serious attempt at establishing centrist or leftist populist forces," and populism emerged in the right with Fidesz and Jobbik. At the same time Hungary has an older discourse on populism, which treats irresponsible economic policies for short-term electoral gains as macroeconomic populism.[8] From such a perspective left-wing populism was also clearly present after 2002 in Hungary as shown by the previous chapter. While fiscal deficits did not pose an immediate threat to liberal democracy in the way Fidesz's policies do, deterioration of the rule of law and the inability of the government to respect external and internal constraints on its power had already started. The financial crisis and the calls for unorthodox measures of crisis management freed the government even further from limits on its power, and this window of opportunity was utilized to the fullest extent.

Overall, the cases of Greece and Hungary illustrate the claim that the deterioration of the rule of law is both a cause and a consequence of the emergence of populist democracies. The financial crisis only accelerated the negative trends, which could be observed earlier.

Rule of law is also relevant for economic outcomes. Fig. 7.5 summarizes the relationship between the two. Looking at the data from 2004 allows the control for the impact of the financial bubble.

Figure 7.5 reveals a strong correlation between changes in the rule of law and economic growth—countries, which saw a worsening of their rule of law registered weaker economic performance. While there are clearly a number of intervening variables in this relationship, ranging from initial level of development to integration into the global economy, the figure strongly indicates the economic relevance of change in the rule of law indicator.

Overall, the eight cases show that trust, and ultimately the success in crisis management, strongly depends on the government's willingness to accept constraints on its power. These constraints take various forms in a liberal democracy ranging from rule of law, political and civil liberties, as well as the level of state redistribution. Those governments, which respect these constraints, had more constructive program negotiations than those that do not, which clearly influenced the success of crisis management.

* * *

As the previous chapters have shown, trust proved to be decisive in the outcome of crisis management. However, in order to understand what follows from this finding, it is important to consider the sources of trust. This chapter showed that trust does not simply imply benign attitudes toward the negotiating partners, but rather it is based on the willingness of the government for self-restraint.

Governmental self-restraint is a multifaceted concept. Governments are limited by international agreements and external organizations, which they have willingly joined. They are also constrained by non-governmental organizations and the media, which provide information on government actions and hold it accountable. Most importantly governments are limited by the rule of law. Populist governments are unwilling to submit themselves to such constraints, and instead, they point to the democratic majority as justification for their actions. However, as the limits on government are eroded, the possibility for the abuse of power opens up. Trust toward such governments is low—as international partners, the public, and the markets do not believe the promises of the government, cooperation becomes difficult and suboptimal economic outcomes follow.

An important fear during the financial crisis is a trade-off between austerity and the emergence of populism. The experiences from the eight program countries show that there is no straight link between crisis management and populism—responsible economic policies in themselves do not cause populism. At the same time there seems to be a link between deterioration in the rule of law and populist parties gaining power. As respect for the law is eroded, populists have an easier time accelerating the trend. For them austerity and an economic crisis is an opportunity for further weakening the institutions that limit their power. The outcome is a vicious cycle between worsening institutions, populism, and a deterioration of economic performance. At the same time, strong institutions can hold back populists even during difficult economic times.

The concluding chapter discusses the policy implications of these insights.

Notes

1. The concept of populism is highly contested. Here I rely on the definition by Mudde (2004: 543), who conceptualizes populism as "an ideology that considers society to be ultimately separated into two homogeneous and antagonistic groups, 'the pure people' versus 'the corrupt elite', and which argues that politics should be an expression of the volonté générale (general will) of the people." On the debate over the main definitions of the term, see Müller (2016): 7–12.
2. For recent elaborations see Tanzi (2011) or Kahn (2011). They both argue that while it is very difficult to determine the optimal size of the government, there is a strong likelihood that government will grow over that size (Kahn 2011: 6).
3. Rothstein (1998: 167) argues that the universality of welfare benefits is particularly important, as it ensures that everyone in society benefits from state redistribution. By experiencing the high-quality services provided by the government in the fields of health care or education, for example, people are also willing to pay their share of taxes.
4. The text is available at: http://eur-lex.europa.eu/legal-content/EN/TXT/?uri=CELEX:12012P/TXT. Accessed: 2 July 2017.
5. In April 2017 the higher education law was amended to require intergovernmental, federal-level agreement for non-EU universities for further functioning as well as an operating campus in the home country. As CEU is the only American-chartered institution, which operates only in Budapest, the requirements clearly aimed at its closure or re-establishment somewhere else. The law on NGOs, which was passed in June 2017, requires civil organizations, which receive over 24,000 euro from abroad, to register as "foreign-supported," which is reminiscent of the foreign agent law in Russia that aims to stigmatize and weaken NGOs.
6. Concerns over the rule of law in Greece have also emerged in August 2017 due to the freezing of the bank accounts of a leading magazine over a reader's letter as well as the prosecution of a former statistics chief, Andreas Georgiou. See: Hope (2017).
7. Data is available at: http://ec.europa.eu/budget/figures/interactive/index_en.cfm. Accessed: 2 July, 2017.
8. The idea of macroeconomic populism strongly draws on the Latin American experiences. See Csaba (2009): 88.

References

Balcere, Ilze. 2014. Populism in the manifestos of Latvian political parties: Increasingly used but ineffective? *Journal of Baltic Studies* 45 (4): 477–497.

Charalambous, Giorgos. 2015. Ideological and organizational aspects of the Greek Cypriot far right. In *The European far right: Historical and contemporary perspectives*, ed. Giorgos Charalambous, 13–21. Nicosia and Oslo: Friedrich-Ebert-Stiftung and Peace Research Institute.

Chesterman, Simon. 2008. An international rule of law? *The American Journal of Comparative Law* 56 (2): 331–361.

Corbu, Nicoleta, Delia Balaban-Balas, and Elena Negrea-Busuioc. 2017. Romania: Populist ideology without teeth. In *Populist political communication in Europe*, ed. Toril Aalberg, Frank Esser, Carsten Reinemann, Jesper Strömback, and Claes H. de Vreese, 326–338. New York: Routledge.

Csaba, László. 2009. *Crisis in economics?* Budapest: Akadémiai Kiadó.

Enyedi, Zsolt. 2015. Plebeians, citoyens and aristocrats or where is the bottom of bottom-up? The case of Hungary. In *European populism in the shadow of the Great Recession*, ed. Hanspeter Kriesi and Takis Pappas, 235–250. Colchester: ECPR Press.

Freedom House. 2016a. *Freedom of the press 2016 country report Greece*. Available: https://freedomhouse.org/report/freedom-press/2016/greece. Accessed 2 July 2017.

———. 2016b. *Freedom of the press 2016 country report Hungary*. Available: https://freedomhouse.org/report/freedom-press/2016/hungary. Accessed 2 July 2017.

———. 2017. *Populist and autocrats: The dual threat to global democracy*, Freedom in the world 2017. Washington: Freedom House.

Fukuyama, Francis. 2004. The imperative of state-building. *Journal of Democracy* 15 (2): 17–31.

Hope, Kerin. 2017. Minister's court win intensifies fears for rule of law in Greece. *Financial Times*, August 9.

Kahn, James. 2011. *Can we determine the optimal size of government?* CATO Institute Development Policy Briefing Paper. No. 7. Available: https://object.cato.org/sites/cato.org/files/pubs/pdf/dbp7.pdf. Accessed 2 July 2017.

Kaufmann, Daniel, Aart Kraay, and Massimo Mastruzzi. 2010. *The Worldwide Governance Indicators: Methodology and analytical issues*, World Bank Policy Research Working Paper No. 5430.

Kriesi, Hanspeter, and Takis Pappas. 2015. Populism in Europe during crisis: An introduction. In *European populism in the shadow of the Great Recession*, ed. Hanspeter Kriesi and Takis Pappas, 1–19. Colchester: ECPR Press.

Kydland, Finn E., and Edward Prescott. 1977. Rules rather than discretion: The inconsistency of optimal plans. *Journal of Political Economy* 85 (3): 473–491.

Mudde, Cas. 2004. The populist zeitgeist. *Government and Opposition* 39 (4): 541–563.

Müller, Jan-Werner. 2016. *What is populism?* Philadelphia: University of Pennsylvania Press.

O'Malley, Eoin, and John FitzGibbon. 2015. Everywhere and nowhere: Populism and the puzzling non-reaction to Ireland's crisis. In *European populism in the shadow of the Great Recession*, ed. Hanspeter Kriesi and Takis Pappas, 287–300. Colchester: ECPR Press.

Papathanassopoulos, Stylianos, Iliana Giannouli, and Ioannis Andreadis. 2017. Greece. populism between left and right. In *Populist political communication in Europe*, ed. Toril Aalberg, Frank Esser, Carsten Reinemann, Jesper Strömback, and Claes H. de Vreese, 195–206. New York: Routledge.

Pappas, Takis. 2014. Populist democracies: Post-authoritarian Greece and post-communist Hungary. *Government and Opposition* 49 (1): 1–23.

Pech, Laurent. 2009. *The rule of law as a constitutional principle of the European Union*, Jean Monnet Working Paper Series No. 4/2009. Available at https://ssrn.com/abstract=1463242. Accessed: 2 July 2017.

Rothstein, Bo. 1998. *Just institutions matter: The moral and political logic of the universal welfare state*. Cambridge: Cambridge University Press.

Salgado, Susana, and Jose Pedro Zúquete. 2017. Portugal: Discreet populisms amid unfavorable contexts and stigmatization. In *Populist political communication in Europe*, ed. Toril Aalberg, Frank Esser, Carsten Reinemann, Jesper Strömback, and Claes H. de Vreese, 235–248. New York: Routledge.

Sanders, Karen, Rosa Berganza, and Roberto de Miguel. 2017. Spain: Populism from the far Right to the emergence of Podemos. In *Populist political communication in Europe*, ed. Toril Aalberg, Frank Esser, Carsten Reinemann, Jesper Strömback, and Claes H. de Vreese, 249–260. New York: Routledge.

Tamanaha, Brian. 2004. *On the rule of law: History, politics, theory*. Cambridge: Cambridge University Press.

Tanzi, Vito. 2011. *Government versus markets: The changing economic role of the state*. Cambridge: Cambridge University Press.

UNCTAD. 2017. *World investment report 2017*. Annex Table 7. New York and Geneva: UNCTAD. Available: http://unctad.org/en/Pages/DIAE/World%20Investment%20Report/Annex-Tables.aspx. Accessed July 2 2017.

Weiler, J.H.H. 2016. Epilogue: Living in a glass house. In *Reinforcing rule of law oversight in the European Union*, ed. Carlos Closa and Dimitry Kochenov, 313–326. Cambridge: Cambridge University Press.

8

The Future of Europe: Bridging the Gap Between Moral Hazard and Solidarity

The management of the financial crisis carries important lessons for the future of the EU at a time when the community is facing a series of overlapping crises. The atmosphere during the 60th anniversary of the Rome Treaty in March 2017 was far from celebratory. Facing Brexit, security threats from the Middle East and Africa, and the ambivalent attitude of Donald Trump to NATO, as well as long-standing domestic problems such as aging societies and adaptation to technological change, European leaders recognized the pressure to cooperate. The European Commission published a white paper and a series of reflection papers on how to deal with these challenges.[1] The plans to move forward, especially on the area of EMU, share an important similarity with the problem faced during the management of the financial crisis: Northern countries have concerns over moral hazard, while Southern and Eastern member states want solidarity.

The suggestions for a European safe asset, a European deposit insurance scheme, or a European unemployment insurance scheme, which are all parts of the Commission's plans (European Commission 2017: 19–26), raise the same question: who will pay? Since failing banks and unemployed people are unequally distributed across member states, Northern countries assume that their funds would be used for supporting

D. Győrffy, *Trust and Crisis Management in the European Union*,
https://doi.org/10.1007/978-3-319-69212-8_8

undeserving or irresponsible governments. These concerns are well-founded as Csaba (2016: 72) cites the findings of the European Court of Auditors showing that even without an examination of the economic rationality, a significant proportion of the funds are used in an improper manner from a procedural perspective. Persistent distrust however makes deeper integration very difficult.

The experiences of the management of the financial crisis show that distrust can be mitigated through an adherence to the concept of limited government or the strengthening of domestic institutions. The debate on the future of Europe neglects this dimension, which is however crucial to limit government's abuse of power, support economic development and ultimately reduce the reliance on other member states for assistance. In other words, institutions can foster trust and thus bridge the gap between concerns over moral hazard and expectations of solidarity. The main objective of the present chapter is to assess the ways the EU can contribute to strengthening the rule of law in the member states and thus build trust at the domestic and European levels.

In order to answer the above question a theoretical framework is presented based on the global governance literature and the issue of compliance with international institutions. By distinguishing ex ante and ex post as well as top-down and bottom-up measures, the chapter provides an overview of the possible steps the EU can take to encourage the adherence to the rule of law at the national level and thus increase trust in the system. It is argued that although the quality of domestic institutions is primarily determined by national-level variables, the EU can strongly contribute to change the system of incentives. Doing so is critical since the paradox of building trust is that the least willing countries to implement the necessary reforms are also the ones that need them most.

The structure of the chapter is the following. The next part provides the theoretical framework on possible sources of compliance with the rule of international institutions. In the second and third sections, ex ante measures are listed, which aim for capacity building as well as the narrowing of resources for adversaries of the rule of law. The measures include the inclusion of institution-building into the European competitiveness strategy and the regulations of the structural funds, the mitigation of moral hazard problems on the financial markets and the correct pricing of risks, a strong focus on education as well as the fight against the influence of hostile foreign actors such as Russia. Ex post measures relate to the sanctioning possibilities of breaching the rule of law from the European level as well as the domestic level, where the idea of militant democracy is explored. The final section concludes the chapter.

8.1 Theoretical Approaches to Rule Compliance at the EU Level

As it was discussed in the previous chapter, the rule of law is a shared value of various European legal traditions and also a constitutional principle of the EU (Pech 2009). In the Treaty it is listed as a fundamental value of the community. Article 2 of the Treaty on European Union (TEU) states that:

> The Union is founded on the values of respect for human dignity, freedom, democracy, equality, the rule of law and respect for human rights, including the rights of persons belonging to minorities. These values are common to the Member States in a society in which pluralism, non-discrimination, tolerance, justice, solidarity and equality between women and men prevail.[2]

While the above values are clearly proclaimed, their enforcement is very difficult, which became obvious in recent years. As Kochenov (2017: 11) underlines, the key problem of enforcing values is that "unlike in the case of the *aquis sensu stricto*, the high level of the Member States' compliance with the values of Article 2 TEU has been simply presumed, thus seemingly not requiring the opening of Pandora's box of the values enforcement debate." As the Hungarian example shows, the government could lose a number of infringement procedures and change the wording of the law without any substantial change to the effect.[3] When attempting to prevent similar cases in the future, a more comprehensive approach is necessary than strengthening sanctions.

Since international organizations cannot enforce their decisions by having a monopoly on the use of force, a large literature has developed in the field of global governance about how to enforce compliance with international or European law. In their overview of theories of compliance, Börzel et al. (2010: 1368–1371) distinguish three mechanisms of compliance: enforcement, management, and legitimacy. Enforcement determines the costs of non-compliance, which can be mitigated by variations in state power—larger states have more opportunity to get away with breaches than smaller, less powerful countries. Management approaches assume that non-compliance is involuntary and its cause is primarily lack of capacity to comply. Theories based on legitimacy argue that states comply because it is the appropriate thing to do. Based on a large database of over 6300 violation of EU laws, Börzel et al. (2010) show that the most compliant members of the EU are the small member states with efficient bureaucracy, while powerful member states with inefficient bureaucracies are most likely to defy the EU. Interestingly, they do not find evidence for the legitimacy hypothesis or the idea that the popularity of the EU increases compliance—they speculate that countries with weak governance capacities expect the EU to deliver public goods for them instead of their national government, but weak capacities hinder the effectiveness of implementation for EU policies as well (Börzel et al. 2010: 1381). As the power structure in the EU can be taken as given from the perspective of designing policies, these results also provide strong support for the importance of institution-building at the national level.

The question is how this might be done. Based on the experiences of the EMU, Amtenbrink and Repasi (2017) show how various compliance mechanisms can work together. Unlike other approaches to compliance, they distinguish between ex ante and ex post measures—"whereas *ex ante* measures are aimed at preventing cases of voluntary and involuntary non-compliance, *ex post* mechanisms are aimed at dealing with non-compliance" (Amtenbrink and Repasi 2017: 149). Another distinction they make is between top-down and bottom-up perspectives—the former refers to the supranational institutions, the latter means other actors in the system, especially private actors, who internalize the supranational norms (Amtenbrink and Repasi 2017: 150).

Based on the above theories, Table 8.1 summarizes the main measures, which can help fostering an adherence to the rule of law within the member states, provide limits on government power, and increase public trust. The following sections give an overview of the individual recommendations.

Table 8.1 Measures to improve institutions and foster compliance with the rule of law in the EU

	Top-down	Bottom-up
Ex ante	*Supranational strategies for institution-building* Institutional leg for competitiveness strategy Conditionality for structural funds	*Improving incentives for good governance* Countering moral hazard on the financial markets Promoting education Containing foreign [Russian] influence
Ex post	*Sanctioning non-compliance* Strengthening enforcement of values Institutional conditionality of financial support programs	*Fighting backsliding* Militant democracy Supporting (defending) pro-democracy groups

8.2 Supranational Strategies for Institution-Building

Building administrative capacities at the national level should be a top priority for the EU in building trust and fighting non-compliance. Institutional variables are the first pillar of competitiveness in the World Economic Forum *Global Competitiveness Report.*[4] The factors related to public institutions include the protection of property rights are intellectual property, ethics and corruption, undue influence in the judiciary and the government, and public sector performance as well as security from terrorism and organized crime for business (World Economic Forum 2016: 39). Considering their primacy in thinking about competitiveness, their absence from the targets of the Europe 2020 strategy is striking.[5] The omission becomes especially problematic once we consider the results of Pasimeni and Pasimeni (2016), who show that country performance on progressing toward the Europe 2020 indicators is determined primarily by institutions. Improving them would contribute toward the quantitative objectives of the strategy. A similar absence can be noticed in the case of regional policy[6]: institution-building is not part of the policy despite the fact that the quality of public administration is a strong predictor of whether a region needs support for convergence or not.[7]

Given the evidence about the significance of institutions for the objectives of the European competitiveness strategy and regional policy, the question arises why they are omitted even from the discussion. Asking this question in relation to regional development policies, Rodriguez-Pose (2013: 1040) gives three reasons: institutions are very difficult to effectively measure, they are context- and geography-specific, and they also have a temporary quality, which means that their efficiency changes over time. In the context of the EU, one can add the reluctance of the EU to interfere into domestic politics—unlike quantitative targets on R&D spending or CO2 emission, institutions are inherently political and represent the prevailing power relations (North 1990: 86).

In spite of the technical and theoretical difficulties of building administrative capacities at the national level, in the past few years the EU has created a number of mechanisms toward this objective. One such monitoring measure is the CVM established for Romania and Bulgaria. As already discussed in Chap. 6, while initially the CVM seemed inconsequential, once the monitoring was tied to Schengen entry in 2011, both governments became motivated to implement reforms, and governance indicators improved. A similar initiative is the Structural Reform Support Service, which was established by the Commission in June 2015 in order to help Greek institutional reforms. As argued by Ioannidis (2017: 491), the management of the Greek crisis "resulted in the introduction of a general mechanism potentially relevant to all Member States." Indeed, as shown in Chap. 4, competitiveness measures improved in the country eventually.

The above mechanisms indicate that in spite of the clear difficulties of addressing member state institutional weakness, the EU has been accumulating experiences on this field. Using these experiences in the competitiveness strategy could imply technical and budgetary assistance to those countries, which are willing to work on these fields.

In regional policy the EU could provide even stronger incentives to improve the rule of law—ranging from national-level conditionality to context-specific measures aimed to improve regional governance. The German proposal for rule of law conditionality in regional policy

(Bundesministerium für Wirtschaft und Energie 2017) or the proposed requirement to submit to the jurisdiction of the European Public Prosecutor's Office[8] points in the right direction.

Addressing these issues in regional policy is especially important once we consider that any outside aid can easily become spoils for corrupt governments with little improvement in the welfare of citizens.[9] As shown by Svensson (2000), democracies are less likely to experience the corrupting impacts of aid, which in turn suggests that improving institutions of democracy should be high on the agenda when distributing such funds. The Marshall Aid in the 1940s was certainly an effective policy to boost the economy and improve the stability of democracy in Western Europe (Bueno de Mesquita and Smith 2011: 181). At first sight the recipients of regional funds are all democracies, but there are clear signs of backsliding in Hungary or Poland (Puddington and Roylance 2017). Consequently, strengthening the institutions of weaker members, instead of letting national governments feed their clientele with it, should be an important priority. Its significance is even more pronounced once we consider a major finding by Bueno de Mesquita and Smith (2011: 25): in countries, where a relatively small minority can gain power given the electoral system, it is more beneficial to reward essential supporters with private benefits than provide public goods for a wide segment of the population. However, in the absence of distributable funds, autocrats tend to be overthrown by rivals (Bueno de Mesquita and Smith 2011: 152). For countries with weakening rule of law, constraining the flow of money seems to be an essential requirement in any fight against an emerging autocrat.

8.3 Improving Incentives for Good Governance

As it has been shown in several earlier chapters, external pressure in itself is insufficient to bring about change—especially change in institutions. Consequently besides supranational mechanisms to assist institution-building, there is also a need to improve bottom-up incentives for good governance. These include the improvement of market incentives and the promotion of European civic education as well as the fight against foreign forces, which aim to destabilize the EU.

8.3.1 Reducing Moral Hazard on the Global Financial Markets

Access to global financial markets and the fall in interest rates played a key role in the crisis of all eight countries examined. The problems of cheap money discussed in the case of regional policy also apply to cheap loans from the international financial markets. While the fall in global interest rates and the subsequent search for yields created the conditions for increased lending to riskier countries, institutional factors also played a role in this outcome and undermined the disciplinary mechanism of the markets. The consequence was increased indebtedness and the postponement of structural reforms in the EU periphery.

As discussed in Chap. 3, in spite of the no-bailout clause of the Maastricht Treaty (Article 125 TEU), there were reasonable expectations from investors about a bailout in the case of trouble. This was due to the establishment of too-big-to-fail banks following the creation of single market for capital, as well as the interdependence of countries within the euro-zone. Strengthening the no-bailout clause is thus crucial for market discipline to work. Sinn (2014: 341) suggests that "if the collateral fails, be it a government bond, a private security or any other kind of asset, the holders of covered bonds should bear the losses rather then ask community funds to step in." He also recommends restructuring debt for the GIPSIC countries (Greece, Ireland, Portugal, Spain, Italy, and Cyprus) in order to restore transparency and trust (Sinn 2014: 339). Beyond these suggestions, which could signal the level of risk to investors, it is also important to revise the regulations related to government bonds. Gros (2013: 94) calls attention to the practice of assigning zero risk weight for sovereign debt of developed countries. In light of the experiences of the crisis, this is clearly imprudent. Lenarcic et al. (2016) calculate how non-zero risk weights could narrow the financing opportunities for weaker governments. Such a development would have at least three beneficial results: it would reduce the risk of a new financial crisis in these countries; there would be more disciplining from the financial markets, which would motivate them to improve their credibility, while it would also push these countries to official institutions for financing, where mechanisms of conditionality could be activated. Reducing moral hazard on the financial markets is thus crucial for providing the right incentives for institution-building.

8.3.2 Promoting Education

It is a cliché to emphasize the importance of education for democratic governance and trust. The significance of education for democracy has been elaborated in modern political theory by Lipset, who argued that "education presumably broadens men's outlook, enables them to understand the need of tolerance, restrains them from adhering to extremist and monistic doctrines, and increases their capacity to make rational electoral choices" (Lipset 1959: 79). Beyond these mechanisms it is also important to recall that one of the major determinants of interpersonal trust is education—more educated people are also more trusting people, which is a crucial factor in fostering cooperation in a society (Uslaner 2002: 112–113). There is substantial empirical evidence supporting the link between education and democracy,[10] which implies the need to focus on education for democracies to survive.

Recent experiences also support the key role of education in populist surges. Hobolt (2016: 1269) shows that besides age, the most significant predictor of voting for Brexit was education. In the US elections, Silver (2016) found a similar result—comparing the 50 most and least educated cities and counties as measured by the proportion of voters with at least a BA degree, he discovered that Clinton surged in the former and collapsed in the latter group. Compared to education, income was a much less significant factor in voters' choice. Another analysis also shows that the low concentration of college degrees was the strongest predictor of a Trump victory (McGill 2016). Some recent decisions by authoritarian governments further underline the importance of institutes of higher education as bulwarks for democracy and obstacles to authoritarian rule. Universities are threatened in Putin's Russia, Erdogan's Turkey, and

Orban's Hungary.[11] In all these cases academics are viewed with suspicion and animosity by the regime.

In spite of the relatively clear case for the importance of education for democracy, education was a major victim of fiscal consolidation in a number of EU countries. As argued by Darvas and Tschekassin (2015: 14), there was a generational asymmetry in bearing the burdens of crisis management—while the benefits of the elderly were largely kept intact, there were severe cuts in social spending on families and children as well as education. Part of the reason might be the well-known willingness of the elderly to show up at elections as opposed to the low participation rates of young people.[12]

For the EU the above means that channeling funds toward education for exchange programs and the development of universities is probably among the most rewarding investments for its future. Young and the educated segments are the most supportive of European integration as shown by the Brexit vote (Hobolt 2016). In order to nudge them to vote, it is also important to develop European civic education in line with proposals such as AEGEE (2016).

8.3.3 Containing Foreign Influence

When building incentives for good governance and laying the foundation of social trust, it is also important to address forces, which have the opposite objectives and foster distrust. At the time of writing, the Russian interference into the US elections is still an ongoing scandal. Furthermore, evidence has been mounting about the buildup of Russian soft power in the EU to serve Russian foreign policy objectives—to destabilize NATO and the EU.

As elaborated by Braghiroli and Makarychev (2016: 217), "the dominating strategy of Moscow is not to disrupt connections with the EU, but rather to open up the concept of Europe to – and include in it – Russia as a fully fledged European nation." This yields a discursive strategy of four elements, which is spread in the EU (Braghiroli and Makarychev 2016: 218): a rejection of liberal values in favor of traditional Christian-conservative values; return to the Westphalian system of state-to-state relations without supranational forces; increasing distance from the United States and NATO; acceptance of Russian concerns about neo-fascism in the Baltic States and Ukraine. In order to spread these messages, Russia has built up relationships with the far-left and far-right parties within the EU.[13] It is also conducting international media campaigns through its state-owned media network in a range of languages as well as utilizes the social media to influence public opinion (Oliker 2017: 18).[14] As shown by the outcome of the 2017 presidential elections in France, Russian campaigns are not always effective, but they can be decisive in close elections such as the 2016 US presidential elections.

The illiberal, authoritarian model of Putin's Russia clearly stands in contrast with the idea of liberal democracy and the rule of law. Fighting Russian propaganda is thus indispensable to preserve these fundamental values of the EU. Such fight includes the debunking of false information, exposing the pro-Russian narratives, and educating citizens about the way propaganda works (Smolenova 2016: 29). In the French elections it was also critical that the French media did not report stolen information from the Macron campaign in sharp contrast to the US media, which provided a strong platform for Russian objectives.[15]

8.4 Sanctioning Non-compliance with EU Laws and Values

The idea of sanctioning non-compliance with EU values is relatively recent. As recounted by Kochenov and Pech (2015: 2), it was only in 2013 when Commissioner Viviane Reding called attention to a "rule of law crisis" in the EU and mentioned French, Hungarian, and Romanian examples. The enforcement mechanism of the value of rule of law is Article 7 TEU, which threatens with the suspension of voting rights in case of serious breach of values listed in Article 2. However, as Bugaric (2016: 91) calls attention, the EU has been rather unwilling to invoke the procedure given the unanimity required for the sanctioning mechanism to be activated.[16] Since it is very difficult to implement, Article 7 is often called a nuclear option—a mechanism of enforcement, which essentially cannot be used leaving only traditional infringement procedures in place (Kochenov and Pech 2015: 3).

The absence of a clear mechanism for sanctioning the breaching of EU values has left the EU impotent in dealing with breaches of values in Poland and Hungary. In order to resolve the problem, Kochenov (2017: 18) summarizes eight proposals, which include systemic infringement procedure and the establishment of a Copenhagen Commission. A systemic infringement procedure is suggested by Scheppele (2016), who suggest the bundling up infringement cases in order to establish the breach of Article 2 and suspending EU funds as a sanctioning mechanism. The Copenhagen Commission is suggested by Müller (2017: 242) as "a guardian of Europe's a*quis normative*, … analogous to the Venice Commission – a body, in other words, with a mandate to craft comprehensive and consistent legal and political judgments." However, as noted by Müller (2017: 250), such changes would require treaty change, which is unlikely at a time when several member states would feel threatened by such new institutions. Given these difficulties, Jakab (2017: 262) believes that it is the European Court of Justice, which has to act and "reassert its responsibility in both enhancing European integration and promoting the values of the EU."

At the time of finishing this book (July 2017), ideas abound about how to sanction the breaches of rule of law more effectively. However, the matter is far from resolved, and renitent countries continue to oppose the interference of EU into their democratic processes. While this may sound as a highly opportunistic argument, Weiler (2016: 322) also argues that the EU is in a difficult position to take action in these areas given that "the two most primordial norms of democracy, the principle of accountability and the principle of representation, are compromised in the very structure and process of the Union." This leads him to the conclusion that when fighting "gross violations of the Rule of Law … it should simultaneously hurry up and put its own democratic house in order lest it be reminded again that those living in glass houses should be careful when throwing stones" (Weiler 2016: 326).

The difficulties of sanctioning renitent states within the current framework underline the importance of pre-empting breaches of values in the EU. Regarding sanctions, a trial-and-error approach is probably the most likely scenario given the challenges arising from member states. Such an outcome however is unlikely to offer fast solution to the above problems. It appears that real and timely solution can be achieved only in countries, which are financially constrained by a financial assistance program (Greece), or have not joined to desirable European projects such as Schengen (Bulgaria, Romania). In these cases institutional conditionality is a realistic option. As it was discussed above, countries dependent on regional funds might also be constrained by enhanced conditionality. The EU has the least leverage over powerful net contributors—however, so far they also seem the least likely to disavow the values of the EU. Consequently, making progress with the three groups of countries mentioned would be a powerful contribution to the respect of rule of law in the EU.

8.5 Militant Democracy

Given the difficulties of imposing sanctions on belligerent states, domestic actors have a key role in sanctioning such regimes. Citizens, who can vote in an election, have the opportunity to dismiss governments, which breach the values of the EU. However, in order to make it possible, there needs to be a greater reliance on the concept of militant democracy.

The original idea relates to fascism and was elaborated by exiled German philosopher Karl Loewenstein in 1937. He argued that fascism is not a coherent ideology but rather a highly effective political technique to gain power: "colossal propaganda is launched against what appears as the most conspicuously vulnerable targets. A technique of incessant repetition, of over-statements and over-simplifications, is evolved and applied. The different sections of the people are played off against one another" (Loewenstein 1937: 423). Loewenstein's most important insight is that fascism preys on the weaknesses of democracy—given its inherent tolerance of different opinions, the system has difficulties in denying the full opportunities of democratic institutions from a legal organization (Loewenstein 1937: 423–424).

As Loewenstein was writing in 1937, the world had yet to see the full horrors of fascism. In light of the later history of the fascist movement, it would be rash to define the current wave of populism as a case in fascism.

However, the regular attacks on the rule of law as well as the similar use of propaganda techniques make the suggestions of militant democracy relevant today. Loewenstein (1937: 429–431) proposes political and legal remedies against fascism: exposure of the fascist technique, which loses its effectiveness once it becomes well known, as well as anti-extremist legislation at the level of the constitution, which makes the application of the fascist technique legally very difficult. In fighting fascism, democracies should show a unified front rather than fight independently. Eighty years later, anti-extremist legislation is widely present at the national and the EU level. However, exposure of the populist technique appears much less effective. Besides outside influences, knowledge about propaganda techniques also seems crucial in the defense of democracy and rule of law. Building critical thinking into education and applying the tools listed in the fight against foreign propaganda are important elements in this struggle.

Müller (2017) also uses the concept of militant democracy to justify the suggestion about the establishment of a Copenhagen Council. At the same time, he offers a paradox about militant democracy (Müller 250–251):

> Skeptics about militant democracy will always be tempted to say that countries which can have militant democracy probably do not need it, whereas those which need it cannot have it. Why? Because any country where the most powerful actors can agree on what the genuine threats to democracy are (irrespective of whether these threats emanate from the right or the left, or from religion or secular ideologies), probably has such a strong democratic consensus that challenges to democracy will fail by themselves. Conversely, in highly polarized and unstable polities characterized by deep moral disagreement, militant democracy might make some sense – but the very fact of polarization and disagreement probably prevent the creation of a militant democracy.

Countries which are most endangered by groups trying to undermine democracy are the least able to defend themselves. Consequently internal mechanisms of defense are weaker, and these countries are more dependent on outside intervention. The EU thus has a particularly important role in protecting agents of democracy such as civil society and the independent media from government inference.

8.6 Conclusions

The problems of militant democracy extend to the problems of building trust as well. In countries, where policy-makers strengthen institutions in order to foster trust, there is probably little cause for concern. In contrast, governments, which aspire to rely on trust in the leader, attack institutions responsible for constraining the executive in the name of improving policy efficiency. If such countries are members of the EU, their problems are problems of the community. The trampling upon the values of the European community can set dangerous precedents for other countries as well. Not protecting citizens in EU countries in the name of non-interference into domestic politics is untenable in a community of values.

Building institutional trust through increasing the commitment of the government to checks and balances in the society is certainly a complex task. Blueprints for such endeavors are present such as the recommendations of OECD (2017). However, it is the motivation to implement such reforms, which is missing in problematic countries such as Greece or Hungary. The EU can strongly contribute to improve their incentives for these reforms. While certainly none of the suggestions offer easy or quick solutions, a trial-and-error approach to these problems can go far. What seems important is to reject false references to European solidarity, domestic sovereignty, or confusing the populist leaders with the country. All these contribute to the status quo and the keeping of populists on power.

The importance of domestic institutions is often missing from the debates on the future of Europe. However, as we could see in the various cases of crisis management, the willingness of governments to comply with their international obligations was a reflection of their willingness to obey domestic rule of law. Strengthening institutions, which serve to limit government discretion, allows the making of credible commitments and thus builds trust domestically and at the European level as well.

As Europe is facing serious challenges and plans for deeper integration, trust is essential. Proposals for the completion of the economic and monetary union entail greater solidarity and greater interdependence. Possibilities for abusing solidarity should be limited, and some sort of institutional convergence is essential for this purpose. Sovereignty cannot be a reference when the rule of law is threatened. The external enforcement of this principle is also the obvious interest of the member states concerned given the fundamental role of institutions in economic development.

The management of the European financial crisis provided important lessons for the future of Europe. As creditors and debtors struggled around their concerns for moral hazard and solidarity, common ground could be found if the partners trusted one another. This trust however had deeper sources than personal sympathies—the ability for self-binding and adhering to the concept of limited government proved to be crucial. Strengthening domestic institutions is a way to build trust. As Europe moves forward from the crisis and addresses the challenges of the future, this lesson from the crisis should not be forgotten.

Notes

1. The papers are available at: https://ec.europa.eu/commission/white-paper-future-europe_en. Accessed 2 July, 2017.
2. The text of the Treaty is available at: http://eur-lex.europa.eu/LexUriServ/LexUriServ.do?uri=OJ:C:2008:115:0013:0045:en:PDF. Accessed 2 July, 2017.
3. Szente (2017: 466) mentions the 2011 case of reducing the retirement age of judges, which made most leadership positions vacant within a year. While the government lost the case at the European Court of Justice and the judges received compensation, their position had been already filled.
4. See the methodological discussion in World Economic Forum (2016): 35–41.
5. The main targets of the Europe 2020 strategy relate to employment, research and development, climate change and energy, education, as well as poverty and social inclusion. The targets are available at: https://ec.europa.eu/info/strategy/european-semester/framework/europe-2020-strategy_en. Accessed 2 July, 2017.
6. The main targets of the current regional policy are research and innovation, information and communication technologies, making small- and medium-sized companies more competitive, moving toward a low-carbon economy. The targets are available at: https://europa.eu/european-union/topics/regional-policy_en. Accessed 2 July, 2017.

7. Charron et al. (2015: 325) provide a map of institutional quality in the European Union and Turkey, which shows the link.
8. This is the suggestion of Věra Jourová, European Commissioner for Justice. See the report by Cooper (2017).
9. There is an enormous literature on the effectiveness of foreign aid, which I do not cover here. For an extensive elaboration of the problem, see the classic book by William Easterly (Easterly 2006).
10. See the overview of studies in Glaeser et al. (2007): 79–81.
11. For an overview of these cases, see Redden (2017).
12. The generational divide is analyzed by Smets (2012), who show that delayed entry into adulthood is probably responsible for this trend.
13. For an extensive overview of these relationships, see Klapsis (2015).
14. According to Veebel (2016: 16) such campaigns have the following objectives: "demonize the adversary, deter and demoralize the adversary, legitimize one's own activities to the general public, mobilize target populations, promote one's own political elites."
15. See the reporting of *Independent*: http://www.independent.co.uk/news/world/europe/emmanuel-macron-email-hack-leaks-election-marine-le-pen-russia-media-ordered-not-publish-commission-a7721111.html. Accessed May 22, 2017.
16. At the time of writing Hungary became the first country, where the European Parliament started this procedure. Poland is also threatened, and the two countries have already promised to defend each other and veto any punishment.

References

AEGEE [European Students' Forum]. 2016. Policy paper on civic education. Available: http://www.aegee.org/policy-paper-on-civic-education/. Accessed 2 July 2017.

Amtenbrink, Fabian, and Rene Repasi. 2017. Compliance and enforcement in economic policy coordination in EMU. In *The enforcement of EU law and values: Ensuring member states' compliance*, ed. András Jakab and Dimitry Kochenov, 145–181. Oxford: Oxford University Press.

Börzel, Tanja, Tobias Hofmann, Diana Panke, and Carina Sprungk. 2010. Obstinate and inefficient: Why member states do not comply with European law. *Comparative Political Studies* 43 (11): 1363–1390.

Braghiroli, Stefano, and Andrey Makarychev. 2016. Russia and its supporters in Europe: Trans-ideology *á la carte*? Southeast European and Black Sea Studies 16(2): 213–233.

Bueno de Mesquita, Bruce, and Alastair Smith. 2011. *The dictator's handbook: Why bad behavior is almost always good politics*. New York: PublicAffairs.

Bugaric, Bojan. 2016. Protecting democracy inside the EU: On Article 7 TEU and the Hungarian turn to authoritarianism. In *Reinforcing the rule of law oversight in the European Union*, ed. Carlos Closa and Dimitry Kochenov, 82–102. Cambridge: Cambridge University Press.

Bundesministerium for Wirtschaft und Energie. 2017. *Stellungnahme der Bundesregierung zur Kohäsionspolitik der EU nach 2020*. Available: http://g8fip1kplyr33r3krz5b97d1.wpengine.netdna-cdn.com/wp-content/uploads/2017/06/170511-Stellungnahme-BReg-zu-künftiger-Kohäsionspolitik-final.pdf. Accessed 2 July 2017.

Charron, Nicholas, Lewis Dijkstra, and Victor Lapuente. 2015. Mapping the regional divide in Europe: A measure for assessing quality of government in 206 European regions. *Social Indicators Research* 122 (2): 315–346.

Cooper, Harry. 2017. EU's Jourová wants funds linked to new prosecutor's office. *Politico*, June 8. Available: http://www.politico.eu/article/eus-jourova-wants-funds-linked-to-new-prosecutors-office/. Accessed 2 July 2017.

Csaba, László. 2016. The EU at sixty: A watershed or business as usual? (comparing Grexit and Brexit). *Acta Oeconomica* 66 (S1): 63–77.

Darvas, Zsolt, and Olga Tschekassin. 2015. *Poor and under pressure: The social impact of Europe's fiscal consolidation*. Bruegel policy contribution no. 2015/04.

Easterly, William. 2006. *The white man's burden: Why the West's efforts to aid the rest have done so much ill and so little good*. New York: The Penguin Press.

European Commission. 2017. *Reflection paper on the deepening of the economic and monetary union*. Brussels: European Commission.

Glaeser, Edward, Giacomo Ponzetto, and Andrei Schleifer. 2007. Why does democracy need education? *Journal of Economic Growth* 12 (2): 77–99.

Gros, Daniel. 2013. Banking union with a sovereign virus: The self-serving treatment of sovereign debt. *Intereconomics* 48 (2): 93–97.

Hobolt, Sara. 2016. The Brexit vote: A divided nation, a divided continent. *Journal of European Public Policy* 23 (9): 1259–1277.

Ioannidis, Michael. 2017. Weak members and the enforcement of EU law. In *The enforcement of EU law and values: Ensuring member states' compliance*, ed.

András Jakab and Dimitry Kochenov, 476–492. Oxford: Oxford University Press.

Jakab, András. 2017. Application of the EU CFR by national courts in purely domestic cases. In *The enforcement of EU law and values: Ensuring member states' compliance*, ed. András Jakab and Dimitry Kochenov, 252–262. Oxford: Oxford University Press.

Klapsis, Antonis. 2015. *An unholy alliance: The European far-right and Putin's Russia*. Brussels: Wilfried Martens Center for European Studies.

Kochenov, Dimitry. 2017. The *aquis* and its principles: The enforcement of the 'law' versus the enforcement of 'values' in the EU. In *The enforcement of EU law and values: Ensuring member states' compliance*, ed. András Jakab and Dimitry Kochenov, 9–27. Oxford: Oxford University Press.

Kochenov, Dimitry, and Laurent Pech. 2015. *Upholding the rule of law in the EU: On the Commission's 'pre-article 7 procedure' as a timid step in the right direction*. EUI Robert Schuman Centre for advanced studies working paper no. 2015/24.

Lenarčič, Andreja, Dirk Mevis and Dóra Siklós. 2016. *Tackling sovereign risk in European banks*. ESM discussion paper series no. 1/2016. Luxembourg: European Stability Mechanism.

Lipset, Seymour Martin. 1959. Some social requisites of democracy: Economic development and political legitimacy. *The American Political Science Review* 5381: 69–105.

Loewenstein, Karl. 1937. Militant democracy and fundamental rights, I. *The American Political Science Review* 31 (3): 417–432.

McGill, Andrew. 2016. America's educational divide put Trump in the White House. *The Atlantic*, November 27. Available: https://www.theatlantic.com/politics/archive/2016/11/education-put-donald-trump-in-the-white-house/508703/. Accessed 2 July 2017.

Müller, Jan-Werner. 2017. A democracy commission of one's own, or what it would take for the EU to safeguard liberal democracy in its member states. In *The enforcement of EU law and values: Ensuring member states' compliance*, ed. András Jakab and Dimitry Kochenov, 234–251. Oxford: Oxford University Press.

North, Douglass. 1990. *Institutions, institutional change and economic performance*. Cambridge: Cambridge University Press.

OECD. 2017. *Trust and public policy: How better governance can help rebuild public trust*. Paris: OECD.

Oliker, Olga. 2017. Putinism, populism and the defense of liberal democracy. *Survival* 59 (1): 7–24.

Pasimeni, Francesco, and Paolo Pasimeni. 2016. An institutional analysis of the Europe 2020 strategy. *Social Indicators Research* 127 (3): 1021–1038.

Pech, Laurent. 2009. *The rule of law as a constitutional principle of the European Union*. Jean Monnet working paper series no. 4/2009. Available at https://ssrn.com/abstract=1463242. Accessed 2 July 2017.

Puddington, Arch, and Tyler Roylance. 2017. The freedom house survey for 2016: The dual threat of populists and autocrats. *Journal of Democracy* 28 (2): 105–119.

Redden, Elizabeth. 2017. Academic freedom front lines. *Inside Higher Ed*, March 30. Available: https://www.insidehighered.com/news/2017/03/30/hungary-and-russia-western-style-universities-are-under-threat. Accessed 2 July 2017.

Rodríguez-Pose, Andrés. 2013. Do institutions matter for regional development? *Regional Studies* 47 (7): 1034–1047.

Scheppele, Kim Lane. 2016. Enforcing the basic principles of EU law through systemic infringement actions. In *Reinforcing rule of law oversight in the European Union*, ed. Carlos Closa and Dimitry Kochenov, 105–132. Cambridge: Cambridge University Press.

Silver, Nate. 2016. Education, not income, predicted who would vote for Trump. *FiceThirtyEight.com*, November 22. Available: http://fivethirtyeight.com/features/education-not-income-predicted-who-would-vote-for-trump/. Accessed: 2 July 2017.

Sinn, Hans-Werner. 2014. *The euro trap: On bursting bubbles, budgets and beliefs*. Oxford: Oxford University Press.

Smets, Kaat. 2012. A widening generational divide? The age gap in voter turnout through time and space. *Journal of Elections, Public Opinion and Parties* 22 (4): 407–430.

Smolenova, Ivana. 2016. The pro-Russian disinformation campaign in the Czech Republic and Slovakia. *Per Concordiam: Journal of European Security and Defense Issues* 7 (S1): 26–29.

Svensson, Jakob. 2000. Foreign aid and rent-seeking. *Journal of International Economics* 51 (2): 437–461.

Szente, Zoltán. 2017. Challenging the basic values – Problems in the rule of law in Hungary and the failure of the EU to tackle them. In *The enforcement of EU law and values: Ensuring member states' compliance*, ed. András Jakab and Dimitry Kochenov, 456–475. Oxford: Oxford University Press.

Uslaner, Eric. 2002. *The moral foundations of trust*. Cambridge: Cambridge University Press.

Veebel, Viljal. 2016. Estonia confronts propaganda. *Per Concordiam: Journal of European Security and Defense Issues* 7 (S1): 14–19.

Weiler, J.H.H. 2016. Epilogue: Living in a glass house. In *Reinforcing rule of law oversight in the European Union*, ed. Carlos Closa and Dimitry Kochenov, 313–326. Cambridge: Cambridge University Press.

World Economic Forum. 2016. *The global competitiveness report 2016–2017*. Genève: World Economic Forum.

Index[1]

[1] Note: Page number followed by 'n' refers to notes.

D. Győrffy, *Trust and Crisis Management in the European Union*,
https://doi.org/10.1007/978-3-319-69212-8

F

The manufacturer's authorised representative in the EU is Springer Nature Customer Service Centre GmbH, Europaplatz 3, 69115 Heidelberg, Germany. If you have any concerns regarding our products, please contact ProductSafety@springernature.com

Printed and bound by CPI Group (UK) Ltd, Croydon, CR0 4YY

01/10/2026

02225952-0002